"**An exciting, wonderful book rivaling anything yet written about the battle of Gettysburg**. It is mandatory reading for Civil War buffs. I have always wondered why General Lee ordered that fateful attack when and where he did. Now I know. Thanks to Tom Carhart's exemplary new research and his knowledge of military matters, *Lost Triumph* presents the first comprehensive view of Lee's previously unknown plan to win the battle."

—Bruce Lee,

author of *Marching Orders: The Untold Story of World War II*

"History is seldom page-turning; here the true events of Gettysburg compose a thriller. Dr. Carhart makes the case for revolutionizing our understanding of the decisive engagement of the Civil War; elevates the renown of Robert E. Lee; improbably reanimates the reputation of George Armstrong Custer; and shows us how history should be analyzed, challenged, proven and taught. On the way, he condenses the complexities of the military art into entertainingly digestible bites."

—Gus Lee,

author of *China Boy*

"Written with verve and a keen eye for a telling detail, *Lost Triumph* brings to life both the battlefield and the remarkable men who fought there."

—Rick Atkinson,

author of *An Army at Dawn*

"Few generals were as brilliant as Robert E. Lee, and few battles as titanic—and puzzling—as Gettysburg. Why did Lee fail? In *Lost Triumph,* Tom Carhart offers a bold and provocative new assessment. Agree or disagree, it is sure to stimulate debate among even the most seasoned Civil War buffs."

—Jay Winik,

author of *April 1865: The Month That Saved America*

# Lost Triumph

## LEE'S REAL PLAN AT GETTYSBURG—
## AND WHY IT FAILED

## Tom Carhart

A Berkley Caliber Book, New York

THE BERKLEY PUBLISHING GROUP
**Published by the Penguin Group**
**Penguin Group (USA) Inc.**
**375 Hudson Street, New York, New York 10014, USA**
Penguin Group (Canada), 10 Alcorn Avenue, Toronto, Ontario M4V 3B2, Canada (a division
of Pearson Penguin Canada Inc.) • Penguin Books Ltd, 80 Strand, London WC2R 0RL,
England • Penguin Ireland, 25 St Stephen's Green, Dublin 2, Ireland (a division of Penguin
Books Ltd) • Penguin Group (Australia), 250 Camberwell Road, Camberwell, Victoria 3124,
Australia (a division of Pearson Australia Group Pty Ltd) • Penguin Books India Pvt Ltd,
11 Community Centre, Panchsheel Park, New Delhi–110 017, India • Penguin Group (NZ),
Cnr Airborne and Rosedale Roads, Albany, Auckland 1310, New Zealand (a division of
Pearson New Zealand Ltd) • Penguin Books (South Africa) (Pty) Ltd, 24 Sturdee Avenue,
Rosebank, Johannesburg 2196, South Africa • Penguin Books Ltd, Registered Offices:
80 Strand, London WC2R 0RL, England

Copyright © 2005 by Tom Carhart
Book design by Michelle McMillan
Interior maps by Jeffrey L. Ward
Cover Design by Bradford Foltz

PRINTING HISTORY
G. P. Putnam's Sons hardcover edition / 2005
Berkley Caliber trade paperback edition / April 2006

Berkley Caliber is a registered trademark of Penguin Group (USA) Inc.
The "C" design is a trademark belonging to Penguin Group (USA) Inc.

The Library of Congress has cataloged the G. P. Putnam's Sons hardcover as follows:

Carhart, Tom.
Lost triumph: Lee's real plan at Gettysburg—and why it failed / Tom Carhart.
p.   cm.
ISBN 0-399-15249-0
1. Gettysburg, Battle of, Gettysburg, Pa., 1863.   2. Lee, Robert E. (Robert Edward),
1807–1870—Military leadership.   3. Military planning—United States—History—
19th century.   4. Strategy—History—19th century.   I. Title.
E475.53.C275     2005               2004060065
973.7'349—dc22

PRINTED IN THE UNITED STATES OF AMERICA

10   9   8   7   6   5   4   3   2   1

FOR JAN, TOMMY,
AND JASON

# Contents

# List of Maps

# Foreword

JAMES M. McPHERSON

EVERY YEAR nearly two million people visit Gettysburg to walk the fields where the largest battle in the history of the Western Hemisphere took place on the first three days of July 1863. Fewer than 2 percent of these tourists, however, find their way to the East Cavalry Battlefield site three miles east of the "high-water mark" at the climax of the Pickett-Pettigrew assault on July 3. Unless specifically asked, the licensed guides who give thousands of battlefield tours each year never take visitors to East Cavalry Field. Most tourists are not even aware that these 750 acres of rolling farmland are part of Gettysburg National Military Park. They leave Gettysburg after driving around the rest of the park without realizing that they have missed an essential part of the battle. As Tom Carhart makes clear in this innovative and important new book, one cannot understand the battle of Gettysburg without understanding what happened at what was then known as East Cavalry Battlefield.

On July 1 the Army of Northern Virginia won a clear victory and drove outnumbered Union defenders back to a defensive position on Cemetery and Culp's hills and Cemetery Ridge. The next day, Confederate attacks on both Union flanks made additional gains but achieved no breakthrough. Having invaded Pennsylvania, looking for a showdown battle and a war-winning victory, General Robert E. Lee believed that renewed assaults on July 3 would produce that victory.

Contrary to common understanding, however, Lee's plan for July 3 was not merely to send 13,000 men spearheaded by Pickett's fresh division against the Union center on Cemetery Ridge. Some visitors to Gettysburg learn that a renewed attack against Culp's Hill by Lieutenant-General Richard Ewell's corps was also part of Lee's plan for July 3. Now we also learn that there was a crucial third component to Lee's July 3 tactics. Thanks to Tom Carhart's painstaking and absorbing reconstruction of events, we now have a clear comprehension of what Lee planned for July 3—and why it went wrong.

While Pickett attacked the Union center and Ewell rolled up the right, Lee intended the 6,000 troopers of Major-General "Jeb" Stuart's cavalry to circle around north of the Union right flank and come in on the rear of the Union position to give the coup de grâce to the Yankees desperately engaged by Pickett and Ewell in their front. It might have worked, even though Union infantry had forced Ewell into a premature firefight on the morning of July 3 and repulsed the Pickett-Pettigrew assault in the afternoon. If Stuart's horsemen had charged the Union rear as scheduled, Ewell could have renewed his attack and Pickett might have broken through. But Stuart never got closer than three miles to the Union rear. His previously undefeated cavalry was intercepted and fought to a standstill by 2,500 Union troopers—principally a Michigan brigade commanded by George Armstrong Custer, newly promoted to brigadier general.

One of the chief merits of Tom Carhart's fast-paced narrative is the new light it sheds on Custer. Almost all Americans have heard of Custer, but most associate him with one disastrous day in 1876 at Little Bighorn in Montana when his entire command was wiped out. Few realize that he emerged—beginning at Gettysburg—as one of the best

Union cavalry commanders in the Civil War. Now, thanks to Tom Carhart, we will have a new understanding of Custer, who led two mounted charges against Stuart's horsemen, shouting, "Come on, you Wolverines," to the men of the First and Seventh Michigan cavalries.

Why haven't we known all this before? Careful students of the battle *have* known some of it. But until now we have not understood how the fight at East Cavalry Field fit into the larger picture of Gettysburg. Most important, we have not previously comprehended Lee's full tactical plan for July 3 in which Stuart's cavalry was to have an essential part. No historian before Tom Carhart has pieced together the whole story from the scattered bits of evidence. Lee's and Stuart's after-action reports on the battle provide only vague and incomplete references to the plan—understandably so, since success has a thousand fathers, but failure is an orphan. From his own experience as a combat officer and military historian, Carhart has combined evidence and plausible inference to reconstruct Lee's plan and the reasons for its failure. Given the vast number of writings on Gettysburg, it seems impossible to come up with new information and insights about the battle. But Tom Carhart has done it.

# Lost Triumph

# *Introduction*

For every Southern boy fourteen years old, not once but whenever he wants it, there is the instant when it's still not yet two o'clock on that July afternoon in 1863, the brigades are in position behind the rail fence, the guns are laid and ready in the woods and the furled flags are already loosened to break out and Pickett himself with his long oiled ringlets and his hat in one hand probably and his sword in the other looking up the hill waiting for Longstreet to give the word and it's all in the balance, it hasn't happened yet, it hasn't even begun yet, it not only hasn't begun yet but there is still time for it not to begin against that position and those circumstances which made more men than Garnett and Kemper and Armistead and Wilcox look grave yet it's going to begin, we all know that, we have come too far with too much at stake and that moment doesn't even need a fourteen-year-old boy to think THIS TIME. MAYBE THIS TIME with all this much to lose and all this much to gain: Pennsylvania, Maryland, the world, the golden dome of Washington itself to crown with desperate and unbelievable victory.

—WILLIAM FAULKNER, *Intruder in the Dust* (1948)

THAT HOT, sunny afternoon, General Robert E. Lee sent 13,000 Confederate soldiers, led by Pickett's fresh division, into a grassy field soon to be spattered with their blood. Their goal was a clump of trees nearly a mile away at the center of Union defenses on Cemetery Ridge. But as they moved into the Yankees' range, their gray lines suddenly shuddered as flaming sheets of rifle fire and bursting artillery shells ripped ragged holes in their ranks. Yet they grimly closed up and kept moving forward.

While many of these men did reach their goal and even broke through federal lines, they were so weakened by that point that they were unable to hold. Forced to retreat, they were assailed once again by enemy fire as they crossed that open slaughter field. When the shaken remnants finally got back, Lee is said to have been there to greet them with his well-known apology line: "It's all my fault!"

But was it really?

The conventional wisdom over the last century and a half has been that Lee risked everything that day—a much-needed stunning victory over the Army of the Potomac in Pennsylvania, the survival of his own army, even, yes, the very life of the Confederacy—on a foolish attack by nine of his forty-three combat brigades launched against ranks of riflemen and clusters of cannon awaiting them in the Union line. If true, that means he was willing to gamble it all on the ability of those 13,000 men to cross a wide and open field under constant artillery and rifle fire, their attack hurled into the teeth of the Union defenses while his other 50,000 men sat quietly by and waited.

As the title suggests, I have a different understanding of Lee's full plan that day. In particular, I hope to change the rather common but seldom considered perception that generals during the Civil War made no tactical plans the night before a battle, that they simply moved their forces forward without any specific intention beyond attacking the enemy's forces where they found them. But Lee was a lifelong student of military history whose battlefield actions closely resembled those of the Napoleon whom he had so carefully studied and absorbed. I believe the detailed planning that consumed Lee the night before a battle was the most important action he performed as an army commander.

The implementation of Lee's plans, of course, was up to his subordinate commanders, and so his ultimate goals were not always realized.

But aside from what has widely been seen as his one great failure at Gettysburg, Lee's battle plans, as any careful review of his personal military history will show, are generally acknowledged to have been both bold and masterful. Despite the contrary popular perception, however, I believe I can show that to have been true at Gettysburg as well.

I want readers to take a fresh look at the Battle of Gettysburg, a fight that most agree was the centerpiece of the Civil War. But it is important at the outset to see it as a Union victory that came after Robert E. Lee had sequentially thrashed and humiliated Generals McClellan, Pope, Burnside, and Hooker on the battlefield, causing them all to be replaced by President Lincoln as he sought desperately for a general who could defeat that Confederate colossus.

It is now clear that General George C. Meade, a man who only reluctantly took command of the Army of the Potomac just a few days before the battle, was no better than those who had preceded him. In this greatest test of his military career, he knew going in that he was outgeneraled, and when looking at all his actions at Gettysburg, it seems apparent that he only hoped to somehow survive. During the three days of battle, awed by the myth of Lee's invincibility, he cowered with his well-armed and bountifully supplied army in hastily prepared defenses, allowing no significant offensive actions by his hunkered-down army of 94,000 surrounded by 70,000 free-ranging Rebels. These are only rough estimates of the army sizes before the battle, of course, and precision here is elusive. Because of the destruction of records, arrival or departure of certain units, and casualties suffered during the first two days of the battle, on the morning of the third day, July 3, 1863, Meade's army had shrunk to about 80,000, while Lee's force was roughly 63,000 men.[1]

After the massive Confederate assault remembered today as "Pickett's Charge" failed to permanently pierce the Union line on July 3, 1863, the Rebel soldiers who had made that attack returned to their positions on Seminary Ridge. No Union counterattack pursued them. On July 4, 1863, after three days of vicious combat, the two badly bled armies simply glowered at each other across a mile of open fields as they licked their wounds. That evening brought a downpour, and on the morning of July 5, Meade awoke to find the gray sky brightened by the absence of Lee and his Army of Northern Virginia.

Somehow, against all odds, Lee and his army were gone. Meade could scarcely believe what this meant: he had taken on the greatest Confederate general, maybe the greatest American general ever, in a major battle, and he had repelled his final attack and so had not been beaten. Indeed, although the Confederates had not been driven off, the naked fact that Lee had left the Army of the Potomac in control of the battlefield meant that Meade had won the battle.

Over the 140 intervening years, many people have reviewed the evidence and, virtually without exception, decided that, on the third day of this three-day battle, Lee made some profoundly wrong decisions. Central to his failures was Pickett's Charge, launched against the center of the Union defenses. And while Lee's battlefield mastery before and after the third day of the Battle of Gettysburg is undeniable, historians so far have been at a loss to explain this dramatic failure. Virtually all history books since that time, therefore, have simply reported that, on July 3, 1863, Lee just had one very bad day.

But I think a better understanding of Lee offers other explanations.

Most of the "facts" of Gettysburg are widely known today, in particular the failure of Pickett's Charge, the "high-water mark of the Confederacy." But I intend to show that Pickett's Charge against the western side of the Union defenses was, at least in part, a massive distraction, that Lee had also planned two other contemporaneous attacks against the Union defensive position involving the other 50,000 men in his army, attacks that, had they been carried off, would have divided the blue force in half and allowed it to be readily defeated in detail. Seen in that light, Pickett's Charge makes perfect sense, and had the other elements of Lee's plan been enacted, it not only would have succeeded, but would have done so at a far less bloody cost to the Confederates.

Using the same information available to other historians, I will develop what I believe Lee truly had in mind by reviewing and interpreting the evidence, which includes private correspondence and institutional records as well as official reports. An important source of information here is *The Bachelder Papers,* personal accounts of the battle written down after the war by a wide array of participants. Sought and collected after the war by a caring civilian, John B. Bachelder, they have been published in a three-volume set as recently as 1994.[2] But as much as possible, I have made use of books and other secondary sources that interested readers might more readily be able to find on their own.

Had his full plan been carried out, it seems probable that Lee would have destroyed the Army of the Potomac in Pennsylvania, and no sizable Union army could have been brought to face him within weeks, perhaps months. Indeed, after such a shattering triumph, what Union general would have dared to face him? The result, with Washington, Baltimore, and Philadelphia helpless before Lee's ebullient army, probably would have been a quick armistice to end the fighting and return things as much as possible to the *status quo ante bellum,* the situation as it existed before the war.

This would have meant the return of peace, for the basis of an armistice would have been the Confederacy's freedom to exist as a separate state, a fact the Union would have been forced to recognize. And that, after all, was the goal for which every Confederate soldier was fighting, that was what Lee was really hoping to win when he ventured north—a triumphant victory over the Army of the Potomac that would have shattered it as the fighting force protecting the Union capital in Washington and an event that would have forced the Union to recognize and accept the Confederacy.

The reason this didn't happen is attributable to the actions of two generals whose clash at Gettysburg changed everything, one Confederate and the other Union: James Ewell Brown (J.E.B., or Jeb) Stuart and George Armstrong Custer. Remembered in modern times only for one day in 1876 when he and his entire unit of more than two hundred men were killed by Sioux and Cheyenne Indians, Custer was one of the brightest stars in the Civil War, a fact that has been obscured by his death on the high plains. While Custer has been roundly condemned by generations of Americans who learned only that he cruelly punished innocent Native Americans, there is another Custer whose record at Gettysburg should at least be noted, for as I will show, it was his raw personal courage alone that prevented a Confederate victory at Gettysburg and thus truly preserved the Union.

I have carefully avoided controversial issues for the large part. Most of the evidence I present in support of my argument is widely accepted and can be found in general world and American history books. Probably the only exceptions are the details of certain incidents that occurred in the lives of the principals, some of the individuals who affected them, and perhaps some facts about West Point during its early days.

At the end, however, it will be the readers who must decide: Did Lee just have one very bad day on July 3, or was his plan for one of the greatest victories in history frustrated by the almost chance presence of a fearless young hero who stood in Stuart's path and would not move?

If I am right, Lee's full plan would have been a very bold stroke indeed. But Lee was a very bold general, and he needed a stunning triumph this time, for the entire game hung in the balance.

## 1

# In Mexico

H E WALKED SLOWLY OUT of the trees and into the clearing, then stopped and listened. Only birds and insects, nothing unusual. Was that a spring on the far side of the clearing? Had someone cleared the brush here? Was I being watched?

He took a step forward, then paused again. Nothing. In a few long strides he reached the pool by the spring, squatted down, and held his canteen underwater. As it began to fill, he looked around and noticed what seemed like a heavily beaten trail entering the clearing in front of him, coming from the south. That was where the Mexican left wing must be, wasn't it? Had he gotten behind them already?

He had spent the last few hours creeping up that steep, brushy ravine from the east, and he was tired. He drank cool water from his hand as the canteen filled, and it refreshed him. But as he was drinking, he suddenly heard noises of something coming through the trees off to the south. He froze as he heard voices, soft Spanish voices, a conversation between Mexicans. Must be soldiers. He slipped his canteen up out of the water, then dove over a fallen tree trunk at the edge of the clearing and pressed into the underbrush below it.

He dared not look, but their voices were loud now. Then they were moving in his direction, and he pressed against the felled tree trunk that concealed his torso. The two Mexicans called out to someone, and he heard voices in response, then laughter. The other voices grew closer, and he realized that this spring must be the watering hole for the left wing of Santa Anna's army. Would they notice his boot prints, or were there too many others? If they found him, hiding behind a log in a U.S. Army captain's uniform, there was no doubt they would shoot him, for their countries were at war. And if that happened, there would be no reconnaissance report, his wife back home would find herself a widow, and their children would lose their father. But he had few options, so he lay there frozen.

Within a short time, two of the Mexicans who had been drinking at the spring came over and actually sat on the log above him, chattering only a few feet away yet oblivious to his presence. Eventually, they rose and left, but he heard others talking or moving around in the clearing for the rest of the afternoon and evening. Finally, long after the last human voice or other man-made noise had faded, he slowly stood in the dark night. Hearing nothing, he carefully crept across the clearing and made his way back down the ravine. When he got back to his own lines, he gave the password to the guard posted on picket, then found his way to the commander's tent. As he stepped inside, a sudden half-surprised silence fell over the staff officers. Then Captain Robert E. Lee was warmly welcomed back from his reconnaissance mission by General Winfield Scott.[1]

After war broke out in 1846, there was a great stirring in the north, and three American columns invaded Mexico by land. Eventually, on March 9, 1847, another expeditionary force was landed at Vera Cruz under General Winfield Scott, and this was to be the army that would take Mexico City and finally win the war.

Robert E. Lee was a bright captain of engineers in Scott's entourage, and although he had graduated from West Point eighteen years earlier and had just had his fortieth birthday, he was still a rather junior officer. But Scott had learned that he was very competent in a wide array of fields, and as the expedition debarked, he learned to rely on Lee much more than on some of his other, more senior staff officers.

Soon after landing, Scott's force started by besieging the town of Vera Cruz, and Lee was one of the key officers who placed the siege artillery. After three days of heavy bombardment, the port city capitulated on March 27, and the column of American soldiers started up the narrow road that led to Mexico City.

On April 12, after having moved about thirty miles, Scott's force was stopped by intense fire from Mexican guns covering a mountain pass above which towered the peak of Cerro Gordo. Scott had 9,000 men in his force, and he was opposed by Santa Anna and an estimated army of 12,000 Mexican soldiers arrayed in strong defensive positions. Initially, Scott found himself stymied, and he asked for a personal reconnaissance by Captain Robert E. Lee, a most trusted member of his staff.

The son of a Revolutionary War hero, "Light Horse Harry" Lee, young Robert's childhood was marked by his father's unfortunate inability to manage his finances. Driven out of his country by relentless creditors when Robert was still just a boy, Light Horse Harry never returned home, dying penniless in the Caribbean. But his mother was able to use family connections to win Robert an appointment to West Point in 1825, and it was there that his star truly began to rise.

He graduated in 1829 ranked second in his class academically and first militarily, and his professional future as an army engineer seemed quite secure. But some of the uncertainties of his boyhood may well have endured and even played a role when, as a young officer, he pursued, wooed, and wed Mary Custis, the only daughter of one of the wealthiest planters in Virginia and the granddaughter of George Washington's wife, Martha, from an earlier marriage. His career in the peacetime army had been predictably dull. But now, at the very tip of the

American lance in Mexico and called on by the commanding general, his moment was at hand.[2]

His reconnaissance had been conducted on April 15, and when he explained what he had found, other officers doubted that the army could climb up the rough ravines on the Mexican left flank, so Lee asked for a pioneer team to clear a road. All day on the sixteenth, Lee and his men worked on a path up which horses and light artillery might be moved, and by dark he returned with news that they had gotten far beyond the spring he had discovered on April 15.

The next morning at dawn, Lee led the division commanded by General Twiggs up the precipitous trail he had carved the day before. Meanwhile, General Pillow would demonstrate against the Mexican right wing, which was poised atop sheer cliffs and was therefore entirely safe. But the rest of Scott's force had to wait along the main National Road that led up through the pass but which was now completely blocked by heavy Mexican defensive works and arrays of dug-in cannon. Everything depended on Lee and his flanking movement: If they succeeded, the way up the National Road would soon lie open; if they failed, then Scott's entire column would be thrown back, and Twiggs's division was itself in considerable peril in the event they were prematurely discovered by the Mexicans.[3]

But of course the flank attack by Twiggs's division was a complete surprise, and Scott ended up capturing about 3,000 Mexican soldiers and virtually all of their cannon. The success was perhaps best described by General Scott himself:

*Reconnaissances were pushed in search of some practicable route other than the winding, zigzag road among the spurs of mountains, with heavy batteries [of artillery] at every turn. The reconnaissance were conducted with vigor under Captain Lee at the head of a body of pioneers, and at the end of the third day a passable way for light batteries was accomplished without*

*alarming the enemy, giving the possibility of turning the extreme left of his
line of defence and capturing his whole army, except the reserve, that lay a
mile or two farther up the road. Santa Anna said that he had not believed
a goat could have approached him in that direction. Hence the surprise and
the results were the greater.*[4]

This victory opened the National Road and allowed the rest of
Scott's army to ascend it, after which Santa Anna's main force, attacked
front and flank, retired with great loss. In the wake of this victory at
Cerro Gordo, Lee received the brevet promotion to major, one way in
which exceptional performance of duty was sometimes recognized.

Scott's column pressed on with little opposition until it reached a
point barely twelve miles from Mexico City, where they confronted
two strong Mexican fortresses, San Agustín and San Antonio, whose
cannon covered the National Road. Well manned and defended, these
massive redoubts also lay behind a lava bed several miles wide, known
as the Pedregal, that was considered by the Mexicans, once again, to
be "impassable." And with the successful plans that had taken Cerro
Gordo still fresh in his mind, Scott turned once again to Captain Lee
for help.

This, of course, was an even greater challenge than had been Cerro
Gordo, for behind the jagged lava rock field of the Pedregal the Mexicans were blocking their path from two formidable walled installations.
Lee's first inclination was to look for a way to bypass the fortresses. But
after he had gone on both day and night reconnaissance runs and made
some narrow escapes from detection and capture or death, he realized
that simple passage would be impractical, that the Mexicans would have
to be defeated where they were. But he got very close to both positions
and discovered ways to bring American forces across the Pedregal while
remaining concealed from the Mexican defenders.

This was welcome news to Scott, and he allowed Lee to formulate the attack plans and then lead the forces into position. After taking troops across the Pedregal during the night to attack both fortresses on the morrow, Lee again crossed the forbidding ground twice to keep Scott apprised of his progress and to ask for a diversionary attack while the men who had crossed the Pedregal hit San Antonio from the rear.

As Scott's main force moved out on the National Road at dawn and began trading long-range artillery shots with San Antonio, Lee and the men he had shepherded across the Pedregal during the night burst into the rear of San Antonio like a thunderbolt. This was an utter shock to the Mexican troops, who, once again, were routed, including the terrified men who had defended San Agustín. Now Scott's force found itself at the very gates of Mexico City. Lee was brevetted to the rank of lieutenant colonel for his service, and General Scott mentioned him in his official battle report, a rare accolade at the time:

> *I am compelled to make special mention of Captain R.E. Lee, Engineer. This officer was again indefatigable during three operations in reconnaissance as daring as laborious, and of the utmost value. Nor was he less conspicuous in planting batteries and in conducting columns to their stations under the heavy fire of the enemy.*[5]

At this time, Santa Anna commanded some 15,000 Mexican troops inside the high walls of Mexico City, while Scott's command on the outside was no more than 9,000 men. But before they could take the city, Scott's men would have to deal with one last obstacle: a castle that perched atop the steeply sided pinnacle known as Chapultepec, inside which eight hundred of the very best Mexican troops awaited the Americans.

On the morning of September 13, three American columns went across the causeway and began the arduous climb, all the while under fire from above. Lee was once again at the front, although this time he was wounded and was forcibly withdrawn because of loss of blood. But Scott mentioned him again in his dispatches, saying, "Captain Lee, so constantly distinguished, also bore important orders from me (September 13th) until he fainted from a wound and the loss of two nights' sleep at the batteries."[6] Right after his wounding, however, Chapultepec fell, the Americans blew through the gates of Mexico City, and Mexico surrendered.

After the war, Scott would say that Lee's actions at Contreras were "the greatest feat of physical and moral courage performed by any individual, in my knowledge, pending the campaign."[7] Needless to say, the courage, insight, and military genius Lee had shown in Mexico became widely known throughout the army as well as to many national political leaders.

# 2

# Building Up to the Civil War

IN ORDER TO UNDERSTAND Lee's full plan at Gettysburg, one must first know much more about Lee, Stuart, and Custer, and about the country in which this bloodbath between brothers had erupted. It is important to start with some common shared information about, and understanding of, the forces that turned Americans into adversaries. Said another way, how is it that a group of immigrants drawn primarily from the British Isles could evolve, over less than one hundred years, from fervent allies in the fight for freedom from England into two armed camps eager to kill each other?

It seems important to review some American history, that we might try to get a better feel for sentiments on both sides in the American Civil War. That means the feelings not only of citizens, but also of soldiers who offered their lives for the survival of the Confederacy as well as those who made similar offerings for the endurance of the Union.

In early American colonial law, slavery was nothing more than a property issue, but it was to become the central issue around which our nation's politics turned for several hundred years. The first African slaves arrived in Jamestown, Virginia, in 1619, and as agriculture developed in some parts of the United States, slavery grew with it. The first such major regions were the Chesapeake Bay area of Virginia and Maryland, where tobacco was grown and exported in ever-growing volume, and the coastal lowlands and sea islands of the Carolinas and Georgia, where rice and indigo became major agricultural products. The land in these regions was flat, the soil rich in nutrients, and many navigable rivers provided ready access to the coast for trade. The sizable profit margins allowed by the use of slavery resulted in steadily growing tracts of land under cultivation by ever more slaves. As settlements moved inland, cotton was planted and quickly flourished, growing in importance during the 1840s and 1850s until many Southerners believed that "Cotton is King." Given the enormous productivity of their "peculiar institution," Southern colonies that at first had only tolerated slavery soon transformed themselves into slave-dependent societies.

But in the North, slavery had a different impact. While the argument has long been made that the heavily forested rocky hills and difficult winters of New England made slavery impractical there, other forces also played a major role. Generally forming into small, family-focused and church-centered communities, the residents of these colonies often brought the fundamental religious opposition to slavery that had grown up in England across the Atlantic. The Society of Friends, or Quakers, for instance, had required members to free their slaves, and Quakers were to provide much of the antislavery leadership in this country. Over time, other religions joined in, and eventually an abolitionist fervor swept through the North. Though held by only a minority of the population, it resulted in the gradual abolition of slavery in the North: by the early part of the nineteenth century, all Northern states either had banned slavery or were passing through gradual stages of emancipation.

During our first days as a nation, the political tolerance of slavery became a source of great discomfort to many Americans on both sides of the issue. During the summer of 1787, a Constitutional Convention made up of representatives from the states met in Philadelphia, where they drew up the Constitution. And despite the careful way in which the institution was never called by its proper name, slavery was validated in places where it then existed by the wording of that document. The Constitution was also the first great compromise between northern and southern states on the issue of slavery: Congressional districts were formed based on the number of white citizens living in a given area, but partial credit was also given for the number of slaves living there.

That same summer of 1787, however, also saw the production of the Northwest Ordinance, which included the first great legal triumph for antislavery forces. In formally organizing land west of the Appalachians, north of the Ohio River, and east of the Mississippi River, Congress expressly stated that slavery would not be allowed in the Northwest Territory, out of which would come the states of Ohio, Indiana, Illinois, Michigan, and Wisconsin.

By the early nineteenth century, slavery was gone from the North, but it was growing like wildfire in the South. The Louisiana Purchase of 1802 brought in territory where slavery had been legal under French rule and whose inhabitants had ranged as far north as St. Louis with their slave property. And as settlement spread to the open West, slave owners and their abolitionist opponents sought to advance their own political causes on the ever-expanding frontier. The representational compromise established by the Constitution helped the South offset the larger and faster-growing citizenry in the North and its population-based power in the House of Representatives, but the South's crucial check was found in the Senate: as long as the number of slave states equaled the number of free states (after the admission of Alabama in 1819 there were eleven of each), the presence of two Senators from each state enabled slave owners in the South to use that body to block abolitionist legislation coming from the House of Representatives, and

they would also use their power there to control the antislavery sentiments of men nominated for appointment to the United States
Supreme Court.

The first post-Constitutional crisis over slavery occurred in 1819
when Missouri sought admission as a slave state. New York Congressman James Tallmadge attached abolitionist language to the bill that
passed the House of Representatives, but this was defeated in the Senate. Serious threats of secession were heard from both North and
South, but eventually agreement was reached that Maine, just separated
from Massachusetts, would be admitted with Missouri, thus maintaining twelve slave states and twelve free. But most important, agreement
was also reached that, other than in Missouri, slavery would not be
allowed in territory north of Missouri's southern border, latitude 36
degrees, 30 minutes. This was the so-called Missouri Compromise,
passed by Congress in January 1820. Both sides believed they had
gained from it, the South prizing the admission of Missouri as a slave
state with the prospect of Florida and Arkansas joining their ranks in
the near future, while the North was able to prohibit slavery in the
larger part of the territories and also maintain the principle of 1787
that Congress could keep slavery out of the territories if it chose
that path.

As settlers moved west, pro- and antislavery pressures continued to
build across the nation. The education of slaves was forbidden by law in
most slaveholding states, and abolitionist publications in the North
encouraged slaves to flee their masters. Helped whenever possible by
the "Underground Railroad" to make good their escape, they were
promised safe refuge in the free states of the North, or even in Canada,
which was beyond the reach of American laws. While often condemned in the North on humanitarian, socioeconomic, and religious
grounds, slavery was defended in slaveholding regions by plantation

owners, political leaders, and clerics who found economic, social, and even scriptural justification for it. The North was castigated as the home of wage slaves toiling under the yoke of the wealthy upper class, while the South professed itself to be made up of only two classes: the whites, all of whom were considered to be the upper class, and the blacks, all of whom were described, whether slave or free, as the lower class, the "mud sills of society."

The crisis of power between North and South took a new turn in 1833 with the reawakening of the battles between state and federal power. The South Carolina state legislature was unhappy with burdensome national tariffs on imports that protected Northern industry at Southern expense. They consequently passed an ordinance in November 1832 that was to take effect in February 1833 stating that the tariffs not specifically authorized by the Constitution were null and void and would not be enforced by the government of South Carolina. The ordinance then stated that, in the event federal officers tried to collect tariffs in South Carolina or force was used by the federal government, South Carolina would immediately secede from the Union.

Responding to this challenging piece of state legislation, President Andrew Jackson, a Tennessean, said this nullification ordinance seemed to be based on the unacceptable proposition that South Carolina could remain in the Union while being bound only by those national laws she chose to obey. He then confronted the threat of a state's secession from the Union as follows:

*The Constitution of the United States, then, forms a government, not a league; and whether it be formed by compact between the states or in any other manner, its character is the same. It is a government in which all the people are represented, which operates directly on the people individually, not upon the states; they retained all the power they did not grant. But*

*each state, having expressly parted with so many powers as to constitute,*
*jointly with the other states, a single nation, cannot, from that period,*
*possess any right to secede, because such secession does not break a league*
*but destroys the unity of a nation; and any injury to that unity is not only*
*a breach which would result from the contravention of a compact but it is*
*an offense against the whole Union.*[1]

This was precisely the doctrine on which President Lincoln acted in 1861 when South Carolina, followed by other Southern states, did secede from the Union. In 1833, many South Carolinians were still hot after hearing Jackson's response, but they allowed cooler heads to prevail: South Carolina's legislature reconvened and repealed the nullification ordinance. But as the burgeoning American population moved west, more trouble was in store.

During the 1830s, the present states of Texas, New Mexico, Arizona, and California were all thinly populated provinces of Mexico. A large number of white Americans had been attracted to Texas by generous land grants, and many of them were Southern planters who brought their slaves to work the land for them. While slavery was forbidden by Mexican law, it was tolerated until 1835, when President Santa Anna proclaimed a unified national constitution that did away with the local rights of Texans. This brought about formal secession of Texas from Mexico, followed by Santa Anna's arrival there at the head of some 3,000 men. They besieged the San Antonio fortress known as the Alamo, and eventually killed all two hundred occupants, including the wounded men they captured. The triumphant Mexicans then rode on deeper into Texas until they arrived near the San Jacinto River, where they were crushed by Sam Houston's army shouting "Remember the Alamo!" The Texans then demanded of Washington either their acceptance as another state or their recognition as a republic. But because of the turmoil in Washington over issues of slavery in territories, no action was taken until 1837, when the Lone Star Republic was recognized by Congress and, on March 3, 1837, his last day in office, by President Andrew Jackson.

Back in Texas, however, whose white population of emigrants from the United States was only about 50,000, a threat still loomed large from some 6 million Mexicans. The prospects of the Lone Star Republic remaining independent of Mexico seemed dim. Only the United States standing behind them kept their republic safe, many believed, and statehood was earnestly sought but long denied because of the domestic political turmoil in Congress over slavery. Then, in 1845, southern interests were able to get a majority vote in both Houses of Congress favoring annexation of Texas as a state. On his last day in office, February 28, 1845, President Tyler sent notice to Texas that only her consent was required to make her the twenty-eighth state in the Union, a consent she quickly gave.

President Polk had not been in office long when Mexico formally protested the admission of Texas as a state and broke diplomatic relations with the United States. Polk's response that summer was to send American troops under General Zachary Taylor to the banks of the Nueces River, which had long been accepted as the southern border of Texas. When Polk's efforts to buy California were rebuffed yet again, he ordered these troops to move on to the Rio Grande River, where they arrived on March 23, 1846. But this latest act was seen by many, including then-Congressman from Illinois Abraham Lincoln, as an unjustified invasion of Mexico and an act of war.

On April 25, Mexican cavalry crossed the Rio Grande and attacked Taylor's men, an act that resulted in a declaration by Congress that "by act of the Republic of Mexico, a state of war exists between that government and the United States." This was the beginning of the

Mexican-American War, and most senior military leaders on both sides of the Civil War were to have important combat experiences there.

After two years of fighting, American victory resulted in the acquisition of land from Mexico that ran from Texas to California, the southwestern tier of our country. But early in the war, a Congressman Wilmot from Pennsylvania had proposed an amendment to a bill for the purchase of California from Mexico. This was to be known as the Wilmot Proviso: since Mexico did not allow slavery, Wilmot reasoned, it should not be allowed in any territory acquired from Mexico. Almost all northern state legislatures passed resolutions approving the Wilmot Proviso, and southerners interpreted this action as a pointed insult.

As pressure grew for admission of the newly acquired territories as free or slave states, the Senate rang with the oratory of Daniel Webster, John Calhoun, and Henry Clay, and once again loud and serious talk of secession by southern leaders was heard across the North. Finally, in 1850, Congress decided that: (1) California would be admitted as a free state; (2) territorial governments would be organized in New Mexico and Utah with no mention of slavery; (3) a very strong fugitive slave law would apply throughout the nation; and (4) the domestic slave trade would be abolished in the District of Columbia. This Compromise of 1850 was a desperate effort to avoid the dissolution of the Union. But despite the political peace brokered in Congress, the fires of fervent support for or furious opposition to slavery raged hot through the land. No better evidence for this can be found than the reception accorded the 1853 publication of Harriet Beecher Stowe's *Uncle Tom's Cabin,* an explosive best-seller in the North that was roundly condemned and even banned across the South.

But in 1854, Congress was far from out of the woods on slavery issues. There were three proposed routes for a transcontinental railroad, one northern, one southern, and one in the center. This last route was favored by Senator Stephen Douglas, a powerful Democrat from Illinois who had wide support across the South, for he was perceived as one of the few Northern politicians who were sensitive to Southern concerns. In order to secure the central route, of course, Douglas supported Southern interests—which meant pro-slavery interests—by promoting the Kansas Nebraska Act, signed into law by President Pierce in May 1854.

Despite the fact that both Kansas and Nebraska lay north of the Missouri Compromise line of 36 degrees, 30 minutes, the act authorized the residents of those territories to accept or refuse slavery on the basis of "popular sovereignty," or "squatters' rights," as it became described by its enemies. Congressional leaders who came up with this bill originally thought that the issue of slavery in Kansas would follow the wishes of pro-slavery immigrants from Missouri, while Nebraska would respond to the votes of antislavery arrivals from Iowa. But in fact, the violence this bill spawned played a major role in tearing the Union apart, as brutal murders of their adversaries were committed by both sides across the length and breadth of "bleeding Kansas." Meanwhile, pro- and antislavery conventions in Kansas drafted their own constitutions and then sought recognition and statehood from Congress. Though the pro-slavery Lecompton constitution was accepted by the Senate, Douglas insisted on a vote by the people of Kansas, who overwhelmingly rejected it. The former darling of the South, Douglas was seen as a traitor for taking this position, and it cost him all chance of being elected president in 1860.

By now, the political animosity between North and South raged through both Houses of Congress. On May 16, 1856, Senator Charles Sumner from Massachusetts, a strong antislavery advocate, spoke on the floor of the Senate and condemned Senator Butler of South Carolina over slavery in truly bitter language. Three days later, as he sat at his desk on the Senate floor, he was approached from behind by Congressman Preston Brooks from South Carolina, who proceeded to beat Sumner senseless with a gold-headed cane. Nearly killed in the affair, Sumner went on leave for three years to recover, while Brooks, his praises ringing across the South, was overwhelmingly reelected to the House.

As the seams began to split beyond repair, the U.S. Supreme Court weighed in with the Dred Scott decision in 1857, holding that (1) a Negro could not be a citizen of the United States and therefore could not bring suit in federal court, and (2) a slaveholder who took a slave into territory north of 36 degrees, 30 minutes could not be deprived of his property by Congress without due process of law. This implied that slavery was national while freedom was local, and slavery was theoretically legal in every territory of the United States.

In 1858, Douglas was opposed in the Illinois Senate race by a former Whig member of Congress who had lost his seat because of his opposition to the Mexican-American War, Abraham Lincoln. The two traveled across the state and engaged in a series of much-celebrated debates. And while he repeatedly denied being an abolitionist, Lincoln was a firm enemy of slavery, and some of his words from the opening debate on June 16, 1858, caught the tenor of the times:

*A house divided against itself cannot stand. I believe this government cannot endure, permanently half slave and half free. I do not expect the Union to be dissolved—I do not expect the house to fall—but I do expect it will cease to be divided. It will become all one thing or all the other. Either the opponents of slavery will arrest the further spread of it, and place it where the public mind shall rest in the belief that it is in the course of ultimate extinction; or its advocates will push it forward until it shall become alike lawful in all the states, old as well as new—North as well as South.*[2] *(emphasis in original)*

While he failed in his effort to replace Douglas in the Senate, Lincoln's speeches won him wide national acclaim sufficient to carry him to the White House just two years later. But in 1859, the social wound of slavery still festered.

On October 16 of that year, John Brown and eighteen others, five of them black, captured the federal arsenal in Harpers Ferry, Virginia. The man who had carried out the Pottawatomi massacre in Kansas with his sons, a slightly mad Brown, saw himself as a sort of avenging angel, and he proposed to set up a republic of runaway slaves in the Appalachian Mountains, though with few specifics. Brown killed the mayor of the town and held others captive, but a company of Marines was sent from Washington, D.C., to rescue them under the command of Colonel Robert E. Lee. And Lee brought with him Lieutenant Jeb Stuart as his assistant, a close alliance that was to play a major role in the story of Gettysburg.

Lee's men took Brown captive on October 18, and he was tried and convicted of murder and treason. Refusing to plead insanity, Brown said he was pleased to "die for God's eternal truth." He was hanged on December 2, 1859, excoriated in the South while praised in the North. His extreme image on both sides would endure.[3]

In the spring of 1860, nominees for the presidential election were chosen. Lincoln was selected on the third ballot of the brand-new Republican Party, and the record of his debates against Douglas as well as his image as a canny midwestern lawyer gave hope of victory. But the far larger Democratic Party was still expected to sweep the election.

During the Democratic convention, however, that party shattered over slavery. While Douglas was to become the official Democratic nominee, the cotton states had broken away and held their own convention, where they nominated the sitting vice president, John Breckenridge of Kentucky. And to further complicate matters, the National Constitutional Union—a party formed for this election and pledging only to uphold the Constitution, the Union, and law enforcement—nominated John Bell of Tennessee.

With the admission of Minnesota to the Union in 1858 and Oregon in 1859, the Union in 1860 was composed of eighteen free and fifteen slave states. Breckenridge carried most of the South, while Bell took Virginia, Kentucky, and Tennessee. Despite the fact that he ran a close second to Lincoln in the popular vote, Douglas took only the state of Missouri. Lincoln took every free state, winning not only the popular vote but, more important, 180 out of 303 electoral votes, thus decisively winning the presidency.

As soon as the ballots had been tallied, alarm bells rang loud and furious across Dixie. On December 29, 1860, South Carolina formally seceded from the Union, followed over the next month by Georgia, Florida, Alabama, Mississippi, Louisiana, and Texas. On February 8, 1861, delegates from these states met in Montgomery, Alabama, and formed the Confederate States of America, electing Jefferson Davis, former senator from Mississippi and U.S. Secretary of War, their first president. At the time, newly elected presidents of the United States did not take office until March, and the incumbent Democratic government of President Buchanan, still holding power in Washington, D.C., took no action at all. But even after his inauguration, Lincoln's primary concern was preventing the secession of slaveholding states from the upper tier of the South. To that end, he did little more than promise to "preserve, protect, and defend" the Union, and he told the people of the South that he would not attack them, that they would have no conflict unless they became the aggressors.

That moment arrived on April 12, 1861, when Confederate batteries fired on Fort Sumter in Charleston, South Carolina, harbor. Almost out of food, the U.S. commander surrendered the next day, and the American Civil War had begun. On April 15, Virginia also seceded from the Union, followed by North Carolina, Tennessee, and Arkansas. These eleven states were to make up the Confederacy that fought a bloody war against Union forces over the following four years.

The new Confederacy contained about five and a half million white residents and some four million black slaves. They were facing twenty-three Union states (including West Virginia, which separated from Virginia and became a state during the Civil War), with a population of some nineteen million. The four slave states that did not secede—Maryland, Delaware, Kentucky, and Missouri—had a population of about two and a half million, and their young men fought for both sides in roughly equal numbers.

When joined with the dominant industrial and naval might of the North, these numbers opposing the secessionists can seem quite imposing. But it is important to remember two things: first, the slaves did much of the agricultural and other hard work at home in the deep South, thus allowing able-bodied young white men to join the Confederate forces in large numbers, which they did; and second, in order to maintain the Union and prevent the Southern attempt to secede, federal forces would have to enter the South and defeat Rebel forces on their home turf, while in order to win, the Confederacy didn't even need victory in battle, for all it had to do was endure and survive.

During the spring of 1861, there were only some 16,000 American soldiers in uniform, and Lincoln immediately called for 75,000 volunteers to defeat the Rebels. In the South, similar calls went out from the seceded states. Colonel Robert E. Lee was at the time assigned to a post in Texas, and he wrote on this issue to one of his sons:

*Secession is nothing but revolution. The framers of our Constitution never exhausted so much labour, wisdom and forbearance in its formation, and surrounded it with so many guards and securities, if it was intended to be broken by any member of the Confederacy at will. . . . Still, a Union that can only be maintained by swords and bayonets, and in which strife and civil war are to take the place of brotherly love and kindness, has no charm for me. If the Union is dissolved, the government disrupted, I shall return to my native state and share the miseries of my people. Save in her defense, I will draw my sword no more.*[4]

## 3

# West Point and West Pointers

AFTER THE MEXICAN WAR, Lee returned to the ranks of the Corps of Engineers, and he spent several years directing the construction of defenses around Baltimore. Then, in September 1852, something occurred that was not widely noted at the national level but is rather important to our story: then-Brevet Colonel Robert E. Lee was named superintendent of the United States Military Academy at West Point, New York, the ninth man to fill that role. This is important because it gives us an opportunity to look at why and how Lee knew about great generals of the past, the "Great Captains" of history. Particularly important are Hannibal, Frederick the Great, and especially Napoleon, all of whom were models for Lee as he led the Army of Northern Virginia in battle.

A man who had graduated second in his own West Point class, Lee was well versed in the Great Captains by the time he graduated. We should also note that Lee had a half brother seventeen years older than he, Henry Lee IV, who had served as a major in the War of 1812. Thereafter, he left the service and wrote a number of books, among which was a life of Napoleon, of which only one volume was published, in London and Paris, in 1837 (*The Life of Napoleon Bonaparte*

*Down to the Peace of Tolentino and the Close of the First Campaign in Italy*). This book covered Napoleon's experiences in Italy in 1796, and we know that Robert E. Lee owned a copy and studied it carefully.[1]

Already a hero of the recent war with Mexico, Lee had developed certain ideas about the education of cadets at West Point. Among his primary goals as superintendent was the installation of the highest standards of good character and social grace in them, and he felt it important that he establish a personal relationship with as many cadets as possible. Since there were only about 250 cadets at West Point then, this goal was reasonable.

While classes were also taught on Saturday mornings then, there was no formal schedule for Saturday afternoons, and cadets were allowed to pursue their personal interests. They were not allowed to leave post, however, and even if they had been, New York City was some fifty miles away. There were not many diversions then available to cadets, but Saturday afternoons were the occasions on which Lee generally invited cadets into his home, often to share a meal. Because his oldest son, George Washington Custis Lee, was a member of the class of 1854 (he would graduate first in his class and eventually rise to the rank of major general in the Confederate army), the superintendent had a very easy way of establishing personal relationships with cadets: they simply accompanied Custis to the Lee residence.

Oliver O. Howard from Maine was a member of that class, an outspoken abolitionist who stood his ground despite virulent criticism by many others who either supported or were not so strongly opposed to slavery. But because he took such a decisive stand, which resulted in violent physical fights with other cadets, certain members of the class grew to admire him. Among these was James Ewell Brown Stuart from Virginia. Although Stuart came from a slave-owning family, the two cadets became fast friends.

Howard would later rise to major general in the Union army and after the war became director of the Freedmen's Bureau and then the founder and first president of Howard University in Washington, D.C., which was established to educate freedmen. But as an injured cadet, Howard tells of the warmth and kindness directed toward him by Colonel Lee when he visited him in the hospital. After his recovery, Howard tells us he visited the Lee household with Stuart, where he was warmly received.[2]

But the cadet Lee probably came to know best, after his own son Custis, was Stuart, and the two men soon established a sort of father-son relationship that would endure to the very end of their lives. During the Civil War, Stuart would become Lee's most trusted cavalry leader, and he was to excel at providing information on enemy movements and activities through the expert and aggressive reconnaissance he or his cavalry subordinates were able to conduct.[3]

While Lee was superintendent, there were many other cadets at West Point who, if they survived the Indian Wars (a number did not), would end up fighting on either side during the Civil War. Lee's mentorship of these young men gave him remarkable serendipitous insight into the men who would later play major leadership roles in the Union or Confederate army. In addition to Howard, there were fifty-one other men who were cadets while Lee was superintendent and would later rise to general's rank in the Union army, including names as prominent as James McPherson, John Schofield, and Philip Sheridan. And on the other side, in addition to Custis Lee and Jeb Stuart, twenty men who were cadets during the same period rose to general's rank in the Confederate army, including John Hood, John Pegram, and Fitzhugh Lee (nephew of Robert E.).[4] For Robert E. Lee, that was no doubt an important exposure, one decade before the fact, to men he would either command or face in battle during the Civil War.

Another important goal of Superintendent Lee was the proper education of all cadets in the military art as it was practiced on the battlefields of history by the Great Captains. During his own cadet days from 1825 through 1829, Lee had borrowed books from the West Point library that covered a wide field. Most were oriented around engineering and similar technical subjects, though he also read Voltaire, Machiavelli, and Napoleon's memoirs as well as a history of Napoleon.[5] But since cadets could not leave the West Point military post, where there were limited distractions available, it was common for them, particularly those who stood high in their classes, to spend a lot of their free time in the library reading. And indeed, the library in those days has been recorded as a rewarding refuge by those who sought its benefits.[6]

While the academy records are often not as precise as one would hope, this is in large measure because of a major fire that occurred at West Point on February 19, 1938, in which the USMA Library and several academic departments, with most of their books and records, were consumed. Among the offices and records destroyed in that fire were those of the USMA adjutant, an administrator acting in the name of the superintendent whose duties and responsibilities included academic record-keeping and day-to-day management of the academy and the cadets. The formal records of West Point before 1938, then, were largely reconstructed from books, documents, and other records that existed in Washington, D.C., or other official or unofficial repositories of army records.[7]

Because of the destruction caused by this fire, it is quite difficult or impossible today to determine the content of courses taught or the texts used for instruction during the nineteenth century. Even so, one can easily see that Lee was a student all his life. As superintendent, Lee was an important force in early structured efforts to educate the staff and faculty, as well as cadets, in the military history of the Great Captains.

The vehicle for this instruction was Dennis Hart Mahan, one of the academic bright lights of West Point's early days. After graduating first in the class of 1824, Superintendent Sylvanus Thayer kept Mahan at West Point, where he taught for two years. He then spent the years from 1826 through 1830 at the French military academy at Metz, where he acquired a wealth of knowledge. His primary academic emphasis was on military engineering, including the latest technical military weapons and techniques. But he also fed a growing interest in the art of war as practiced by the Great Captains, in particular Napoleon Bonaparte. After his return to West Point, he began to develop his own textbooks, and within two years was named the Professor of Engineering.

Sometime between 1848 and 1850, Mahan started what became known as the Napoleon Club. This was a voluntary organization of members of the staff and faculty as well as cadets at West Point who met weekly to discuss and debate various actions of Napoleon and his adversaries. Mahan was president of the Napoleon Club, and he ordinarily assigned certain battles or campaigns to specific officers or cadets, who were then given up to six weeks to research their topic and prepare an opening summation that would begin the discussion. It appears that Lee was not only a strong supporter of the Napoleon Club, but as superintendent he arranged for their use of a particularly large room. And he fulfilled Mahan's earlier request to have large-scale maps of Europe and some of the battlefields from the Napoleonic Wars painted on the walls of that room.[8]

These paintings became renowned, especially a large one of Europe, eight feet by eleven feet, depicting the major campaigns of the Napoleonic Wars. When President Lincoln visited West Point in 1863, he was impressed by the map and asked if he could get a copy made for his own use in the White House, a request that was quickly fulfilled.[9]

A letter from Cadet William H. Harris to his father in 1858, written while he was a "plebe," or freshman, indicates that cadets received more education about the Great Captains than is commonly understood:

> . . . *In History we have been studying the French Revolution and Napoleon's campaigns and these have come hard to me as I have never read much about them, but I have "maxed" it so far on them. We have a large room in the Academic Building, on the walls of which are painted very large maps of Napoleon's campaigns. It is called the "Napoleon room" and cadets are taken in there to study his marches and battles. The officers are very particular about the study of all military campaigns and they are generally well "posted" on them, so that the study is interesting.*[10]

The Napoleon Club, which was in full operation during Lee's tenure as superintendent, also covered the campaigns of Frederick the Great and occasionally others, including Alexander, Hannibal, and Caesar. As the name implies, however, the primary focus at meetings and in other relations between members was on the campaigns of Napoleon Bonaparte. Lee's studies at West Point, of course, were focused on engineering, but as a cadet he developed a lifelong habit of studying military history.

Douglas Southall Freeman, in his magisterial four-volume biography entitled *R. E. Lee,* goes into some detail in showing Lee's personal dedication to studying the Great Captains. For instance, he lists the forty-eight books Lee withdrew from the library as superintendent, fifteen of which related specifically to war, and of which seven concerned Napoleon Bonaparte.[11] Several of these were withdrawn more than once, and the books he most commonly borrowed from the library dealt with Napoleon's campaign in Italy in 1796, a point that will become important to us later. In addition to Napoleon, Freeman notes that Lee also studied the campaigns of Hannibal and Julius Caesar.[12]

But in addition to his use of texts found in the West Point library during his years as superintendent, Lee had also begun to accumulate certain titles, his own collection of military history books. These were his personal possessions, books he doubtless read numerous times in the days when reading was one of the few productive pastimes after the sun had set. Sixteen such books are listed by Freeman, all of them in French. And while seven of these are engineering or other technical texts, the rest are devoted to various aspects of the Art of War.[13] Probably the most important of these, in terms of the establishment of his professional war-fighting capabilities and understanding, is Antoine Henri Jomini's *Précis de l'Art de la Guerre,* published in 1838.

While various translations appeared in English, Lee's version was in the original French. In drawing on Napoleon's campaigns therein, Jomini develops many things, including tactics used to attack an adversary fixed in place. These include a flank or rear attack against a defensive line by infantry and cavalry together, by cavalry alone, and an attack by infantry against the adversary's center while cavalry makes a simultaneous attack against one flank.[14]

Consisting of two volumes, this was perhaps Jomini's greatest and most important work, and it was widely respected around the world, all the more so because precious few individuals had ever made such a thorough study of the Art of War. An early acquisition of Robert E. Lee, it would probably not be too great an exaggeration to describe it as his bible, and there seems little doubt that he studied it quite religiously.

In April 1855, Lee received orders to join the Second U.S. Cavalry in Louisville, Kentucky. There were only two cavalry regiments in the U.S. Army at the time, the First and the Second, and most of their officers were to rise to prominence in the Civil War, including such men as Joseph Johnston, W. J. Hardee, William Emory, George Thomas, Earl van Dorn, E. Kirby Smith, George Stoneman, John B. Hood, and, of course, Jeb Stuart.

Jeb Stuart was born on February 6, 1833, in a large, comfortable house known as Laurel Hill in the country of southwestern Virginia, the seventh of eleven children, and the youngest boy. His father was not a wealthy man, and the house, land, and several dozen slaves at Laurel Hill had been inherited from his mother's side of the family.[15]

Always a splendid horseman, Jeb entered Emory and Henry College in 1848, but in 1850, he won an appointment to West Point. He did well academically there, made many friends, and graduated fourteenth in a class of forty-six in June 1854. During his first assignment, he and his men from the Mounted Rifles chased Mescalero Apaches and Comanches through the West Texas wilderness. He quickly learned that it was hard work requiring long patrols, and demanding a constant state of alertness.

The following summer he was reassigned to the First Cavalry Regiment at Fort Leavenworth, Kansas. But in July 1855, soon after he had arrived, he met his destiny: Flora Cooke, the beautiful twenty-year-old daughter of Lieutenant Colonel Philip St. George Cooke, the commander of the Second Cavalry Regiment. Stuart was immediately dazzled, and Flora clearly shared the attraction. After many long rides together, they were engaged in September and in November 1855 were married.

On July 29, 1857, Stuart was part of a cavalry charge directed at a band of some three hundred renegade Cheyenne warriors, and a pistol bullet from one of them was deflected by his sternum and lodged in his chest. The lead was later removed, but this moment marked him as a blooded warrior.

Between campaigns, Stuart also developed two inventions: a metal device to be attached to a leather halter that would allow a cavalryman to more quickly unhitch his horse before mounting, and a brass hook to be attached to cavalry saber belts that would allow the cavalryman, once mounted, to more readily detach his saber from his belt and re-attach it to the saddle. These inventions don't sound terribly complex, but the War Department granted Stewart six months' leave in 1859 to go to Washington, D.C., patent his inventions, and try to sell them to the army.

On October 17, 1859, he happened to be in the office of Secretary of War John B. Floyd when news of some kind of slave revolt at Harpers Ferry arrived. Harpers Ferry was the location of an arsenal and an armory, and the details of the violence were sketchy. Stuart immediately volunteered to take a summons to Colonel Robert E. Lee at Arlington, the plantation just across the river that he had inherited from his father-in-law and whose will he was then attempting to execute. Stuart delivered the summons, then immediately returned to the War Department with Lee. Though the facts remained unclear, it was evident that shots had been fired and the threat was more than could be handled by local forces alone. In an effort to jam a military thumb into the dike, the colonel and the lieutenant soon left Washington on a special train to meet a company of marines just outside Harpers Ferry.

After discussion of their options with Lee, Stuart approached the garage in which John Brown and his co-conspirators were holed up with hostages and demanded their surrender. When he was refused, he signaled the marines to attack, and within minutes they had overwhelmed the building and its occupants. John Brown was later tried and hanged, of course, but by then Stuart was back in Kansas, where he commanded Troop G, First Cavalry. He had made $5,000 from his inventions and had renewed friendships during his six-month trip east, including that he shared with Colonel Robert E. Lee.

At the beginning of May 1861, Stuart learned of the fight at Fort Sumter and that Virginia had seceded from the Union. He immediately left Fort Riley with his family, writing and posting his letter of resignation from the United States Army as they traveled south. Within a short time, he was a lieutenant colonel in the Confederate army.[16]

But Stuart wasn't the only bright young West Point–trained horseman to make his name and fame as a cavalry leader during the Civil War.

In 1840, George Armstrong Custer was born in New Rumley, Ohio. A gleeful blond with piercing blue eyes, George was a rough-and-tumble boy, a spark in the village and the bright light of his family. His older stepsister, Lydia-Ann, was especially taken with him, and she even made him a suit of velvet with brass buttons, a special outfit the young boy wore when his father took him along to militia meetings. But in 1850, life took an important turn.

Lydia-Ann had recently married David Reed, a very successful farmer who specialized in the horse business in Monroe, Michigan. Not too far north of the Ohio border, Monroe was renowned for its excellent school, the Stebbins Academy. Lydia pleaded with her parents to let George live with her so that he might get a first-rate education at Stebbins, an arrangement that would also ease Custer living arrangements back in New Rumley. And so it was that George got most of his education in Michigan before finally winning the political appointment to West Point that he had long coveted.

When Custer first arrived at the U.S. Military Academy, he embarked on a program that had recently been changed from four years to five, this largely at the urging of Secretary of War Jefferson Davis. He was sworn in on July 1, 1857, and so embarked on a somewhat harrowing voyage filled with trial and adventure, rigid discipline and earnest book-learning, and—at long last for him—formal exposure to the realities of military life and close instruction in the secrets of military success on the field of battle, where courage, flexibility, and audacity might carry the day. And this, truly, was Custer: *L'audace, toujours l'audace!*

His years at West Point are remembered primarily because of his not-easily-controlled youthful zeal, which sometimes caused him to stray beyond the bounds of permissible cadet behavior. Yes, he accumulated a large number of demerits for his violations of regulations. But he was young and full of mustard, and he was just the sort of tyro West Point hoped to mold into a skillful battlefield leader. Unruly behavior was expected at first, for that is the way of exuberant youth. But when he was caught in some infraction of the rules, Custer was punished, just as legion others before and after him were. He seemed to have come out no worse for the wear, however, and he learned.

Lincoln was elected president in November 1860, when Custer had begun his fourth year, and by January a number of states had seceded and others threatened to follow them. Then, on April 12, Fort Sumter was fired upon, and cadets from Southern states began to resign in order to join the still-nascent Confederate army. Custer's class reverted from a five-year course back to the traditional four years, and very quickly one class, having completed five years at West Point, graduated in May 1861, while his class graduated a month later, in June 1861.

Custer's academic performance has long been criticized, but this can be a confusing issue. It is true that, at graduation, he was ranked thirty-fourth out of thirty-four graduates. But it is important to remember that he had started as one of seventy-nine members of the class, and during their four years at West Point, twenty-two resigned to join the Confederacy while twenty-three fell by the wayside, most of them for academic reasons. So saying he was "last in his class" is somewhat misleading, to say the least. Class rank was determined by the "General Order of Merit," of which academic performance was the most important component. But other factors, such as the large number of demerits Custer accumulated, also weighed heavily against cadets in the determination of their class rank. Custer's academic performance at

West Point, therefore, might be better captured by the simple statement that he had survived a most demanding experience.

And even after graduation on June 24, he learned that the petty harassment endured. While awaiting his army assignment, Custer was serving as "Officer of the Guard" at West Point one June evening, and as such, he had general responsibility for the adherence to regulations by all cadets. While making his duty rounds of West Point that evening, he was attracted to some noise that turned out to be a fistfight between two cadet candidates, with a large crowd of other cadets and cadet candidates cheering them on. Rather than end the fight, as was his responsibility, he told the observers to stand back a bit, to give the combatants some room so that there might be a fairer fight.

The fighting resumed, with Custer watching, when two officers senior to Custer suddenly stepped out of the shadows. The cadets disappeared like smoke in the wind, but Custer, the officer of the guard, stayed where he was. He was duly reported, of course, then waited to face a court-martial. And while that may sound serious, in the nineteenth century courts-martial were common for cadets, even for minimal offenses such as this.

Had this occurred during peacetime, there is little doubt that Custer would have ended up with a conviction and a minor blot on his record. But the nation was at war with itself, and every young officer was needed to train and lead the mobilized American masses. After a brief period of detention, the court-martial heard testimony from both sides, then found there were insufficient grounds for a conviction and released Custer to the war. He arrived in Washington, D.C., on July 20, 1861, reported to the adjutant general, and through a fluke of fate, he also met with Winfield Scott, the Mexican War hero who was then the commanding general of the United States Army.

# ~ 4 ~

# *Classic Battles of History*

BECAUSE OF THE ROLE PLAYED in it by railroads, steamships, longer-range rifled muskets and artillery pieces, and a generally robust national industrial power, the U.S. Civil War has often been described as the first "modern" war. In that sense, it is often seen as being more akin to World War I than to the Napoleonic Wars that preceded it by only decades. The next obvious question then becomes why we should believe that the military nostrums of Antoine Henri Jomini, drawn primarily from the examples of Napoleon himself, were applied by Lee and other military commanders on both sides of the Civil War. And the answer is very simple: West Pointers applied what they knew, and the works of Jomini and Dennis Hart Mahan and other histories of the Napoleonic Wars were what they had learned.

This point is addressed by Paddy Griffith, a faculty member at the Royal Military Academy, Sandhurst, England, in *Battle Tactics of the Civil War*. In that work, Griffith shows that new, more lethal weaponry, for instance, had virtually no effect on the combatants on either side, who doggedly continued to mimic Napoleon and his armies as closely as possible. Indeed, in his conclusion he even refers to the Civil War as "the Last Napoleonic War."[1]

From 1853, an English translation of Jomini's famous text *The Art of War* was used for instruction at West Point. Earlier partial translations had long been in use, as had much of the entire text in the original French (all cadets in those days studied the French language intensively). That book includes extensive discussion of twenty-four battles from earlier times, including the battles of Cannae, Leuthen, and Austerlitz. Widely accepted in modern times as three of the four greatest battlefield victories in history (the fourth, Alexander the Great at Gaugamela, will be briefly treated later), they were the apogee victories of Hannibal, Frederick the Great, and Napoleon respectively. Lee would have been exposed to them first at West Point, then continued and intensified his reading on these and other battles as he grew into a mature professional. In those days before television and movies, of course, many Americans read in the evening, and while military history was of cardinal importance to military professionals, to the rare soldier like Lee, who was also an intellectual, it was life's very blood.

From his study of Napoleon, Lee was to learn that a commander who wants to retain strategic flexibility and control will generally seek to be on the offensive, for being on the defensive entails certain restrictions and limitations to his possible actions that are not always optimal. In other words, awaiting the attack of an adversary rather than initiating such an attack places the commander in a reactive rather than an active mode, and allowing an adversary to establish where and how a battle will be fought is usually not a good thing.

In this regard, Napoleon had also warned against the fatal attraction of a fortress, an important guideline observed by Lee whenever possible. Nonetheless, when Meade arrived at Gettysburg and faced the enormous military reputation that Lee had built up, he preferred the safety and security of a strong defensive posture rather than the risk of the offensive. But when Lee found that Meade was firmly rooted to his defensive lines in the shape of a giant fishhook at Gettysburg, and that he would be allowed to operate relatively freely outside them, he saw his chance for true triumph.

I believe Lee planned his attack against Union troops at Gettysburg on July 3, 1863, by drawing on his broad base of knowledge of the battlefield performances of the Great Captains. I further believe he used key elements from three specific battles in his plan: Cannae, Leuthen, and Austerlitz. Because I propose that Lee sought a triumphant victory at Gettysburg similar to these three, it is important that readers know more about them in order to understand some of the military history Lee had to draw on when he planned his battlefield actions.

## Cannae

During the Punic Wars, Hannibal, king of Carthage and ruler of Spain, steadily improved the quality of the Carthaginian army, then led it into southern France, over the Alps, and down into today's Italy. There, he repeatedly fought and defeated Roman armies in great battles, bringing Rome close to collapse. The most important of these battles was that of Cannae in 216 B.C.

An army of 70,000 Romans made up of some 56,000 hoplites, or heavy infantry, 8,000 light infantry sharpshooters, and 6,000 cavalry challenged Hannibal. His Carthaginian army consisted of only about 22,000 heavily equipped hoplites, 8,000 sharpshooters, and 10,000 cavalry. When the two armies faced each other, the Romans were arrayed in a rigid phalanx—64,000 armored soldiers standing side by side, many rows deep, their front covered by a row of shields from which loomed menacing lances—and 3,000 cavalry covered each flank.

Hannibal's center facing the Roman phalanx was made up of 20,000 Iberian and Celtic hoplites, and their line seemed to bulge forward at the center toward the Roman army. He had both flanks covered by cavalry, with more than 7,000 of his 10,000 horse on his left flank under Hasdrubal. And concealed behind the cavalry formations on

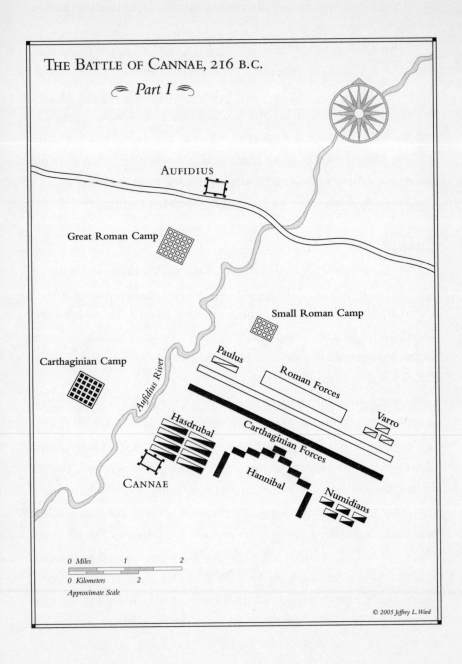

THE BATTLE OF CANNAE, 216 B.C.

Part I

AUFIDIUS

Great Roman Camp

Small Roman Camp

Carthaginian Camp

Aufidius River

Paulus

Roman Forces

Varro

Hasdrubal

Carthaginian Forces

CANNAE

Hannibal

Numidians

0  Miles          1          2

0  Kilometers        2

Approximate Scale

© 2005 Jeffrey L. Ward

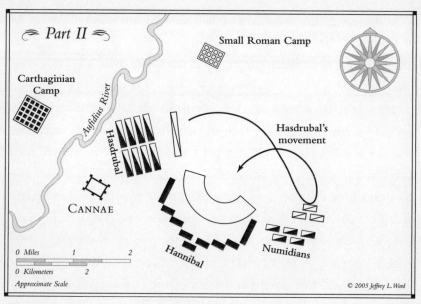

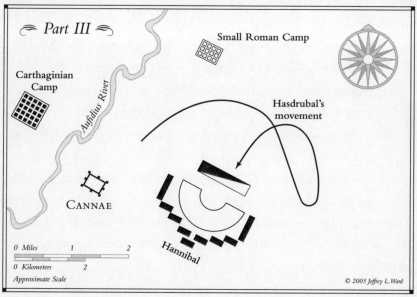

each flank were columns of 5,000 African hoplites, Hannibal's best foot soldiers.

At the outset, the Romans marched forward and attacked the center of Hannibal's line, and the Carthaginians steadily gave ground. Soon enough, the Carthaginian line that had started as convex became concave, and as it fell back, it drew the Roman phalanx between the two columns of African hoplites. Then Hasdrubal attacked the Roman cavalry unit before him on the Roman right flank, a force of only 3,000 against his 7,000. He quickly crushed it and drove its remnants off, then raced around the back of the Roman formation, which was still moving ponderously forward, and attacked the Roman cavalry contingent of 3,000 on the other flank from the rear while it was engaged from the front with the other body of Carthaginian cavalry. Hasdrubal's now-united force of 10,000 quickly killed or scattered the rest of the Roman cavalry, then turned to the rear of the Roman phalanx. Meanwhile, the African hoplites had turned inward on the Roman flanks and launched their own attacks. When the cavalry attacked the rear and sealed it off, they had accomplished the seemingly impossible: the complete double envelopment of a force of 70,000 by a force of 40,000.

As Carthaginian horsemen smashed into the Roman rear, the phalanx ground to a massive, rigid halt. Roman soldiers in the outer ranks turned outward and fought for survival. But their cause was hopeless: because of their weapons, only those on the outside could engage the enveloping forces. For the Carthaginians, on the other hand, virtually every projectile they launched hit a Roman soldier. The Romans were slaughtered that day. Perhaps 8,000 organized themselves and broke out, but only a few prisoners were taken. Cannae was the military high-water mark for Hannibal.

The most decisive factor in the victory was Hannibal's cavalry. Though larger in numbers than the Roman mounted force, it was the skill in their use and their speed and shock value that really won the day. After the very brief time it took them to wreck the Roman cavalry, they then smashed into the undefended backs of the Roman foot soldiers. These men had expected to fight only against a smaller number of Carthaginian foot soldiers in front of them, and the sudden violent attack launched against their unprotected backs by enemy soldiers on horseback had to be the realization of the Roman soldier's worst nightmares.

Cannae is important to us in our study of Gettysburg because it shows how Hannibal was able to completely surround a much larger Roman force (40,000 against 70,000, as compared with Lee's 74,000 facing 90,000 Union troops at Gettysburg) and then defeat it, with the key blow being launched by Hasdrubal's cavalry, who slammed the door and then crushed the Roman rear.

## Leuthen

On December 6, 1757, Prince Charles and his 60,000 Austrians were arrayed in a line of defense, facing west in hilly country. Their left wing was considered weaker because of the terrain, and so their large reserve was positioned behind their left flank, against which they expected Frederick to maneuver because of the open ground. Cavalry protected both flanks.

The army of Frederick the Great, some 36,000 Prussians, approached the Austrian front in a column pointed directly at the Austrian right wing. Deception was the key to this battle, and Frederick wanted the Austrians to believe he would attack there, and it seemed to work: as the Prussians got closer, the Austrians quickly moved their reserve from their left wing to their right wing. But the Prussians would continually slip from view behind hills as they moved in as if to attack, then reappear. On one of these disappearances, Frederick diverted most of the column to the right and marched it straight across the Austrian front, though out of sight. A small force continued to

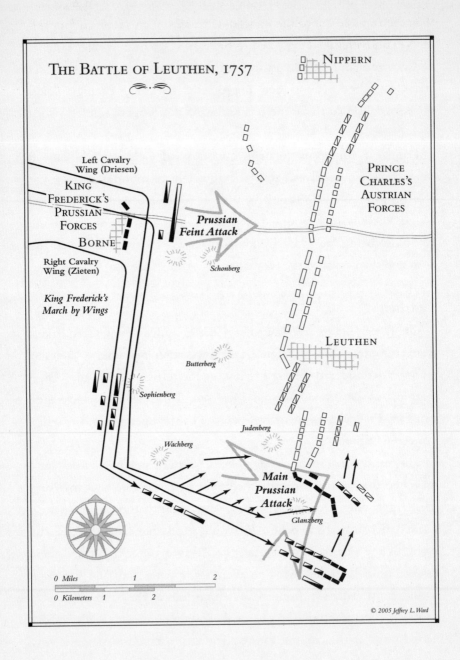

THE BATTLE OF LEUTHEN, 1757

NIPPERN

Left Cavalry
Wing (Driesen)

KING
FREDERICK'S
PRUSSIAN
FORCES

BORNE

*Prussian
Feint Attack*

PRINCE
CHARLES'S
AUSTRIAN
FORCES

Schonberg

Right Cavalry
Wing (Zieten)

*King Frederick's
March by Wings*

LEUTHEN

Butterberg

Sophienberg

Judenberg

Wachberg

*Main
Prussian
Attack*

Glanzberg

0 Miles 1 2
0 Kilometers 1 2

© 2005 Jeffrey L. Ward

march toward the Austrian right wing while the concealed force approached the Austrian left wing, which they suddenly overwhelmed. The stunned defenders of that area simply fell apart as Prussian artillery smashed their center defenses and Prussian cavalry poured through the broken Austrian left wing, pressing it back into the center.

Prince Charles tried to throw the cavalry from his right flank against this force that had surprised his left flank, but they were intercepted by a Prussian cavalry force and badly beaten. Meanwhile, the smaller Prussian force still marching toward the Austrian right wing was counterattacked at first, but then met little resistance as the Austrian army just folded.

Both armies suffered about 6,000 casualties, but the Austrian army had simply dissolved: 20,000 prisoners were taken, 116 guns captured, and all the other Austrian soldiers were routed. Five days after the battle, Breslau surrendered, which ended the campaign. This victory is considered to have been the masterpiece of Frederick the Great, whom many hold to be the most able tactician in military history.

Leuthen is important to us in our study of Gettysburg because it shows how Frederick the Great was able to deceive the commander of the much larger army: Prince Charles believed the Prussian attack would be made at one point and so shifted his defenses there. When the main attack was then made at the opposite extreme in his adversary's defensive line, this major surprise was key to the Prussian victory over an army twice the size of their own. This was an action I believe (as I will show) Lee attempted to replicate in part at Gettysburg.

## Austerlitz

In late November 1805, Napoleon was one hundred miles north of Vienna with his headquarters in the town of Brunn. He was at war with the Russians and the Austrians, and had spent the past few months pursuing and defeating smaller Austrian armies. But now he was going

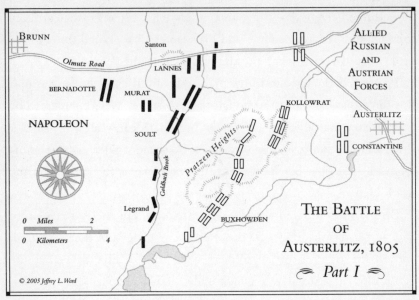

BRUNN

Olmutz Road

Santon

LANNES

BERNADOTTE

MURAT

SOULT

NAPOLEON

*Pratzen Heights*

*Goldbach Brook*

Legrand

BUXHOWDEN

KOLLOWRAT

ALLIED
RUSSIAN
AND
AUSTRIAN
FORCES

AUSTERLITZ

CONSTANTINE

0    Miles    2

0    Kilometers    4

© 2005 Jeffrey L. Ward

THE BATTLE
OF
AUSTERLITZ, 1805

⌒ *Part I* ⌒

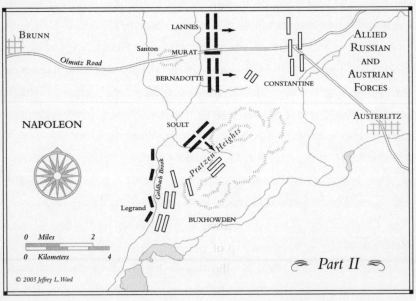

LANNES

BRUNN

Olmutz Road

Santon

MURAT

BERNADOTTE

CONSTANTINE

ALLIED
RUSSIAN
AND
AUSTRIAN
FORCES

NAPOLEON

SOULT

*Pratzen Heights*

*Goldbach Brook*

AUSTERLITZ

Legrand

BUXHOWDEN

0    Miles    2

0    Kilometers    4

© 2005 Jeffrey L. Ward

⌒ *Part II* ⌒

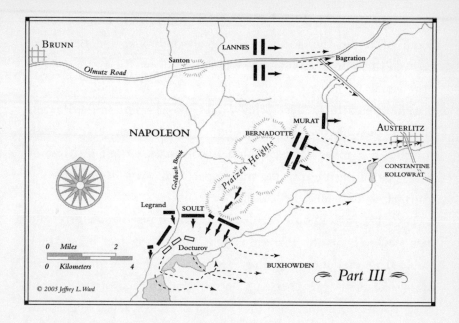

after big game: a combined Russian and Austrian army that was considerably larger than his own.

When he received news that the Allied army was coming toward him from the east on the road to Olmutz, he carefully examined the territory along that road for the ten miles or so between Brunn and the town of Austerlitz. He had a force of 73,000, and would face 86,000 Russians and Austrians.

Napoleon carefully looked for favorable ground on which to meet and defeat the advancing Allies, and he finally selected an area four miles east of Brunn, where, just south of the road, a large hill rose some seven hundred feet. This was known as the Santon, and it had a relatively flat and almost circular top of perhaps a mile in diameter. To the southeast of the Santon was an elliptical plateau of about the same elevation as the Santon, known as the Pratzen Heights, that ran perhaps three miles north and south and a mile or so east and west.

The Santon was to be his strongpoint, on top of and behind which he placed most of his army, to include his artillery and cavalry reserves. South of it ran the north-south Goldbach brook, and he placed Legrand's division of 6,000 men on the west side of that stream and less than a mile from the dominating Pratzen Heights. Napoleon hoped that the approaching Allied army would take position on the Pratzen Heights, then discover his weak southern deployment—one division covering two miles—and launch a major attack against it. Most of Napoleon's army, meanwhile, was hidden from view in his left-wing rear area, on or behind the Santon.

The Allies arrived on December 1, observed Napoleon's force, and then deployed on the Pratzen Heights, just as he had hoped they would. Late that afternoon, they began to adjust their forces so that nearly half their army ended up on the southern end of the Pratzen Heights, an area from which they would obviously attack Legrand in the morning. As Napoleon watched their movement through a telescope, he was almost beside himself with joy, for they had taken the bait.

Dawn on December 2 brought thick mists along the Goldbach, which suited Napoleon perfectly. He immediately deployed the divisions of Vandamme and St. Hilaire along the Goldbach just below the Santon where they waited, well hidden. Within a few hours, Napoleon's scouts told him that some 40,000 Allies were moving down off the Heights to attack Legrand. Davout's division of 6,000 had arrived during the night and reinforced Legrand, but these 12,000 Frenchmen were steadily pushed back by this Allied force. As soon as he was sure the Allied attack force had come down to the level of the Goldbach, Napoleon threw two divisions forward to occupy the center of the Heights. But the last 15,000 Russians under Kollowrat weren't quite gone as the French arrived, and a fierce fight ensued. Within an hour, however, this last Allied remnant collapsed and the French surged forward to truly divide the Allied army in twain. And at that moment, even though a hard day of fighting remained in both the north and the south, Napoleon's triumphant victory was as good as won.

This was the moment he had awaited, and Napoleon lost no time in hurling the corps of Soult and Bernadotte, along with the 7,000 horsemen in Murat's cavalry reserve, into this new opening in the enemy center. He kept Lannes's corps in place on the Santon, and soon enough its massed artillery hammered back a secondary attack there by the Allies. Bernadotte and Murat, meanwhile, turned north to hit the northern segment of the Allied army in the flank while Soult turned south and hit that wing of the Allies in the rear. As the Allies in the north realized what was happening and turned south to face this new attack, Lannes's corps smashed into them from the west.

Napoleon then sent in part of his reserve, Oudinot's division of 6,000 grenadiers along with 6,000 members of the Imperial Guard, to help his southern wing. Soon enough, the Allies in that area found themselves surrounded, with their only path of retreat leading across a frozen lake in their rear. All seemed lost to them as the French pressed in, and many Allied units tried that route of escape. But French artillery fire broke the ice, causing perhaps 2,000 Allied soldiers to drown and only adding to the confusion.

In the north, meanwhile, heavy attacks from front and flank had eventually worn down the Allied army, but as they retreated, they were fiercely pursued by the Imperial Guard cavalry under Nansouty and other elements of Murat's cavalry reserve. But the French army was exhausted, and many Allies got away. Still, there were perhaps 11,000 Russians and 4,000 Austrians left dead on the battlefield, and another 12,000 were captured. This total of 27,000 men lost to the Allied army amounted to nearly a third of the army that had taken the field earlier that day, and there were doubtless many additional thousands of wounded Allies who managed to get away but would be of no further military value. The French numbers were much better, as they lost only

1,300 killed, 7,000 wounded, and perhaps another 500 men lost as prisoners. But the political outcome was most important to Napoleon, and this triumphant close to the campaign of 1805 had brought the Third Coalition to its knees. Other countries would think long and hard in the future before joining alliances against France, at least as long as Napoleon was still there to lead his Grande Armée against them.

The Allies were overly confident at the Battle of Austerlitz because they knew that they outnumbered the French force, and the facts that Napoleon was far from Paris and challenging them on their home territory only added to their self-deception. Their attack plan was based on this overconfidence and on a miscalculation about Napoleon's seemingly weak right wing. The fact that Napoleon encouraged them in this view does not excuse them from the rashness of their actions and the subsequent total destruction of their force that they brought upon themselves.

Austerlitz is important to us in our study of Gettysburg because it shows how Napoleon was able to divide a larger adversary force into two segments and defeat them in detail. I believe Lee attempted something similar on July 3.

# 5

# Infantry, Artillery, and Cavalry in the Last Napoleonic War

AS MENTIONED EARLIER, all West Point graduates who
fought in the Civil War had learned about Napoleon at West
Point, where his methods had been strongly promoted by Professor
Mahan and other officers considered to be authorities by cadets. Since
almost all major armies on both sides were led by West Point graduates,
it should come as no surprise that they applied the tactics, strategies,
and methods of Napoleon, or what they believed them to be, as much
as possible. While discussing the three spheres of the battlefield army
during the Civil War, therefore—the infantry, the artillery, the cavalry,
and how they acted and interrelated—it seems appropriate that we
should also investigate their use during Napoleon's day and try to make
some comparisons.

In both wars, infantry was the arm of decision in which the great
bulk of soldiers served. Normally slow moving but steady and reliable,
the infantry had two basic formations: column and line. They normally
moved on roads or cross-country in columns, then deployed to fight in
long lines of riflemen standing side by side, usually several ranks deep.
Such formations were able to deliver mass fire against targets to their

front, when all the muskets or rifles in the unit could be used, and were lethal at up to two hundred yards in Napoleon's day, eight hundred yards in the Civil War. Taking enemy fire from their flank or rear, of course, was to be avoided at all costs. This was not only because they were unable to return it, but also because of the great psychological effect such flanking fire could have on unit cohesion, which was often a function of unit esprit.

Another Napoleonic specialty was building unit esprit, something he did with "light" as opposed to "line" infantry. Though carrying the same weapons, light infantry became known for its speed and aggressiveness, being rewarded with special blue uniforms and the right to lead all attacks. He also established units based on his soldiers' height— Grenadiers and the Imperial Guard were made up of tall men, while the similarly elite Voltigeurs (which means "vaulters") were all less than five feet tall but quick and agile in battle.[1] They also were very skilled at placing their hand or hands on the hindquarters of a horse and then vaulting up onto it to either attack the enemy rider or catch a free ride from a French horseman (compare the vault and our pommel horse, where the handles represent the saddle, in modern gymnastic competition).

In the American armies of both sides during the Civil War, there were a few attempts at such specialization. Small units of sharpshooters were often effective in their long-range fire,[2] though they usually wore no special patches or other uniform distinction. But the most colorful organization on either side was modeled on the ideas of Charles Ellsworth, who organized a group of Zouave cadets in Chicago in 1859. He sought to introduce recently acquired abilities of infantry *chasseurs à pied* (pursuers on foot) that were popular in France to his cadets and raise their competence in those areas to the highest level. These differences from normal infantry units included practiced and therefore accurate long-range fire with rifled muskets, regular movement of the well-conditioned men in the unit at the *pas gymnastique,* or a steady jog, and certain gymnastic routines.

At the outbreak of the Civil War, Zouave units sprang up on both sides, easily noted by their baggy red pants and red caps known as "kepis." The uniforms and the name came from Algeria, a French colony, while the drills came from French army *chasseurs.* In rather short order, the distinctive physical conditioning and marksmanship skills fell by the wayside in most Zouave units, but many of them continued to wear the red pants and caps for the duration of the war.[3]

The only truly elite infantry units in the Civil War were those that earned renown by their actions in combat. Of particular note in the Confederate army was the Stonewall Brigade, made up of five Virginia regiments whose men were drawn primarily from the Shenandoah Valley. This unit served at what Confederates called the First Battle of Manassas, where, as General Bee said just before his death, they were "standing like a stone wall," thus earning the nickname "Stonewall" for their commander, General Thomas Jackson. In the Union army, the most elite unit was probably the Iron Brigade, which was made up of "western" men in regiments raised in Wisconsin, Michigan, and Indiana. The Iron Brigade wore black hats, but no other special pay, uniform, or formal recognition was accorded either unit by their armies. Their reputations for courage and ferocity, however, were widely acknowledged.

One infantry formation worth noting is the square. If a battalion of five hundred foot soldiers, for instance, was attacked by cavalry during the Napoleonic Wars, they would quickly form an outward-facing square, with each of the four sides made up of 125 men arrayed in ranks. The front rank would normally kneel, and there would be another one to five ranks of men lined up behind them, all pointing their bayonet-tipped muskets outward. This was done because a line of infantrymen, while very deadly to anyone in front of them, would find themselves the helpless victims of any force attacking them from the flank or rear, particularly high-speed cavalry. The square was formed because it automatically eliminated the flank and rear that were most vulnerable, with the added benefit that it is very difficult to get a horse to charge into a row of men standing shoulder to shoulder and extending bayonet-tipped muskets. But even if a large mass of horsemen was able to do that, volleys fired by each row in turn at the cavalry force as it approached one side of the square were lethal and would usually stop the attack.

During the Napoleonic Wars, large masses of cavalry were a very common sight on the battlefield, and they were a very important arm of the commander. When a mass of five or six thousand heavy cavalry, huge horses ridden by men wearing steel helmets and cuirass body armor, came thundering toward an infantry unit in what must have seemed an unstoppable mass, it was a terrifying and effective weapon. And even if the infantrymen were able to form squares, there were other tactics we will see later that could quickly strip them of their seeming safety and once again open them to attack by cavalry.

Infantry units on all sides during the Napoleonic Wars were well drilled in forming squares, and since their lives often literally depended on it, they were able to do so very quickly. This movement was part of the drill in the American army before the Civil War, and the Regular Army units practiced it, as did many of the militia units that were formed. But with the limited threat of cavalry attacking infantry during the American Civil War, it was seldom used.

Muzzle-loading muskets or rifled muskets were standard in both the Napoleonic and American civil wars, though percussion caps replaced the flintlocks and the Minié ball made loading and firing somewhat easier and more accurate for the Americans. Though lines delivered more firepower, columns were more easily controlled, and Napoleon eventually developed what he called a "mixed order," which consisted of a loose group of skirmishers or infantry in line followed into battle by heavy columns of infantry. In both wars, long lines of infantry facing forward were virtually helpless against fire from their side, and fire into their rear tended to spark panic. In both wars and on both sides in the Civil War, infantry forces were reliable, powerful, and durable when not worked or marched or bled to the point of physical exhaustion.

Artillery often played a crucial role in battle. Cannon were very heavy and slow-moving, but once in place and well serviced, they could put out quite a bit of destructive firepower. The cannon in both wars fired solid cannonballs, exploding shells, and, at shorter ranges of less than four hundred to six hundred yards, canister or grapeshot against attacking infantry or cavalry. Canister rounds were cylindrical canisters containing from twenty-seven to forty-eight cast-iron shot, which were basically the same as musket balls. When the round was fired, the canister split open and individual shot would burst from the mouth of the cannon like the projectiles of a giant shotgun. Grape was larger shot, and was originally developed for use against ships. During the Civil War, rifled cannon far outranged their Napoleonic counterparts; at Gettysburg about half the guns on both sides were smoothbores, and half were rifled.[4]

In the best case, ten artillerymen were needed to service each piece, as the guns had no recoil mechanisms and so leaped from their emplacements with each shot, after which they had to be rolled or lifted back into position and carefully relayed. There was a standard drill for laying, sponging out, sighting, loading, fusing, and firing an artillery piece, after the recoil of which the crew would relay the piece and repeat the cycle.[5]

Although ten men were assigned, as few as three or four could handle a gun in a pinch, though at a much slower rate of fire. But great difficulties would be faced by a smaller crew simply because of the weight of the cumbersome pieces and their carriages and the need to relay a gun after every shot fired.

Each gun would normally have from ten to twenty men assigned as its crew, and while many of these men had primary duties of handling and moving ammunition and the horses, caissons, and other wagons that might be involved, they also were trained to fill the roles of various members of the ten-man gun crew. This was important in the not-unusual event that counter-battery or other hostile fire knocked out all or part of the crew but left the gun intact. If that happened, other gun crew members could quickly step in and fulfill the required tasks of the casualties so that the gun could continue to fire.

These artillery gun crews normally carried no side arms in the Civil War, which would have been quite cumbersome. And for all save horse-drawn artillery gun crews operating with the cavalry, such personal protection was virtually never needed, since artillery pieces were normally placed behind friendly infantry lines and thus were well protected from personal threats presented by enemy infantrymen.

During the Civil War, there was no "heavy" armored cavalry, an important battle force in Napoleon's time. The vulnerability of steel helmets or cuirasses to Minié balls is not the reason for this, as heavy cavalry was used by both sides in the Franco-Prussian War of 1870. And these forces were used in that war despite the facts that both armies were armed with rapid-firing breech-loading weapons and that the French had developed a machine gun with a range of two thousand yards and a rate of fire of 150 rounds per minute.[6]

In fact, although some charges made by cavalry units in the Franco-Prussian War were bloody failures, they also sometimes won the day. The last successful cavalry charge in Europe was probably that made by von Bredow's Prussian brigade on August 16, 1870, near Vionville, France. He was ordered to lead his men in a charge against French guns that were pounding the Prussian left flank, guns that were well supported by infantry. Using a depression to mask their approach, the eight hundred cavalrymen were not even seen by the French until they appeared out of the battlefield smoke at a dead run with only hundreds of yards to go. The French did not have time for any organized return fire, and the horsemen quickly overran the gun line, driving the terrified infantry before them. They were stopped only when their flank was hit by two brigades of French cavalry, an envelopment out of which they literally had to cut their way. But this cavalry attack stopped the French advance and saved the Prussian left wing for a period, although at a steep price: only 420 horsemen made it back to their own lines from what was later described as "von Bredow's Death Ride."[7]

Both sides in the Civil War used units of armed horsemen for the traditional "light cavalry" missions: scouting, reconnaissance, raids, screening of forces, pursuit of retreating infantry, turning a line of infantry, or (worst imaginable fate for infantry fighting to their front) attacking infantry from the rear.

Cavalry forces on both sides were based on the squadron formation, which consisted of two companies, or about two hundred men, and they were usually formed in squares. These were not the hollow squares of the infantry, however, but solid masses of horsemen. Since horses are longer than they are wide, such a square consisted of a front of about twenty horses, which was ten horses deep, though commanders could make them wider or deeper as required. For movement, both sides formed easily maneuvered columns of squadrons, which basically meant they lined up one behind the other, like the cars of a railroad train. For attacks in open areas, they shifted into lines of squadrons, in which they were aligned side by side—not unlike the same railroad cars if they could leave their rails and move sideways. Such formations could sweep destruction across a wide swath of terrain, but it was also very easy to lose control of them.

Cavalrymen on both sides in the Civil War carried light weapons (sabers, multi-shot revolvers, carbines) and their primary mission was mounted, although they could dismount and fight on the ground in a limited way (carbines have a shorter range and are less accurate than infantry rifles, and they mount no bayonets for close-in fighting). When mounted, cavalry units would not generally attack a group of infantrymen who faced them in ranks and might fire at them in volleys, though they regularly panicked and destroyed the cohesion of infantry units they attacked from the side or rear.

And their use of revolvers gave them a new deadliness unknown in earlier times. During Napoleon's day, cavalrymen carried "horse pistols," which fired a devastating single shot but were notoriously inaccurate and virtually impossible to reload while mounted and moving. But by the summer of 1863, even Confederate cavalrymen were armed with revolvers, often arms that had been captured from Union supply wagons, the most common type of which was the six-shot Colt .44. Armed with these multi-shot death-dealing weapons, a cavalryman was now a much bigger threat to infantrymen, whose single-shot rifled muskets took twenty to thirty seconds to reload. The only exception to this new lethality delivered by mounted troops against foot soldiers would be the case when the horsemen confronted an infantry formation massed in several rows and firing in volleys. Even armed with multi-shot revolvers, no sane cavalryman would want to charge against such a front, though such charges did occur, some of them successfully, others less so.

By the time of the Battle of Gettysburg, much of the Union cavalry was armed with rapid-fire repeating rifles or carbines, which were two different weapons. As the war dragged on, of course, this superior armament would play an increasingly important role, though cavalrymen had to be careful not to shoot up all their ammunition, which happened too often. Handicapped industrially, the South was never able to produce a repeating rifle or carbine in sufficient quantities to arm an entire unit.

The cavalry's great potential strengths were shock and mobility, which allowed them to make rapid assaults or even to capture key ground, though they would have difficulty controlling it against an infantry counterattack unless supported by their own infantry. Early in the war, neither side used cavalry in these traditional European ways, though after a few years they began to do so, particularly the Union.

Most soldiers assigned to Union cavalry units early in the war were dreadfully incompetent horsemen, and Stuart and his legendary cavalrymen, widely renowned in both North and South as the "Invincibles," usually just ignored them. As newspapers began to follow the fighting, Stuart loved basking in their limelight, and rather than attacking infantry frontally and losing valuable riders, as had happened to him at Bull Run, he much preferred launching raids deep into the Union rear. These raids, he soon learned, brought him personal fame and glory and sent wildfires of naked terror leaping across the North through inflammatory newspaper stories. The newspapers, of course, wanting most to sell copies, only fanned the flames of fear. But unfortunately, these colorful raids meant that Confederate cavalry was not often used in its conventional Napoleonic role, that of attacking en masse and supporting infantry as an important battlefield weapon.

Griffith makes an interesting analogy, that of Civil War cavalry raids to the World War II bombing of cities. He notes that what began as a temporary diversion of German bombing from the battlefront and military targets ended up, as the Allies responded, to a more or less permanent state of affairs, from Dresden to Nagasaki. So, too, in modeling Stuart, the Union cavalry sacrificed much of its potential battlefield use by going on colorful but militarily useless raids deep into enemy territory.

Though infantry, cavalry, and artillery bore a sort of rock–scissors–paper relationship to one another—in other words, under the right circumstances any of them could trump one or both of the other two—some possible shift in this had begun to surface by the summer of 1863. Having observed the successful tactics of Nathan Bedford Forrest in the West, Lee was well aware of his use of mounted infantry as a replacement for both cavalry and infantry: they carried the longer rifles and bayonets of infantrymen, while horses gave them far greater range and mobility. Upon arrival at the battlefield, these soldiers generally dismounted and fought as infantry, although they could also perform limited cavalry operations.

But even if Lee had wanted to model Forrest on a large scale, he simply did not have a reliable source of horseflesh on which to mount large numbers of infantrymen. He did, however, have one brigade of mounted infantry with him at Gettysburg, and that was Jenkins's brigade. When Stuart received his mission to go out the York Pike in a northeasterly direction for several miles on July 3, he also was given Jenkins's brigade of 1,000 mounted infantrymen to add to his three-cavalry brigades of 5,000. Jenkins's brigade was armed with the new Enfield rifle and sword bayonets that had been purchased from England and shipped through the less-than-perfect naval embargo of Confederate seaports. When dismounted and deployed thus armed, Jenkins's brigade could be a fearsome infantry foe.

To demonstrate the different uses of these three mutually supportive branches of a war-fighting army during the Napoleonic wars and the American Civil War, let us look at how Napoleon would typically fight a battle.

His troops were formed in *corps d'armée,* each made up of several divisions that included all arms—infantry, artillery, and cavalry—and they would thus be able to fight on their own independently with no immediate need for support. When he began a campaign, Napoleon almost always chose to attack, even when his force was smaller than that of his enemy. This allowed him to dictate the battle, while his opponent would have to react quickly just to survive. But before a campaign started, he had made the most thorough preparation possible, including consideration of all possible actions or reactions of an adversary under a long list of possible developments.[8]

Another Napoleonic marker was the way in which he spread his troops out while moving toward the enemy. Other armies of the period moved with long trains of wagons carrying their supplies, particularly food for the men and grain for the horses. But this cumbersome tail dramatically slowed army movements, and Napoleon decided that his army would live off the land.

In order to do so, his units had to spread out over a certain area so that they could forage without denuding the countryside. But he very carefully kept his units within a day's march of him, using architectural dividers set at twenty kilometers on the map as he made his plans and moved his forces. When contact was made with the enemy, deployed units could reassemble from many directions and fall on the unsuspecting enemy like a bag of rocks. This maneuver has been called the "Napoleonic Fan," which is spread open while moving but then comes together in a sudden, crushing set of movements to kill the fly that has inadvertently been caught in the web.[9]

In a typical Napoleonic battle his army would be moving in a fan when one of his corps would strike a main enemy force. This corps would immediately launch an all-out attack, even if it faced a much larger army, as its goal was to pin the adversary in place. Other corps would join the fight as they came up, and with the battle growing, Napoleon would send an enveloping force of a corps or more to a point in the foe's rear or flank. Once there, it remained concealed while awaiting the signal to attack, and only after his adversary had committed his reserve did Napoleon launch this usually crushing blow.

Determining the right time to commit these forces through the noise and smoke of battle was a crucial act of generalship at which Napoleon excelled. Few adversaries would survive this *manœuvre sur les derrières* (maneuver on the hindquarters), Bonaparte's favorite battlefield tactic. Designed to crush an opponent who was foolish enough to have gotten too far away from an Allied army to be rescued, it was used by Napoleon no fewer than thirty times between 1796 and 1815.[10]

Whenever possible, Napoleon also used all three arms on each battlefield. If we look at the sort of frontal attack he normally launched against an enemy line, Napoleon would move his forces toward it behind a cavalry screen. Once the location of the enemy's line of infantry had been confirmed, he would rush a large number of massed artillery forward to within about five hundred yards and use them to hammer the enemy. This artillery barrage was a major attack, and he commonly used fifty to one hundred guns to soften up the enemy from short range.

As large openings were being ripped in the defenses, Napoleon's infantry would hurry forward and charge in with the bayonet. At the same time, clouds of cavalry would race past the French guns, forcing the enemy to form squares and so dramatically reduce their firepower against the attack. Horse-drawn artillery would also move forward and, once confronted by an enemy square, blast gaping holes in its sides with canister, holes into which French cavalry or infantry would pour, killing or capturing the enemy soldiers who did not flee.[11] The coordination of these attacks was of crucial importance, but Napoleon was the true battlefield master, and few stood up to his onslaught.

## ~ 6 ~

# The Fighting Begins

AFTER VIRGINIA and the other upper South states had seceded, the new nation's capital was moved to Richmond, Virginia, the most populous state in the Confederacy. Thereafter, the Civil War was to be fought in two wholly different theaters of operation: the East, meaning Virginia, with brief forays into Maryland and Pennsylvania; and the West, a much larger area that ranged through the Tennessee and Mississippi valleys.

The first major battle in the Civil War occurred in northern Virginia, remembered today as the First Battle of Manassas (Confederate) or the First Battle of Bull Run (Union). While Lee was not there and Custer only watched, Jeb Stuart led his first charge of the war.

Both armies intended to attack, but the Union forces made the first move. The Confederates were on the southern side of Bull Run, a steeply banked stream that could be crossed only on bridges or at fords. On July 21, Union forces crossed that stream at several points and drove the Rebels back. Their commanders were able to draw back to the high ground of Henry Hill, where they found General Stonewall Jackson and his brigade in a strong defensive position, which they joined.

Around two o'clock, the Union attack opened, but it was less than overwhelming. Between two o'clock and four o'clock, fifteen Union regiments went up Henry Hill and attacked the Confederates. But they made their attacks piecemeal, with never more than two regiments charging at the same time. The result was their predictable failure to break the Rebel line, and as the Yankees continued to attack, they continued to be repelled.[1]

Jackson, meanwhile, was concerned about his flanks, and when Stuart appeared at the head of his three-hundred-man cavalry regiment, he was told to split it in half and use each element to cover either side of the Confederate line. Once so deployed and watching from the woods, Stuart did not see all the Union attacks. But he did see some of the remnants as they tried to regroup in formation on a road below. The red pants and caps of one regiment convinced him they were Louisiana Zouaves, and he rode out of the woods and called to them, "Don't run, boys, we are here!" But then a glimpse of their Stars and Stripes and a few ragged shots over his head disabused him of this misperception. He raced back to the front of his men, then turned and led them in a charge.

The Yankee Zouaves fired one volley, and Stuart lost nine men and eighteen horses. But as he led his 150 screaming horsemen on a hell-for-leather charge into their formation on the road, the Zouaves simply dissolved and those who could fled for the rear. When they finally pulled their horses up, Stuart and his men turned and repeated the charge. But this time, there were only bodies in the road, and Stuart returned to his line.[2]

As the afternoon wore on, the green Union soldiers tired of their losses. Then, after one withdrawal turned into a rout, the panic spread through the other defeated Union soldiers and streams of blue soldiers crossed Bull Run and flooded north. As the blue lines crumbled and fled, there was no real pursuit, but none was possible, for most of the

Confederate soldiers were also green, and they were both too tired and too disorganized to follow up their splendid success of simple survival that day.

McDowell's failure at Bull Run was roundly condemned in the North, and Lincoln wanted most of all to have a winner lead his troops into the next battles. George McClellan, the "young Napoleon" of high repute, had recently won a minor clash in a region that would soon become the new state of West Virginia, and despite the small scale of his victory, he was the only proven winner available. Quickly brought to Washington and appointed to take command of the Army of the Potomac, he soon found himself in command of the entire Union army. He trained his men thoroughly, and was roundly loved by them. But the only sticking point was that he absolutely refused—a problem he could never shake—to lead his army across the Potomac River into Virginia and attack the Confederate army.

As spring blossomed, however, McClellan was finding himself the butt of much public criticism for not taking his army across the river to fight. While he disparaged such criticism, he knew that Lincoln and his advisers were losing patience, and it soon became clear that he must attack the enemy or he would be replaced.

Under such pressure, the plan he came up with was rather elaborate. He proposed a shipborne movement of his immense army of more than 100,000 men to Fort Monroe, a Union post that had been held at the tip of the peninsula between the York and the James Rivers and less than forty miles southeast of Richmond. Such a bold plan caught his critics by surprise, and so his public image became glamorous once again.

McClellan arrived at Fort Monroe on April 4, and his plan was to move up the peninsula until he was able to besiege and capture Richmond. His immense army was initially successful in driving smaller Rebel forces before it. But the true import of McClellan's movement on Richmond was that it would bring Robert E. Lee forward to command, a superb battlefield commander who was to profoundly affect the conduct of the Civil War.

When Virginia seceded, Lee had resigned his U.S. Army commission to serve his home state and so the Confederate army. When McClellan landed at Fort Monroe, Lee was in Richmond, filling the role of military adviser to President Jefferson Davis. The 60,000 Confederate troops defending Richmond at the time were commanded by General Joseph E. Johnston, and it would be his job to meet and defeat the invading Yankee army.

On March 9, 1862, a column led by Custer's Fifth Cavalry began to march south from Washington toward Richmond. Unbeknownst to its soldiers, this column was only a feint, a ruse intended by McClellan to mask his loading of the huge Army of the Potomac aboard boats for water transport to Fort Monroe. The feint would last only a few days, and during that time Custer was an acting company commander, a fact of which he was very conscious and a set of responsibilities to which he was strongly committed. As far as Custer was concerned, they were, in the parlance of the time, moving "on to Richmond," and spirits were high.

There was no enemy contact on their first day of movement, so they stopped short of Bull Run and camped in the countryside. The next morning, scouts came racing back with news that they had seen Confederate pickets stationed on the next rise. When word came down to drive in the pickets, Custer immediately asked Whiting if his company could have the honor of carrying out that order, a request which was quickly granted.

Custer rode back to his men and led them to the front of the column. They then moved down the road in a column of fours until Custer spotted the Confederate picket, men on horseback atop the next ridge, dressed in farmer's clothing but carrying firearms. Custer ordered segments of the fences on either side of the road removed and had his company spread out side by side in the fields, then started them forward at a walk, a hundred horsemen spread out in a line several hundred yards wide.

There is no doubt that the young leader of this host felt some anxiety, for this would be his first moment under fire. Those men up on the ridge were enemy soldiers carrying weapons, and they would certainly shoot at the approaching line of blue horsemen before withdrawing. Custer knew he would soon learn whether or not he had the requisite courage of a professional soldier in combat—not the absence of fear, but the ability to overcome that normal fear of death and still perform his mission.

Tongues of flame from the hands of those anonymous butternut horsemen, that was exactly what Custer wanted to face and so to test himself, to prove that he could be what he wanted to be. For this, after all, was war, this was what he had so long trained for at West Point. He now intended to live out the motto that had been bandied about among his young officer contemporaries for so long: "Glory and promotion or a coffin!"

When Custer and his men got to the foot of the ridge, the Rebels could no longer be seen, though their gunfire cut through the air above their heads. As they began moving up the hill, the sound of bullets whistling by became quite unsettling. But the young commander never even flinched, for he was planning.

When fighting from horseback, his men had the option of using pistols or sabers, and he did not want them stopping their horses in a charge in order to take better aim. Many of them, he had noted, were carrying pistols in their right hands, so he ordered them to fire their pistols just to break the tension, then holster them and draw sabers. As they neared the summit, he yelled, "Charge!" and dug spurs into his horse's side.

When they reached the crest, the enemy was gone, but they didn't even slow down. As they galloped down the far side of the ridge and across the meadow before them, they saw no enemy activity at all. But as they approached a creek at the edge of the field, a volley flashed from the woods on the far side, and Custer's men all drew rein. He led them back out of rifle range, then stopped to assess the damage.

One man had his scalp cut open by a bullet, and one horse had been wounded. When they rejoined the column, Custer's men were jubilant as he reported "mission accomplished." But by this time, the transports were loading for the trip to Fort Monroe, and so the cavalry column rode back to Alexandria, where they embarked.

After arriving at Fort Monroe, Custer's regiment was marched north along the James River, but within days, all forward movement stopped at fortified Yorktown. McClellan mounted a siege, and after a month, Confederate forces abandoned the town and the slow Union move up the peninsula started once again. But the weather was cold and wet and the dirt roads soon became almost impassable quagmires. While the main column struggled, Custer was allowed to ride out in front to search for solid detours that would get them to Williamsburg, where the Confederates had also built solid defenses.

As he approached a bridge over Skiff Creek, Custer saw that it was on fire, so he spurred his horse forward. As he got close, he ducked when he heard a bullet whistle over his head, then pulled out his pistol and fired back blindly as he jumped from his horse and ran onto the bridge, kicking the kindling wood away while stamping out the flames, then tossed the burning sticks and other debris into the water with his bare hands. He saved the bridge and was cited for gallantry, the first in a long series of such citations.[3]

A little later that day, General Winfield S. Hancock and his brigade were sent to try to turn the left flank of the Rebel defenses east of Williamsburg, and Custer went along. After a march of a few miles, they came to a typical defense on the peninsula, a series of dams covered by Confederate redoubts. Hancock's men moved against them and took the first two unoccupied forts with virtually no resistance. The third was heavily defended, however, and Hancock sent for reinforcements, saying he needed them to turn the enemy line.

But despite repeated requests, Hancock heard nothing for several hours. Finally, a large Confederate force came out of the last redoubt and formed for an attack on Hancock's men. As the enemy came forward, the Rebel yell now keening through the air, Hancock ordered his own men to attack them with the bayonet. They formed up to follow orders readily enough, but then the screaming, gray horde lunging their way simply paralyzed them.

Then Custer was out in front of them, waving his hat, shouting encouragement, urging them forward. It was terribly incongruous, a young boy with long yellow hair and a laughing face, out in front of them on a horse where he was much more vulnerable to enemy fire than they were at ground level, cavorting up and down the line and calling them to join him on the battlefield. It was overwhelming, and a deep roar came bellowing out of their mouths as they rushed forward. The Rebel line stopped, then broke and ran. In doing so, they abandoned that last redoubt that protected the end of their line, and they left behind a Confederate battle flag, the first one taken by the Army of the Potomac.

After this Union victory, the Rebels were flanked at Williamsburg, so that night they withdrew from the defenses they had carefully constructed there. Hancock won great credit for his brigade's actions, and he also wrote up Custer for bravery, his second citation of the day.[4]

McClellan continued to move his army forward cautiously, and Custer was one of the scouts who rode out in front. By the last week in May, the Union force was lined up along ten miles of the banks of the Chickahominy River, one flank close enough to Richmond that the men were able to hear the church bells on Sundays. One morning, the chief engineer in McClellan's army, Brigadier General John G. Barnard, took Custer down to the banks of the Chickahominy River, between the picket lines of the two forces, and had him try to ford the river at a bend.

Custer found the water was over his shoulders as he crossed, but he was able to stay on his feet, keeping his pistol dry by holding it above his head. Once on the other side and armed with only that pistol, he crept some distance into enemy territory, discovering not only pickets walking their assigned posts but also the main post where they rested between tours of duty. Since this post was also caught within the bend of the river, it was clear that a federal raiding party might swoop down on them, capture a handful of Rebel soldiers on picket duty, and then make it back across the river before any Confederate command would be able to react.

Barnard took Custer back to headquarters with him, and despite the fact that he was still soaking wet and muddy from crossing the river and crawling around behind enemy lines, he was asked to explain what he had found to General McClellan. Custer, like most other soldiers in his army, simply adored McClellan, and he must have felt just the slightest trepidation because of his appearance. But Little Mac listened patiently.

After Custer had given him a detailed report of what he had seen and answered some questions, McClellan ordered a crossing by the Fourth Michigan Infantry Regiment, which Custer accompanied. They returned with fifty Confederate prisoners, having shot and left behind more, all at a cost of two Union soldiers killed and six wounded.

After the raid, McClellan called Custer back to his headquarters and told him he was just the sort of officer he was looking for. He then invited him to join his staff, which meant a brevet promotion to captain, and Custer was little short of deliriously happy.[5]

At the confused Battle of Fair Oaks on May 31, the Confederate field commander, General Joe Johnston, was wounded. He was replaced by Robert E. Lee, and both sides spent the next several weeks entrenching, fortifying, and planning.

On the night of June 8, Stuart went on a ride northeast of Richmond, through an area that the Union army should have been covering, but from which they were largely absent. He then met with a local man who gave him some information about the area, and returned to camp outside Richmond. Stuart then told Lee that the Union right wing was totally unprotected and just hanging out "in the air" with no covering force or attachment to a strong defensive geographical feature. And once you got around the Union right wing, he said, the Union supply line ran over a totally unprotected road.

Lee then tasked Stuart with the mission of taking a thousand horsemen and confirming these glaring weaknesses in the Union deployment. But Stuart said that if they went out on a raid and came back the same way, the Union might anticipate such a move and set an ambush for them. In order to avoid that potentially fatal danger, he suggested that he take his force around the Union army right flank and then just continue on, making an entire circuit of McClellan's army. He would return by passing around the Union left from its rear, cross the Chickahominy, and return to Richmond.

Lee did not specify which return route the party should take, believing that should be up to Stuart's discretion as things developed during the raid. But he made sure Stuart understood what he wanted to know about Union arms dispositions.

Stuart selected twelve hundred of his men and told them to cook three days' rations. At two A.M. on June 12, Stuart and his men headed north. They moved twenty-two miles that day, with no sighting of Union troops, before stopping on a farm near Ashland. Next morning, Stuart turned their column to head due east. As they got closer to

Hanover Court House, Stuart's force was suddenly behind the Union army, and they began to move southeast. And as they continued their movement, they would continually hit Union picket forces posted in the small towns and villages they passed. The Confederate column was big enough that there was no threat of these men delaying them, but they spread word of this large Rebel cavalry force loose in the Union rear.

Stuart said he hoped the Union cavalry would be sent to challenge him, for McClellan's cavalry force was commanded by General Philip St. George Cooke, his father-in-law. Despite being a Virginian, Cooke had stayed loyal to the Union, which had enraged Stuart. He told his wife, Flora, that her father would regret that decision, but only once—implying that he would regret it as he died at Stuart's hand.

About twenty miles southeast of Hanover Court House, they passed through Old Church and drove off a few hundred Union cavalry. Stuart then sent two squadrons to Putney's Ferry on the Pamunkey River, where they found and burned two large transport ships loaded with supplies. Ten miles southeast of Old Church, they came to Tunstall's Station, which was on the east-west railroad line between the port city of White House on the Pamunkey River and Richmond. McClellan used that line to transport supplies from White House forward to his forces, which were only about six miles east of Richmond.

There were many rail cars on sidings filled with supplies in Tunstall's Station, some of which Stuart's men looted before burning them. They also captured a wagon train of about seventy-five wagons, which had a similar fate. Before moving on, Stuart felt a strong urge to move four miles down the rail line to capture the Union storehouse at White House, clearly a treasure trove of supplies. But while the temptation was great, he knew he could never hold that position when counter-attacked, and given the size of the nearby Union army, such a counter-attack could easily destroy his force. So they kept trotting south, ever aware that intelligence reports on them were racing through McClellan's command and growing blue forces were on their trail.

Among these forces, of course, was the Union cavalry under General Philip St. George Cooke. But alas, false reports about Confederate infantry regiments being with Stuart had made him hesitate, and when he finally got more accurate information, it was far too late for him to do anything. On the other hand, there is always the chance that he just let his daughter's husband get a free pass this time; there was sorrow enough in this war, why bring more on your own flesh and blood? And for all his private protestations of anger at his father-in-law's disloyalty to the South in her hour of need, wouldn't Jeb Stuart himself also have had mixed feelings about actually facing him on the field of battle? But whatever the truth in either case, they managed to avoid each other for a crucial period in June 1862 measured only in hours. Had they met, Flora Cooke Stuart's heart would surely have been broken, whatever the outcome.

It was full dark when Stuart left Tunstall's Station and headed south. After five miles, he came to Talleysville, where he stopped for three hours to allow his column to close up and rest. Then at midnight his men moved south again.

About ten miles later, as dawn was breaking, the lead horsemen came to a ford over the Chickahominy that was on private land, a ford they were led to by one of Stuart's men who had grown up nearby. But the river was high and raging, and it looked to them like it was too dangerous to cross here. When Stuart himself rode up, he groaned: suddenly, things did not look so good. The last thing he wanted was to have made a successful transit around the Union army, only to be trapped and captured when his passage back to safety was blocked by a river too wild to ford.

After stroking his beard for a few minutes, Stuart sent scouts to look for other bridges or even possible fording sites. Soon enough, he learned that there had been an old bridge downstream about a mile, most of which had fallen apart. But the abutments were still in place, as were a few of the spans. He quickly moved his force down there, and a large abandoned warehouse nearby became the source of timber he would require. A large workforce dismounted and went to work, and within about three hours, the bridge was ready for passage not only of cavalry but also of his four towed cannon.

It was around noon when the entire column was on the west side of the river, and as they put this reconstructed bridge to the match, Union riders appeared on the eastern side. But the men in blue were too late, and Stuart's horsemen were both exhausted and elated at their undeniable triumph of having bearded the lion in his lair and gotten away clean. They rode another ten miles, then stopped near Charles City Court House, close to the banks of the James River. The men had been in the saddle for thirty-six hours straight, and neither they nor their horses could go much farther without rest. After a few hours of sleep, Stuart rode on to Richmond alone, reaching Lee's headquarters on June 15. And his information about the Union right wing being "in the air" was most welcome news.[6]

Stuart did not know, of course, about further plans Lee was making. His information about the weakness of the Union right would be very important a few weeks later, for Lee would use that knowledge in an attempt to bring Jackson down from the Shenandoah Valley and have him fall on the Union right and rear. Those plans were frustrated because of factors that are unimportant here, for the spectacular hero of the moment, renowned in press north and south, was Jeb Stuart. With his "invincible" cavalrymen, Jeb had ridden completely around McClellan's army, thumbing his nose at him as he went. And that act had so captured the image of romantic hero nationwide, even among his most bitter enemies, that it would live beyond him and never die. No matter the objections one might hold to the Confederacy, one could not deny the dash, the romance, the glamour of Stuart's feat. It was a bold challenge to the Yankees that he would repeat twice again on different ground, and the reputation, the aura won by Stuart in those wild rides, even beyond his success as a fighting cavalry leader, were to win him the immortality he and his other romantic fellows so desperately chased all their lives.

With this new information, Lee had preparations to make, defenses to build, deceits to prepare. Then, almost two weeks after Stuart's triumphant return, the new commander of the Army of Northern Virginia made his move. On June 26, he launched the first of a series of attacks that would be remembered as the Seven Days battles. And even though he lost most of these battles in terms of blood and flesh—some 20,000 Confederate casualties, as compared to 16,000 for the Union—it was readily apparent that his constant aggression simply terrified McClellan.

The first attack was launched on June 26 against Porter's corps north of the Chickahominy at Mechanicsville, and it was a Union victory. But Lee attacked again the next day and broke Porter's line, forcing him to flee across that river. These two attacks so scared Little Mac that he issued hurried orders to change his supply base from the York to the James River, then immediately began to retreat. On the twenty-ninth, Lee attacked again at Savage's Station, and Jackson's slow movement resulted in another Union victory, but one from which the victors, yet again, fled.

On June 30, Lee hit the Yankees at Frayser's Farm, and despite fighting into the night, he gained little. Union troops retired into a strong position on Malvern Hill, and on July 1, Lee smashed into them again. But this time, the Union had heavy artillery lined up in support of strong infantry defenses, and the main results of Lee's attacks that day were massive Confederate casualties.

Even so, McClellan was still scared, and he retreated again the next day into strong defensive lines at Harrison's Landing on the James. Lee moved his army back to Richmond, but McClellan's force took no further offensive action. Lincoln, however, lost his patience with McClellan and ordered his army to return to Washington by water.

As it turned out, Lee paid a price for his constant aggression, and Confederate casualties suffered during the Seven Days were much larger than those of the Union army. But this was much more than just a Pyrrhic victory, for if Johnson had not been wounded and replaced by Lee, it appears that Richmond would have fallen and the Confederate army in the east eliminated as a factor. Had that occurred, it seems that the seceded states would have recognized their predicament and soon returned to the Union fold. But the crucial aspect of this was that their return would have been made with slavery intact, for the Emancipation Proclamation would not be announced until September 1862 and would not take effect until January 1, 1863. Seen in that light, one could make the ironic point that Lee fought for the freedom of the slaves, since his arrival on the battlefield resulted in a dramatic extension of the Civil War, an extension sufficient to ensure the announcement and enactment of the Emancipation Proclamation.

# ～ 7 ～

# *Early Confederate Victories*

ON JUNE 26, just as the Seven Days battles of the peninsula were about to begin near Richmond, Lincoln decided that command from Washington of Union forces trying to parry Stonewall Jackson in the Shenandoah Valley was an unacceptable threat to the nation's capital. Accordingly, he created the new Union "Army of Virginia," made up of these forces and a few other units drawn from the defenses of Washington and elsewhere. He gave this army to General John Pope, a man junior to many of the generals in the East, but a battlefield commander who had known success in the West.

Pope's orders were to protect Washington, to eliminate any Rebel threats from the Shenandoah Valley, and ideally to draw southern troops north from the Richmond defenses. As he took the field, Lee found himself caught between two massive blue armies, and he soon decided that McClellan would stay quiet while he took care of this new Union army to his north. He therefore began moving his forces to join Jackson and maneuver against Pope. To ensure that McClellan stayed in place, he also ordered diversions launched against Harrison's Landing, mostly artillery fire directed at certain points.

On the twenty-fourth, Lee's army faced that of Pope across the

rising Rappahannock. Lee knew he had to act before any more reinforcements arrived for Pope, and on July 25, he sent Jackson and half
his army northwest along the Rappahannock for some twenty-five
miles, where they crossed to the northern side in the upstream area.
Jackson drove his men hard and got to his target town of Salem that
night. The next morning, he started his force directly east and, unop-
posed, they arrived in Manassas that night, a railhead deep in Pope's
rear that contained a mountain of supplies. Longstreet, meanwhile, left
5,000 men across the river from Pope and followed Jackson with
25,000 men. He spent the night of the twenty-sixth near Salem, then at
dawn on the twenty-seventh moved east to join Jackson.

Pope had found out about Jackson's movement on the twenty-fifth,
but was confused about where he was going. Then, in the evening of
the twenty-sixth, the telegraph line north went dead, and by ten that
night, scouts reported that Jackson was in Manassas. On the twenty-
seventh, the hungry Rebels had an orgy of looting and gorging themselves on the abundant Union supplies. That evening, Jackson ordered
his men to carry away four days' rations, filled wagons with ammunition, and had the rest of the enormous stockpile burned. After ripping
up some rails, his divisions moved off on separate routes of march
northeast and northwest that would be circuitous, this to confuse the
Yankees. But that night, his 25,000 men were reunited at Stony Ridge,
ten miles northwest of Manassas Junction, where they set up in a strong
defensive position along a railroad cut facing the Warrenton Turnpike.

The twenty-eighth found Pope's army pursuing Jackson relentlessly.
But with no cavalry available to him, he had difficulty divining Jackson's movement, and he made some bad guesses. Finally, about 5:30
that evening, King's Union division was moving east on the Warrenton
Turnpike when they passed directly in front of Jackson's men. The
temptation was too great, and the Rebels opened up.

As Pope learned of Jackson's location, he sent orders to all his corps to concentrate. But when he prepared to attack Jackson that night, he apparently had forgotten about Longstreet, who was approaching from the west with his 25,000 men. During the next day's fighting, while Pope was throwing his 56,000 men at Jackson, Longstreet came up within a mile of Pope's left but remained concealed and inactive. On three separate occasions Lee told Longstreet to attack, but reluctantly gave in to that man's pleas that the time was not yet right. If Lee had been more insistent, it is very probable that Pope's army would have suffered a more crushing defeat.

The next morning, Pope was convinced that the Confederates were retreating, and it wasn't until the early afternoon that he renewed his attack from the previous day. Badly used over three days of steady fighting, Jackson's men were starting to crumble when Longstreet's five divisions crashed in on the Union left, driving all before them. Pope quickly withdrew units from his right flank to try to stem the tide, but this allowed Jackson's men to launch their own counterattack. Pope's men fell back in some disarray, but finally were able to set up in a strong defensive position on Henry House Hill. At seven o'clock that night, Pope's army retreated north, with no pursuit from Lee. They were soon back inside the defenses of Washington, but Lee was off pursuing other bold plans.

The campaign of the Second Battle of Bull Run provides a good example of Lee's use of the Napoleonic fan: divide units and confuse the enemy, then have them join suddenly together again, crashing into the flanks of a shocked adversary.

After this Union debacle at Second Bull Run, Pope was sent to Minnesota to fill an administrative role, and his army was absorbed into McClellan's Army of the Potomac. But the men in blue and their commanders, burned again by Lee in northern Virginia, planted themselves in Washington in a purely defensive, reactive mode.

Lee, meanwhile, was flushed with victory and he and Confederate

President Jefferson Davis agreed that the Army of Northern Virginia should cross into Maryland, where they would seek battle. There were many reasons for this, including the hope for foreign recognition, the prospect of fomenting an uprising in Maryland, the need to retain the initiative, and the desire to let the devastating scourge of battle fall on another state.

On September 4, 1862, Lee began crossing the Potomac north of Washington, and by the seventh, his forces were near Frederick, Maryland. McClellan began his pursuit very slowly on September 6, and on the thirteenth, he also reached Frederick, from which the Rebels were long gone. But someone had inadvertently left a treasure in a long-since-abandoned Rebel campsite. Wrapped around three cigars and lying on the ground, a copy of the entire Confederate plan and the proposed deployment across Maryland of various Rebel units was found by a Union soldier. When these papers were brought to him, McClellan was beside himself with joy, and he loudly proclaimed that he now had what he needed to defeat Lee.

Such news traveled fast through camp followers as well as spies, and Lee soon learned of it. But even with his startling discovery of Confederate plans and dispositions, McClellan was still cursed with the "slows." When his Union army of 70,000 finally caught up with Lee, the Confederate general had reassembled most of his force of less than 40,000 that had been spread out in Napoleonic fan style and deployed it in front of the town of Sharpsburg and behind the Antietam creek.

On September 17, 1862, McClellan launched attacks against the Confederate left, then the center, and finally their right wing. Just as Union forces under Burnside were finally breaking through the Confederate right, they were hit in the flank and driven back by A. P. Hill's Confederate division as it got to the battlefield from Harpers Ferry, the last element in the fan to arrive. After the bloodiest day in American history (26,000 casualties for the two armies combined), McClellan pulled back. On September 18, both armies watched and waited, but no fighting occurred. The Potomac River ran behind Sharpsburg, and that night, Lee's army slipped over a ford and back into Virginia.

After Antietam, Stuart's force was spread across the northern end of the Shenandoah Valley, acting as a wide screen between the Army of Northern Virginia moving south in the valley and any potential direct pursuit by McClellan's Army of the Potomac. But McClellan was still in Maryland, and despite having been ordered to cross the river and engage the enemy on October 6, he dawdled for several more weeks.

Stuart kept his headquarters at "the Bower," which was the name of the large estate of a Mr. A. S. Dandridge some fifteen miles west of Harpers Ferry. In Stuart's entourage, there were perhaps one hundred people, including staff officers, couriers, and servants, and their two hundred or so horses grazed near the staff's tents. Dandridge had several beautiful young daughters and nieces, and they happened to have invited a number of other young female friends to come and stay with them.

The daily routine of Stuart and his staff was taken up with administration, coordination, inspection, and other organizational tasks. The fact that his cavalry force was so spread out meant that brigades and regiments operated pretty much on their own, and that meant less work for Stuart and his staff. Many of them found time to fish, others to hunt, wild turkeys being their most sought-after game, but hares and pheasant and grouse from the neighboring countryside usually supplemented the fare served in their small army camp. And in late afternoon every day, Stuart and his staff were always invited to afternoon tea, which was usually the opening social event of the evening. After that, there were songs, dances—with music provided by Sam the banjo player and Bob the violinist, who were always kept close by Stuart—and various games, even skits. On October 7, the Dandridges threw a ball, to which many guests were invited from far and near. It was a great success, but to Stuart's staff, every night there was as pleasant as the softest dream.[1]

The house was transformed every evening into a glowing light in the night from which sprang intermittent gales of laughter. The pleasure that exuded from that structure was almost palpable, the raw joy of men taking a break from the war in the company of beautiful young women, all hosted by a most gracious and generous man.

The night was often capped by moonlight strolls or even rowboat rides. But all this was done very innocently, for that was the morality of the day. Stuart and his staff never spoke of themselves as the Knights of the Round Table, but the image was too real, the aspirations to that role they all felt in their breasts too strong. And for those knights, forbearing temptations of the flesh outside of marriage was a natural, and sacred, aspect of the persona they presented to the public as well as of their own self-image. A fair damsel in need of protection from the Yankees and other dragons somewhere in the woods, no higher duty exists—or so they would have us believe.

Stuart and his entourage would spend a month at the Bower, and it was clearly an interlude of uninterrupted bliss they relished long after. There were many visitors to Stuart's headquarters, of course, and among the most welcome were correspondents from various newspapers in the South as well as in England and elsewhere. Stuart was beginning to build his reputation, and his cavalry was regarded as vastly superior to that fielded by the Union, a sentiment shared by those in both North and South.

But the war was always there, and on October 8, Stuart told his acting adjutant to prepare all papers that needed his signature, an unusual act. The next day, he had his subordinates select eighteen hundred of the most reliable and best-mounted men for an expedition, the details of which he kept to himself. The evening of the ninth, Stuart led this force up near the Potomac some twenty miles north of Harpers Ferry, and at dawn on the tenth, they crossed over and headed north.

Lee was sending Stuart on a raid deep into Pennsylvania, with directions to destroy a bridge near Chambersburg, twenty miles north of the Maryland–Pennsylvania border. He was also to gather as many horses as he could, while taking care to give their owners receipts, that they might seek repayment from the Union government. They were also to capture a number of public officials—sheriffs, postmasters, judges—for use by Richmond as ransom for southern officials then being held prisoner in the North. And he was also to gather as much intelligence as he could about the dispositions of the Army of the Potomac and any other Union forces he might uncover. The emphasis, of course, was on speed, that he might elude the Union soldiers who would no doubt soon be put on his trail. Because of that potential threat, Stuart was given the authority to decide when in Chambersburg whether to return the way he had come or to turn east and go all the way around McClellan's army, crossing the Potomac on the way home well south of Harpers Ferry. But for the man who had first flown to fame on the wings that had carried him around McClellan's army on the peninsula, this was not a difficult decision to predict.

By midafternoon, the advance guard for the main column had reached the town of Mercersburg, where they surprised a local merchant by crowding into his store and ordering boots and shoes. It wasn't until it came time to pay that he discovered they were Confederates, for they simply gave him the receipts they had been directed to render in return for private property.

As they continued north, it began to rain. Members of the advance guard, of course, were very happy with their new Mercersburg footwear, but the raiders on either side of the column were stripping the countryside of horseflesh, and that slowed forward movement. Finally, at eight o'clock the evening of the tenth, they reached Chambersburg.

There were no Union army troops there, and the town was turned over to Stuart by a group of citizens. He made one of his brigade commanders the "governor" for the night, and then his riders not only took all horses in the city but they also began to visit nearby farms for the same purpose. He sent a body of riders to burn the bridge they had been sent to destroy, who soon returned with the unfortunate news that the bridge was made of iron and they were simply unable to destroy it.

Most of the Rebel riders slept in town that night, though Stuart was too busy to get much rest at all. At dawn on the eleventh, the column headed out of town directly to the east rather than retrace their steps to the south. Stuart explained his reasoning to several of his staff officers, and indeed, it seemed very probable that the Union troops would either be awaiting his return or were swarming in his pursuit. Thereafter, he would redirect his men east, then south, steadily working his way down to the border into Maryland. At the state border, the column stopped and Stuart reminded his men that no horses or other private property would be taken in Maryland.

When they arrived in Emmittsburg at sunset, they had traveled over thirty miles from Chambersburg, and they still had about forty-five miles to go to get to one of the fords across the Potomac twenty-odd miles southeast of Harpers Ferry. As they rode into town they were greeted by many loud fans, for Maryland was one of the four slave states that did not secede. Stuart's cavalcade had collected about twelve hundred horses in Pennsylvania and they were led by some four hundred men in the middle of the column, each holding the reins of three to five horses.

Despite the loud welcomes, Stuart kept moving through Emmittsburg and headed in the general direction of Rockville. Although man and beast were exhausted, they couldn't take the chance of stopping, for alarms were flying across Maryland. The Yankees knew he had been in Pennsylvania and was apparently heading back to Virginia, but they didn't know exactly where he was or where he planned to cross the Potomac. There were many who saw his column, however, both civilian and military, and they no doubt spread the news to whatever military authority they could find. McClellan was clearly on their trail, but he was just a few hours behind them.

Stuart's men could not rest themselves, but they did have the comparative luxury of changing to a fresh horse several times during the night, and they trotted steadily south through the dark. By about eight in the morning, they reached Hyattstown, and the sun was well up in the sky. And in the last twelve miles, Stuart moved his column down an old road in the middle of a forest that took him to a ford several miles upstream from the one toward which he had been heading. This was a final blow to Yankee intelligence, and when Stuart and his men got to White's Ford, they found about two hundred Union infantry soldiers well placed above the ford.

Colonel W. H. F. "Rooney" Lee commanded the lead brigade, and when he saw the strong Union position, he wasn't sure what to do. Before launching a time-consuming and no doubt bloody attack, however, he decided to try to bluff the commander. He sent a lieutenant forward under a white flag with a note telling the Union commander that Stuart was there with his entire command, but in the interest of avoiding unnecessary bloodshed the Union unit would have fifteen minutes within which to surrender. If they failed to lay down their arms in that time frame, they would be attacked and overwhelmed.

After fifteen minutes, there had been no white flags or anything else from the Union position, so Lee prepared his men for the attack. But then several of his men called out to him, and he looked where they were pointing. Sure enough, the blue soldiers were marching out of their little fort and heading downstream, leaving the ford wide open.

Stuart was able to get his entire command across and back into Virginia in a very short time, and he was simply elated with his success. He returned with about twelve hundred fresh horses, thirty-odd public functionaries; none of his men had been killed, and only a few had been lightly wounded. Two of his riders had gotten separated and, he later learned, ended up prisoners of war. But he had been able to move 120 miles in forty-eight hours through the heart of the North, gathering up splendid horseflesh and politically valuable prisoners, and all without losing a single man to Yankee fire. The last thirty-six hours had been ridden without a stop or a break, and it was basically this that kept Stuart from being caught by the Army of the Potomac, which was hot on his heels. General George McClellan, the commander of the Army of the Potomac, is recorded by his cousin, Major Henry McClellan of Stuart's staff, as having later said, "I did not think it was possible for Stuart to recross, and I believed that the capture or destruction of his entire force was certain."[2] But they never caught him, and his self-confidence must have been virtually unbounded.

Stuart was soon back at the Bower with his entourage, and the celebration was all about him. What a tremendous ride this had been, and it was all directly attributable to him. On October 15, there was a ball in his honor, and guests came from far and near with gifts, including the presentation to him of a pair of golden spurs by the ladies of Baltimore. After this, a private *nom de guerre* he adopted for his occasional use was "Knight of the Golden Spurs," and he sometimes signed letters simply "K.G.S."[3]

McClellan was following Lee's army with what seemed to Lincoln to be almost glacial slowness. Finally, Lincoln had had enough, and on November 7, he replaced McClellan as commander of the Army of the Potomac with Burnside.

Within a few days, Burnside sent Halleck his plan for crossing the Rappahannock at Fredericksburg and then plunging south toward Richmond. It was approved, but before he could even get his pontoon bridges in place, Lee knew of his plans and moved his army to meet

Burnside at Fredericksburg on the western side of the Rappahannock. On December 13, Burnside threw six successive infantry charges against a strongly defended Confederate position atop a ridge known as Marye's Heights, all bloodily repulsed.

The rest of the winter along the Rappahannock passed quietly. But in March 1863, Lee was alarmed at news of federal troops boarding transports at Hampton Roads, Virginia. To stave off what might be a true crisis, Lee sent Longstreet south with two divisions to protect the Virginia–Carolina coast. He was left west of Fredericksburg with some 50,000 troops, facing twice that number of Union soldiers across the river. He also knew that Burnside had been replaced by Hooker, and he expected to be attacked.

# 8

# Chancellorsville

THE NEXT UNION COMMANDER to face Lee was "Fighting Joe" Hooker. On April 27, he began to march the great bulk of his army north and west, then had them crash through Confederate pickets at several fords and move south. Meanwhile, on April 29, a large corps of his army under Sedgwick crossed the Rappahannock and reoccupied Fredericksburg. And so it was that on May 1, a veteran army of some 75,000 was poised around the crossroads of Chancellorsville in Lee's left rear while another 30,000 under Sedgwick threatened him from Fredericksburg.

Lee was aware of this Union movement, of course, and he made a parallel move himself, bringing about 43,000 of his men to the west of Fredericksburg while leaving 9,000 under Early in place defending Marye's Heights. Then, on the evening of May 1, Lee met with Jackson. They discussed the threat of Hooker's army, and then Lee told Jackson that the main Union force was advancing from the west and that he must move around it with 26,000 men in what would be a classic *manœuvre sur les derrières*.

Although Jackson disagreed with Lee about the main Union threat, he did as he was told. Lee showed him on a map the roads by Catherine's Furnace that he should use, and the next morning, May 2, 1863, Jackson was off on his roundabout daylong flanking movement. In an extremely high-risk move, Lee divided his army in the face of a vastly superior attacking force, sending 26,000 men under Stonewall Jackson on a long march south, west, and then back north while he stayed in place facing Hooker's force with the remaining 17,000 men. Once he arrived in a position to the west of the Union's XI Corps, Jackson's men arrayed themselves in a line running north to south that was more than a mile long and several brigades of soldiers deep. The Union XI Corps, meanwhile, was lined up perpendicular to them, facing south along the Orange Turnpike, and many of its men were relaxing and preparing their supper.

It was early evening as Jackson's men came out of the setting sun, hitting the Union line squarely on its exposed wing, their keening Rebel yell striking true terror into the stunned Yankees. The line washed forward, unstoppable as crowds of men in blue ran like barnyard fowl before it. The XI Corps was unable to stop this attack, but units to its east began to turn and prepare for it while it was still approaching. As full dark settled, the Confederate advance was also finally slowed and then stopped.

Stonewall Jackson was mortally wounded during the fighting that evening, and Jeb Stuart, Lee's cavalry commander, took over his command. The next morning, fighting was hard, and ground was given up only grudgingly by both sides. But after a few hours Union forces began to run out of ammunition, and Hooker decided to pull all his forces up into a strong horseshoe-shaped defensive formation.

Lee's reunited Confederate force, having driven Union infantry back after brutal fighting that washed back and forth in both directions, now faced a solid Union semicircular position with both wings tied to the Rappahannock River, a position that seemed quite impregnable. The fighting until this point was the first part of the battle, and it remains the best known by far, particularly Jackson's long roundabout march, his stunning surprise attack on the Union flank at dusk, and his tragic wounding by his own men that led to amputation of his arm, followed in only days by his death. Another very important part of the battle, however, remained to be fought.

After Appomattox, Lee would not write about or discuss the war with virtually anyone. The result was that some newspapers or journals guessed at what Lee had planned or done, and they were often wrong. Still, Lee refused to correct them or even notice their writings, save on two occasions.

The first such incident was a letter he wrote to Stonewall Jackson's widow that was meant to assuage any slight against her late husband she might have felt from an erroneous article. The second occurred because Lee had remained silent about his meeting with Jackson on the evening of May 1, in which he had directed that man's crushing flank attack of May 2. This meeting and its contents were known only to a few staff officers who were nearby, and they had respected Lee's wish for secrecy, with the result that many people, civilian as well as military, had begun to assume that it had been Jackson's idea alone. *Southern Review* even published a story supporting that belief, and this was finally too much for Lee, who wrote the following letter in response:

*Robert E. Lee to Dr. A. T. Bledsoe, October 28, 1867:*

*In reply to your enquiry, I must acknowledge that I have not read the article about Chancellorsville in the last number of the "Southern Review," nor have I read any of the books published on either side since the termination of hostilities. I have as yet felt no desire to revive any recollection of those events, and have been satisfied with the knowledge I possessed of what transpired. I have, however, learned from others that the various authors [R.L. Dabney] of the* Life *[and Campaigns of Lieut.*

*Gen. Thomas J.] of Jackson award to him the credit of the success*
*gained by the Army of Northern Virginia when he was present, and*
*describe the movements of his corps or command as independent of the*
*general plan of operations and undertaken at his own suggestion and on*
*his own responsibility. I have the greatest reluctance to do anything that*
*might be considered detracting from his well-deserved fame, for I believe no*
*one was more convinced of his worth or more highly appreciated him than*
*myself; yet your knowledge of military affairs, if you have none of the*
*events [facts] themselves, will teach you that this could not have been so.*
*Every movement of an army must be well considered and properly ordered,*
*and everyone who knew General Jackson must know that he was too good*
*a soldier to violate this fundamental principle. In the operations round*
*Chancellorsville, I overtook General Jackson, who had been placed in*
*command of the advance, as the skirmishers of the opposing armies met,*
*advanced with the troops to the Federal line of defences, and was on the*
*field until their entire army recrossed the Rappahannock. There is no*
*question as to who was responsible for the operation of the Confederates, or*
*to whom any failure would have been charged.*[1]

This letter should remove all doubt about the source of Jackson's
flanking movement at Chancellorsville. And by extension, it should be
clear that if Stuart were to use his men at Gettysburg in an effort to
burst up Baltimore Pike and into the Union rear, as I suggest, this
would have been possible only if he had been specifically ordered to do
so by Lee. Like Jackson, Stuart was too good a soldier to have tried such
freelancing with his forces on his own.

As mentioned earlier, on May 3 Lee drove three Union army corps
north, where they were reunited with three other army corps and
formed a solid defensive line. Meanwhile, he had left Early in defensive
positions west of Fredericksburg with 9,000 men, a defensive line that

was necessarily thin and strung out. Sedgwick and his 25,000 men quickly broke through Early's defenses, but then moved west at a very slow rate.

Now Lee was faced with a true dilemma: his force of perhaps 55,000 men was separated into two main bodies, the 43,000 he controlled at Chancellorsville and another 9,000 under Early that had just been thrust rudely aside by Sedgwick. Now his main body of 43,000 was threatened from the north by 75,000 under Hooker and from the east by 25,000 under Sedgwick. At present, only Sedgwick was moving forward and menacing him, but the very real threat was that Hooker might also advance and the two Union armies would then crush Lee's force between them. What should he do? Were there any lessons available to him from military history that addressed such a situation?

An almost identical situation faced Napoleon in northern Italy in 1796, one with which Lee was no doubt intimately familiar. That campaign is remembered mostly for the Battle of Arcola central to it, but it remains one of the most renowned of Napoleon's many triumphs, for it showed his military genius when he was only twenty-six years old.

France and Austria were at war, and Napoleon commanded France's Army of Italy. In September 1796, he had defeated Wurmser's Austrian army, and now some 24,000 Austrian soldiers were besieged in the walled city of Mantua, though 10,000 of these were sick and unable to fight. The city was surrounded by a French force of only about 9,000, but the Austrians made no sign of coming out to fight.

In November, the Austrian Supreme War Council ordered Alvintzy to advance on Italy, with the goal of relieving the siege of Mantua. Napoleon's army of some 40,000 was spread widely over northern Italy, and the Austrian plan was to take advantage of that. It involved one force of 28,000 moving west into Italy under Alvintzy, while another force of 18,000 under Davidovitch came south down the

Adige River valley through rough mountainous terrain. They would meet near Verona, then sweep south some thirty miles by road to Mantua, where their combined force would break the French siege and relieve Wurmser's force. This movement into northern Italy by Austrian forces is today remembered in military history as "Alvintzy's First Advance."[2]

On November 2, Davidovitch ran into 10,000 Frenchmen under Vaubois, and after heavy fighting, the French withdrew. Napoleon was surprised when he heard that such a large force threatened him from the north and he sent word that Vaubois was to hold Davidovitch. Then he raced north with Masséna, his wily mountain fighter, to try to solidify Vaubois in a defensive position.

He found Vaubois's army in Rivoli the night of November 7–8, only some twenty miles northwest of Verona and in considerable disorder. But he fairly blistered them with a strong rebuke, then ordered Masséna to restore order and establish them in a strong defensive position. This caused Davidovitch to pause while allowing Napoleon to return to Verona and consider his options. Caught between two large forces, he had some 22,000 men in Verona, and as Alvintzy advanced from the east with 28,000, Davidovitch gave signs of breaking through from the north with his 18,000. But Napoleon refused to adopt a passive defense, for the much larger Austrian force would eventually crush him unless he did something.

His choices, however, now seemed quite limited, for if he attacked Alvintzy's force in the open, he would be inviting disaster. If he kept his men in Verona, Alvintzy would advance and eventually besiege them. If he retreated to the south, Davidovitch and Alvintzy would unite and follow him, this time with overpowering numbers. If he retreated south of Mantua, Alvintzy would then relieve the siege there, which would add even more more Austrian soldiers to their force. What was he to do?

And this is where Napoleon's true genius really showed itself. The Adige River flowed through Verona in a southeasterly direction. As Alvintzy moved west, his left was a large marshy area many miles wide until it reached the river. Near the river was the town of Arcola, sited behind a smaller north-south river, the Alpone.

On the night of November 14, Napoleon left a force of twenty-five hundred men to hold Mantua, then secretly moved the other 19,000 under his command southeast for perhaps eighteen miles, until they were near the juncture of the Adige and the Alpone. He built a pontoon bridge across the Adige and at dawn on the fifteenth, he got his men on the north side, only a mile or so south of Arcola and about five miles south of Villanuova.

Alvintzy's supplies and rear area were located in Villanuova, Napoleon's true target that was defended by 8,000 Austrians. There were another 3,000 Austrians in Arcola, covering Alvintzy's left flank, and the area for many miles west and north of that town was a heavy marsh with few roads through it. This was an advantage to the French, for Alvintzy's larger numbers would be of no use to him in such terrain.

After a fierce fight, Napoleon's men forced their way over the bridge across the Alpone and took Arcola. But the Austrians they drove out of that town were reinforced by an Alvintzy who was now growing worried about his southern flank, and Napoleon could get no farther north toward Villanuova.

Napoleon, of course, had other issues that he had to deal with as well. Concerned at dusk that Davidovitch might have broken through Vaubois's position, he withdrew all his forces south of the Adige. Relieved to learn from couriers that night that there had been no movement by Davidovitch on the fifteenth, Napoleon led his men back across the Adige in the morning of the sixteenth.

But the Austrians had returned to Arcola, and this time the French were unable to even get over the bridge that crossed the Alpone there.

After another day of heavy but inconclusive fighting, a Napoleon still worried about Vaubois and Davidovitch crossed to the south side of the Adige. And once again, he learned that night that Davidovitch had made no move on the sixteenth.

At first light on the seventeenth, Napoleon's men were again across the Adige and advancing aggressively. But the Austrians in Arcola were by now well prepared, with artillery covering the roads and the bridge across the Alpone that the French would have to use to attack them. Frustrated once again, Napoleon turned to a bit of trickery, something he was not to use often. He sent a small group of his elite Guides and four mounted buglers across the Alpone far downriver and out of sight of the Austrians. As the French attacked the bridge across the Alpone once again, the Guides and the buglers east of town made so much noise that the Austrians were sure they had been turned and were being attacked from the rear. Shaken by two days of heavy fighting and many losses, the Austrians in Arcola panicked and fled north toward Villa-nuova, and Alvintzy's worst fears were confirmed: Napoleon was loose in his rear. Not waiting to be tested, he turned his troops around and headed them back to the east.

As Napoleon began his pursuit, couriers told him that Davidovitch was driving Vaubois back. Leaving his cavalry to pursue Alvintzy, Napoleon force-marched his infantry toward Rivoli. That afternoon, Davidovitch had pushed Vaubois some distance and it was looking like he would soon overpower him. But his scouts saw the large force marching his way, and realizing that he would soon be facing Napoleon's entire army, he turned his army around and immediately started a forced march to the north.

Napoleon's men were quite exhausted, so he let Davidovitch get away. But over the past few days, he had done something quite stunning: faced by an army of 18,000 moving south and another army of

28,000 moving west, both poised to crush his army between them, Napoleon took the initiative from his adversaries and attacked them. First he feinted north, freezing a hesitant Davidovitch. Then he attacked Alvintzy's army coming from the east and struck it in the flank, eventually driving it back in disorder and confusion. Finally, he turned on the army threatening him again from the north and so frightened Davidovitch that he turned and fled.

Now, in early May 1863, Lee found himself confronting a similar challenge at Chancellorsville. After Sedgwick broke through Early's thin defenses, Early did what Lee had told him to do in this eventuality: he withdrew his force south on Telegraph Road, thus staying between Sedgwick and the Confederate supply point at Guiney Station. Another brigade, that of Wilcox from McLaws's division, found itself on the northern side of the Union breakout. But as Sedgwick proceeded deliberately and somewhat cautiously westward on the Orange Plank Road, Wilcox saw his opportunity, and he raced west, then south to block that road.

With barely 2,000 men, Wilcox could not hold long in one place, but he made a slow, stubborn retreat, fighting for every foot he gave up. That Confederate aggression, combined with Sedgwick's reluctance to advance into the unknown, consumed several important hours. Lee, meanwhile, had pulled McLaws's division out of the line and sent it down the Orange Plank Road to help Early and Wilcox delay Sedgwick. At the same time, he ordered Trimble's division to threaten Hooker's left flank near the U.S. Ford. He also moved Anderson's division north to the River Road, thus presenting another threat to Hooker's left flank.[3]

By three o'clock, Lee was sure that Hooker had heard of Sedgwick's breakout from Fredericksburg, and the movements by Trimble and Anderson were intended to freeze Hooker, preventing him from either advancing to meet Sedgwick or withdrawing north across the Rappahannock. And they had their desired effect: Hooker saw the demonstrations against his line as a real threat and his men stayed locked in their defenses, sure they were about to be attacked.

Wilcox, meanwhile, was doing his best to delay Sedgwick, playing for time as McLaws and his four brigades approached from his rear. After several miles of constant firing with, in some places, only hundreds of feet between blue and gray forces, they came to a clearing near the Salem Church. As the Union forces drove Wilcox through that open area and over a rise, they followed aggressively, only to confront Wilcox joined by the first of McLaws's men to arrive. The sheet of rifle fire that screamed out from the long butternut line was balanced by the thunder of cannon pouring canister into their blue ranks and stopping them dead in their tracks. Then the Rebel counterattack drove the stunned blue soldiers back across the clearing in desperate, confused disorder.

Sedgwick's force hurriedly dug in as night fell, and the soldiers of McLaws and Early also spent the night where they were. Soon after dawn on the morrow, Early marched north and got between Sedgwick and Fredericksburg. Gibbon's Union division had been left on Marye's Heights by Sedgwick, but Early handled him roughly, driving him off the heights and back into town. Early posted Barksdale's Mississippi brigade on Marye's Heights to ward off Gibbon, then turned his men west to hit the Yankees from the rear.[4]

Back at Chancellorsville that same morning of the fourth, Lee saw that the Army of the Potomac had significantly improved its defenses during the night. Now he was even more confident that Hooker was frozen in place. He soon received messages from McLaws asking for reinforcements, so he pulled Anderson's division out of line and sent it to support McLaws and Early by stretching between their lines on the southern side of what had become Sedgwick's U-shaped perimeter.

But by the afternoon of the fourth, the Union soldiers were prepared for Confederate attacks, their perimeter shrewdly enclosing a long segment of the Orange Plank Road. This positioning prevented the Confederates from using that main road to move their troops, a limitation that cost them many frustrating hours of cross-country marching. And at the northern end of Sedgwick's perimeter, a pontoon bridge across the Rappahannock had been built, giving them an open door through which to slip on any dark night.

Anderson's men thus handicapped necessarily moved slowly, and of course both McLaws and Early awaited their arrival before launching their unified attack. Lee soon appeared on the scene, having left Stuart in charge of the rest of his army, some 25,000 men facing Hooker's 75,000. And although Lee had only some 21,000 men arrayed here to confront Sedgwick's 19,000, his constant aggression made him impatient with his subordinates, McLaws in particular. It wasn't until six o'clock in the evening that all the guns were in position and the cannon shots signaling the attack were fired.

Early's force moved forward aggressively, as did some of Anderson's men. General McLaws, however, did not advance his units, keeping them where they were and doing virtually nothing. Then fog crept in, further obscuring the countryside. But Lee's ire was up and he wanted to continue the attack on Sedgwick, so he ordered his first night attack of the war.

The soldiers of all three divisions, however, were exhausted, and they made very little headway in the dark. The artillery, for their part, fired all night, both at assumed enemy locations and more particularly at where they thought the pontoon bridge was located. But these guns were literally firing blind, and they did little damage to Union forces.

The next morning, Lee learned that all of Sedgwick's men had gotten across the bridge, whereupon the southern end had been detached from the bank and the entire pontoon structure pulled back over to the northern side of the river.

Lee was not happy that Sedgwick had gotten away as he sent his three divisions back to Chancellorsville, and he was determined to fall on Hooker and crush him. But Hooker, too, refused to take his blade: on the night of May 5, Hooker issued the order for the Army of the Potomac to withdraw to the northern bank of the Rappahannock.[5]

This battle has been compared to the Battle of Arcola by many people since then. In a *Military History and Atlas of the Napoleonic Wars* by Esposito and Elting, a book used for instruction of cadets at West Point during the 1960s, we find the following:

> *The campaign of Alvintzy's first advance is somewhat reminiscent of the Chancellorsville campaign in the American Civil War. Bonaparte, like Lee, caught between two superior forces, utilized superior mobility and a central position to exploit enemy delays and to seize the initiative. Similarly, both campaigns were largely battles between the wills of the opposing commanders. As Lee did with Hooker, Bonaparte overcame Alvintzy and Davidovitch through determination, superior energy, impetuosity, tenacity, and the ability to analyze situations and calculate the chances under the most difficult conditions. In the words of General Patton: "Weapons change, but man changes not at all. To win battles, you do not beat weapons—you beat the soul of the enemy man."*[6]

Given his focused study of Napoleon ever since he was a West Point cadet, it seems reasonable to look at the similarities Lee might have detected between the circumstance he faced at Chancellorsville and those faced by Napoleon during Alvintzy's First Advance. With this background it becomes self-evident that Lee used Napoleon's brilliant success in that moment as his model when he also found himself squeezed between two enemy forces that wanted to crush him. And in the end, Lee, too, realized a spectacular success, thus reinforcing the efficacy and the power of his use of Napoleon's triumphs to guide his own battlefield plans and actions during the American Civil War.

# 9

## Lee Moves North

DESPITE THE TWO great victories at Fredericksburg and Chancellorsville within five months, all was not well with the leadership of the Confederacy. Grant threatened Vicksburg in the west, and if that last bastion fell, it would mean all open connections to the states of Texas, Louisiana, and Arkansas would effectively be cut by Union gunboats. Lee and others knew that the South was far outstripped by the North in all the essentials of war: manpower, horsepower, matériel, industrial capacity, weapons and ammunition production, railroads, ships, and many other factors as well. With the blockade locking down the South's access to the markets of Europe, it would be only a matter of time until all life had been squeezed out of the Confederacy.

And with so much of the war being fought in northern Virginia, the land was becoming scraped bare. Lee not only couldn't feed his horses there, he couldn't even feed his men. He knew that he had to do everything he could to raise their morale, to fill them with the sense that they were on a moral mission, truly fighting the good fight and showing the world that they were far better soldiers than their adversaries, even though that was just plain no longer the case. Lee no doubt remembered Napoleon's famous maxims "In war, the moral is to the physical as three is to one" and "A man does not have himself killed for a few half-pence a day or for a petty distinction; you must speak to the soul in order to electrify the man."[1]

And Lee did speak to his men's souls. Throughout the war and for the rest of his days, all the men who served under his command simply adored him, as, indeed, did many of his adversaries.

Now the time was at hand for a bold move. Lee, more than anyone else, could see that the glimmer of extended life for the Confederacy was there, right there, you could almost reach out and touch it. But it would be a fleeting opportunity. Now was the moment for him to act. Now, in the wake of Chancellorsville, he would lead his army north, into the Pennsylvania countryside, where he would fight the last major battle of the war. He did not want another inconclusive battle, from which the defeated Union army could retreat to refurbish itself and then return to battle on another day. No, what he wanted was a triumph in the north such that he killed, captured, or scattered the soldiers of the Army of the Potomac. If that happened, with his victorious army poised above Washington, Baltimore, and Philadelphia, he could not only humble his adversaries, he could force the Union to concede southern independence and so bring about the end of the war. That was his real goal.

After his triumph at Chancellorsville, Lee began to make serious plans to invade the North. Back in February, he had asked Jackson's master cartographer, Jedediah Hotchkiss, to prepare a set of maps that would show the roads and terrain all the way north from the Shenandoah Valley to Harrisburg and east to Philadelphia. Hotchkiss finished the maps in March, and now Lee was ready to use them.[2]

Lee argued strongly with the political leadership of the Confederacy that he should be allowed to lead the Army of Northern Virginia, now at the peak of its strength, into Pennsylvania, where he hoped to win a climactic battle. And eventually, Jefferson Davis and Secretary of War James Seddon approved Lee's proposal.[3]

The first week of June had been almost pure bliss for Jeb Stuart. He had moved his headquarters to Fleetwood Hill above Brandy Station in Culpeper County, Virginia, and recruits had flooded into his camp on fresh horses until he had some ninety-five hundred men under his immediate command. His horse-drawn artillery had not only been expanded but had new horses as well, and Stuart was proud as punch of his command. There seemed to be almost an air of gaiety on Fleetwood Hill, and their commander felt so good that he directed a celebration and invited hundreds of civilians from surrounding areas.[4]

There was a ball in the county courthouse on the evening of June 4, and the next day began with a review of the entire force accompanied by music from three bands. Then Stuart presented a series of mock battles in which his waves of horsemen flashed across the meadows, their silver sabers shining in the sun while horse-drawn artillery fired rounds of noise-only gunpowder and no ball. The noise, the speed, the glamour, the dash were almost too much, and ladies lining the reviewing area on a hillside sighed and squealed and even fainted in sheer delight. The pageant lasted until around four in the afternoon, and it was followed by another ball that evening.

The Confederate cavalry rested the next few days, but on June 8 they repeated the performance, though without the ladies. This time, the reviewing position on the hillside was occupied by Robert E. Lee and the 10,000 infantry in Hood's division. And once again, Stuart put on quite a show. Lee was quite pleased at the seeming strength of Stuart's command, and he complimented him before leaving that evening. That night, the Rebel horsemen, pleased and exhausted, fell into a heavy and well-earned sleep.[5]

But unbeknownst to Stuart, Hooker had ordered his cavalry commander, General Pleasonton, to cross the Rappahannock and try to punish the Confederate cavalry. He was also to try to learn whether Lee was moving north. Rumors said a large body of Rebel infantry was nearby, some twenty miles northwest of Chancellorsville in northern Virginia. If true, it was powerful evidence of Lee's impending move north.

On June 9 at 4:30 A.M. (there was no daylight saving time in the nineteenth century), just as the first shades of gray began appearing in the eastern sky, Custer accompanied Colonel Benjamin Davis, who was leading the column of Pleasonton's right wing across the Rappahannock River at Beverly Ford. Some 11,000 Union cavalrymen crossed the river that day, at both Beverly Ford and Kelly's Ford. The Eighth New York Cavalry was the leading regiment, followed by the Eighth Illinois and the Third Indiana Cavalry, but Custer and Davis rode up front with the first horsemen to enter the water. Coming out of the river in a dark fog just before dawn, they were challenged by a Confederate sentry, but their response was to dig in their spurs and fire their pistols.

A cloud of blue horsemen followed them, rushing past the picket line and clattering up a wooded slope. Bursting out of the tree line and into the fields beyond, they were suddenly among what seemed like a thousand Confederate cavalrymen, some still rolled in their blankets but up and running for their horses.

Custer and Davis got several hundred horsemen of the Eighth New York all the way across the field, then stopped while other members of the regiment behind them rounded up prisoners and herded them back toward the ford. A few hundred yards to their front was a stone wall, and behind it, they could see hundreds more Confederates massing in a wood. They probably were not infantry, for many horses could be seen in the trees as well. Once those men in gray got organized, they looked like trouble.

Davis turned this advance element of the Eighth New York and followed the prisoners back to the edge of the Rappahannock. Meanwhile, the Eighth Illinois and Third Indiana came up from the river, out of the woods, and lined up for a charge across the field toward the stone wall. While the Union force was being aligned, Custer and Davis learned from the prisoners that they were part of Jeb Stuart's cavalry force, the so-called Invincibles that had never been defeated by Union cavalry.

Davis and Custer joined the three regiments of some twelve hundred Union horsemen, all straining at their bits. Then Davis gave the signal and they flooded across the field, over the stone wall and through another band of woods. As they charged across the following field, driving scattered clumps of Confederates before them, Custer noticed a large band of gray cavalry forming off to his left as if to cut them off. As he galloped on, a rider caught up with him and shouted the news that Colonel Davis had been shot and killed.

When he heard this, Custer stopped the entire brigade and turned them around. Now a heavy line of Confederate horse was arrayed between them and Beverly Ford, but he never even hesitated. Raising his sword again, he dug in his spurs as his voice rang out:

*"Cha-a-a-a-a-rge!"*

They slammed into the waiting gray line and hacked their way through it, then stopped short of the ford. Looking back, Custer could see that large elements of the Confederate force were leaving, spurring off to the south where loud gunfire reverberated from what must be the rest of Pleasonton's force attacking Jeb Stuart. It would do no good for him to cross the Rappahannock again now, so Custer had his men turn and launch attacks with two-hundred-man squadrons against the apparent weak points in the Confederate lines. The result was that gray squadrons that had spurred off came rushing back to avoid disaster, and the Confederate crisis was made more severe.

Stuart and his Prussian cavalryman friend Heros von Borcke, who acted as an unofficial aide, courier, and companion, were cherishing rare cups of coffee at Stuart's headquarters on Fleetwood Hill when they were startled by gunfire. They didn't know what it was, believing the Yankees to be far away, but it came from the northeast, the direction of Beverly's Ford. Then an orderly arrived at the gallop with news that large Yankee mounted forces had crashed through the pickets at Beverly's Ford.

Stuart brought his scattered brigades forward to the area of Fleetwood Hill, but the tired troopers were slow in assembling. As the men arrived by regiment, Stuart attempted to form them in a line of battle, then ordered them forward. He sent Robertson's North Carolina brigade down to cover Kelly's Ford to their southeast almost as an afterthought, then went down off Fleetwood Hill with most of his staff to direct the fighting.

Unbeknownst to them, Stuart and his men were facing only Buford's division, which had come across Beverly's Ford, backed by a brigade of infantry under Ames, which was less than half the entire Union force. Two other cavalry divisions, under Gregg and Duffie, were scheduled to cross at Kelly's Ford at the same time, though they were delayed. Once out of the water, however, Gregg and Duffie moved directly west, and Robertson's brigade somehow missed them entirely. Gregg turned his division north at the right place and moved toward the south slope of Fleetwood Hill while Duffie was apparently confused and kept his force going west.

At the time, there were only a few men left on Fleetwood Hill, including Stuart's adjutant general, Major Henry B. McClellan, a handful of couriers, and one artillery gun for which there were only a few rounds. McClellan saw Gregg's force headed toward him in the distance and sent riders off with the panicked message to Stuart that his headquarters was in peril. He then coolly had the single gun wheeled forward and ordered its crew to begin a slow, methodical fire on the approaching blue column.

His bluff worked perfectly, for Gregg, a less-than-aggressive cavalry leader, suddenly became worried about what he was risking with his division. He stopped forward movement to bring his own guns up and had them commence a measured counter-battery fire. But this didn't last long, for McClellan's gun soon ran out of ammunition and was pulled back. Then, just as Colonel Wyndham's brigade from Gregg's division was moving up the hill, two regiments of horse sent by Stuart arrived, plunged over the edge, and slammed into them.

Stuart had pulled his men in the northern section back to form a defensive line that ran across the front slope of Fleetwood Hill. On the northern flank, W. H. F. "Rooney" Lee led a charge that stopped Buford. But he suffered a serious wound to his thigh in the process, a wound that would keep him from leading his brigade to Gettysburg and caused command of the unit to pass to Colonel Chambliss.

The lines continued to move back and forth over several hours, but finally Stuart began to get the upper hand. And it was the blue that finally gave way on Fleetwood Hill, Gregg's men driven off by Hampton's. During that time, however, Pleasonton got to Brandy Station, where he saw railroad cars coming down the line from Culpeper and unloading regiments of Confederate infantry. This must mean that Lee had moved his main army northwest from Chancellorsville, and that was important news for Hooker to have. Pleasonton knew he could not stand against a major combined force of Confederate infantry as well as cavalry, so in late afternoon he ordered all his troops back across the Rappahannock. And that was the end of the Battle of Brandy Station.

Union forces had suffered more casualties than Stuart's men had—some 900 casualties out of 11,000 Union cavalrymen, versus 500 casualties out of 9,500 Confederate horsemen from Stuart's command. Still, it was fair notice that the Union cavalry of the Army of the Potomac could almost match that of Stuart.

Pleasonton heard about Custer's actions and decisions in handling a cavalry regiment on the battlefield, a performance that pleased him greatly. In his after-action report, Pleasonton said Custer "charged with Colonel Davis, in the taking of Beverly Ford, and was conspicuous for gallantry throughout the fight."[6] More than even Custer himself suspected at the time, his star was starting to rise high.

Lee had begun to move his army north in earnest, choosing a route that would take him down the Shenandoah Valley to the Potomac. He intended to plunge north into Pennsylvania, but wanted a good head start. After Brandy Station, therefore, Stuart was told to prevent Yankee reconnaissance by keeping Union cavalry east of the Blue Ridge Mountains, which parallel the Shenandoah River.

Stuart brought three of his cavalry brigades up to the east of the Blue Ridge Mountains, where he was repeatedly attacked by Union cavalry and infantry. At Hooker's orders, they were trying to learn if Lee's army was massing in the Shenandoah Valley and perhaps preparing to invade the north. On June 17, 19, and 21, battles were fought at Aldie, Middleburg, and Upperville, and although the Union force continually pushed Stuart's men back, this was largely because they had the advantage of infantry support. But the Confederates were playing a delaying game, and Stuart's mission was to prevent the Yankees from getting past the Blue Ridge Mountains, a mission he accomplished.

Still, the fights were vicious, with casualties on both sides in the hundreds, though none approached the scale of Brandy Station. But since these engagements were brought on by Union forces and Stuart's men were only trying to slow and hinder them rather than defend certain ground, the troops in gray usually had the ability, when things looked bad, to simply ride away and set up another delaying defensive position on the next ridgeline to their rear. While sometimes the fighting was heated, in the light of the Battle of Gettysburg that would soon follow, these were only bloody skirmishes.

When Lee's army moved across the Potomac River into Maryland, the cavalry brigades of Jenkins and Imboden went with them. The brigades of Robertson and Jones were to follow Lee, who had authorized Stuart to decide what route to take with the other three brigades of Hampton, Fitzhugh Lee, and Rooney Lee (commanded by Colonel Chambliss on this operation), just so that he came up on the right flank of the Army of Northern Virginia. Stuart decided to lead his men in another ride completely around the Army of the Potomac, after which he would join Lee's army somewhere in Pennsylvania.

But as soon as he started on June 25, problems developed. First of all, his path to the river was blocked by large Union army units and he had to swing far to the east before getting across the river, a delay of two days. Then, while riding north through Maryland, he had captured 125 Union supply wagons filled with much-needed supplies, and his movement was delayed as he escorted these valuable but slow-moving vessels along. Once he entered Pennsylvania, he even came close to Lee's army without realizing it. Then, on June 30, a line of blue horsemen suddenly blocked his path in the town of Hanover.

# ~ 10 ~

# *The Gettysburg Fight Begins*

A s the army of the Potomac followed Lee north, it went through some important transformations. On the morning of Sunday, June 28, Meade received the order to replace Hooker as commander of the Army of the Potomac.[1] But other changes were also to spring from this, as Pleasonton, in consultation with Meade, decided to shake up the command of the cavalry divisions in the hope of improving their effectiveness.[2]

In the Union army at the time, a division of cavalry was made up of three brigades, and each brigade contained from three to six regiments. By July 1863, the average Union cavalry regiment was probably around 350 men, which means that brigades averaged between 1,000 and 2,000 men, and a division consisted of 3,000 to 5,000 mounted men. Custer's brigade at Gettysburg, nearly 2,000 men strong, was quite large by Union standards. Confederate cavalry regiments and brigades were somewhat larger than their Union counterparts.

Pleasonton wanted men of action in front of his cavalry brigades, commanders who were prepared to fight, to personally lead mounted attacks against the enemy. At the time, he had several men who, for political reasons, commanded brigades they had raised back in their home states. But once they were actually at war, he had found that some of them were little better than tired old men. While they may well have loved the title and authority of brigade command, they tended to shy away from combat or any other risks, particularly those in which they might be in personal danger. And if the Union was to win this war, such behavior just wouldn't do.

But Pleasonton had an immediate solution to this problem. He had observed several of his aides in combat, and three of them were just the sort of aggressive fighters that he sought: Wesley Merritt, Elon Farnsworth, and George Custer. Custer in particular had shown his courage, style, and levelheaded judgment, most recently at Brandy Station, where he had led a New York regiment into combat after its colonel had been killed in action. Pleasonton had gotten numerous reports on Custer that day, and his performance in battle had been superb.

Although these three men were only captains at the time, Pleasonton sent their names to Meade requesting their promotion to brevet brigadier general. Such a leap was virtually unprecedented, passing over the ranks of major, lieutenant colonel, and colonel, all of which were normally held for many years each in peacetime. But war sometimes calls for bold strokes, and Pleasonton assured Meade these men had shown their capability and that he was confident they would be aggressive and reliable brigade commanders.

Meade accepted Pleasonton's assessment, and at midday on the twenty-eighth, he wired their names on to Halleck, the commanding general of the U.S. Army back in Washington, D.C., requesting their immediate promotion. Within hours Pleasonton received orders from Meade promoting the three men as requested. Custer and Farnsworth were given brigades in Kilpatrick's Division, while Merritt became a brigade commander under Buford.[3]

The news soon reached Custer, along with notice that the brigade he was to command was made up of the First, Fifth, Sixth, and Seventh Michigan cavalries. His new brigade was some forty-five miles ahead of him when he received his promotion, and he didn't catch up to them until late that night. But before he set out for them that evening, he took care of his uniform, for the appearance of a new general officer taking over command is of crucial importance.

Despite the short time he had, he somehow managed to replace the simple blue jacket he had worn as Pleasonton's aide with a black velvet coat adorned by a double row of gold buttons down the front and large loops of gold braid on the lower sleeve of each arm. He also wore a silver star on each collar, a large-brimmed black hat with gold braid and a star pinned to it, and a bright red scarf tied around his neck.

In later years, one aspect of Custer that was heavily criticized was his gaudy uniform, with many feeling that was just further evidence of his boundless ego and lack of common sense. But this whole uniform issue deserves some context.

General officers were always given wide latitude in choosing their own uniforms, and with gold braid being rather common among Civil War general officers on both sides, Custer's outfit might have been a bit extravagant, but it was far from outrageous. His model, of course, was the renowned Marshal Murat, Napoleon's chief of cavalry, whose uniform was primarily bright colors offset by feathers, gold braid, or anything else that might catch his fancy.

But the point of a showy uniform for Custer was one of command presence on the battlefield: to his men, he wanted to be readily distinguishable at first glance from all other soldiers. He intended to lead from the front, and to him it was a crucial issue of unit morale that his men be able to look up in the middle of a charge, or at any other time on the battlefield, and instantly see him leading the way into danger. And as we shall see, it worked.

On the very next day after Custer had joined his unit, June 29, his brigade led Meade's army into Pennsylvania. There was no serious contact with Rebel forces for the first thirty-six hours or so of his command, and in the late morning of the thirtieth, Custer and the First and Seventh Michigan Cavalries rode through the small town of Hanover, while the Fifth and Sixth were still some seven miles behind them at the village of Littlestown. The First and Seventh were armed at the time with revolvers, sabers, and single-shot carbines, while the Fifth and much of the Sixth, in addition to their sabers and revolvers, were able to put out far more rapid firepower from their seven-shot Spencer repeating rifles.

Custer was only a few miles down the road past Hanover when the noise of battle suddenly erupted from that direction. Custer had turned his two regiments around and started moving them back toward Hanover when a courier arrived, with the news that Farnsworth's brigade had been in the middle of town when a column of gray cavalry burst upon them from a side street and smashed through one of his regiments, cutting it in half. After a brief flurry of gunfire, the Confederates had pulled back into the surrounding farm fields, but there was now a large host of mounted gray troopers exchanging fire with Farnsworth's reassembled unit.

As he reentered town, Custer quickly saw that these attacking Confederates were a sizable force—certainly many hundreds, maybe even thousands—and they therefore had to be part of Jeb Stuart's force. The Fifth and Sixth had fortunately moved forward toward the sound of the guns, and Custer's brigade was quickly reunited in Hanover. Then he received the order from Kilpatrick to array his troops on the northeast end of town near the railroad station and engage the enemy.

That is precisely what he did, ordering the First Michigan to support his artillery battery on a nearby hill, then directing the Sixth to dismount and advance on the enemy, engaging them with their rifles while the Fifth and Seventh were held in reserve. The commander of E Troop, Sixth Cavalry, was Captain James H. Kidd, and he later recorded his first exposure to Custer:

*As the men of the Sixth, armed with their Spencer rifles, were deploying forward across the railroad into a wheat field beyond, I heard a voice new to me, directly in rear of the portion of the line where I was, giving directions for the movement, in clear, resonant tones, and in a calm, confident manner, at once resolute and reassuring. Looking back to see whence it came, my eyes were riveted upon a figure only a few feet distant. . . . At first, I thought he might be a staff officer, conveying the commands of his chief. But it was at once apparent that he was giving orders, not delivering them, and that he was in command of the line. . . . A keen eye would have been slow to detect in that rider with the flowing locks and gaudy tie, in his dress of velvet and gold, the master spirit that he proved to be. That garb, fantastic as at first sight it appeared to be, was to be the distinguishing mark which, during all the remaining years of that war, like the white plume of Henry of Navarre, was to show us where, in the thickest of the fight, we were to seek our leader—for, where danger was, where swords were to cross, where Greek met Greek, there was he, always. . . . Showy like Murat, fiery like Farnsworth, yet calm and self-reliant like Sheridan, he was the most brilliant and successful cavalry officer of his time. Such a man had appeared on the scene, and soon we learned to utter with pride the name of—Custer.*[4]

Although this description was written much later, it shows that Kidd liked Custer a great deal, as did his men. But their affection was based on his battlefield performance, and that implies a true respect and admiration for this young commanding general that was earned in battle. Custer's boyish good looks were also a compelling feature of his appearance, for as he became a triumphant hero, he was painted in the newspapers of the north as "the boy general with the golden locks."

From the Hanover railroad station, Custer's men of the Sixth Cavalry advanced, firing steadily, against the much larger Confederate force. But after only ten or fifteen minutes, the Rebels turned and withdrew, riding off to the northeast. Custer reported this to Kilpatrick, and they agreed it seemed strange, as they were certain Lee was still somewhere out to the west in front of them with his main army. Kilpatrick's division tried to pursue these Rebel riders, but they lost contact after dark.[5]

This first exposure to combat with Custer as their leader had a dramatic effect on the whole brigade. Again, Kidd conveys that rather clearly:

*Under his skilful hand the four regiments were soon welded into a coherent unit, acting so like one man that the history of one is oftentimes apt to be the history of the other. . . . The result of the day at Hanover was that Stuart was driven still farther away from a junction with Lee.*[6]

They camped that night somewhere in the Pennsylvania countryside well north of Hanover, and the next morning, July 1, 1863, Custer led his men through Abbottstown, then on to the Harrisburg Pike. Though he sent scouts out in all directions, no Confederate forces were detected. Then, in late morning, they heard gunfire from the direction of Gettysburg, still some ten miles away. They knew Buford's cavalry division was over in that direction; perhaps they had found something.

The firing seemed to last most of the day, echoing in the distance as they moved on an assigned course that did not seem to take them much closer to the battle. Although they did not know it at the time, the gunfire they were hearing came from the first day of the three-day Battle of Gettysburg.

THE BATTLE HAD BEGUN on the first of July, just to the northwest of that key town. An element of Buford's Union cavalry division had fired upon the lead infantry units of A. P. Hill's III Corps of the Army of Northern Virginia as it moved down the Chambersburg Pike toward Gettysburg. As the Confederate infantry brigades of Archer and Davis deployed and moved against them, the Union cavalry was suddenly in serious trouble. But then Meredith's First Brigade and Cutler's Second Brigade of the First Division of the I Corps of the Army of the Potomac—the First Brigade being the famous "Iron Brigade"—replaced the cavalry. The Iron Brigade threw Archer's brigade back south of the Chambersburg Pike, even capturing General Archer himself. North of that road, however, Cutler's men were driven back by Davis's men.

The two forces paused in a sort of stalemate atop McPherson's Ridge and Heth removed the brigades of Archer and Davis. These well-used units were moved out to the flank while two fresh brigades replaced them at the center and the gray line pressed forward once again. More of the Union I Corps had come to the front to help stem the tide, but then it was flanked on its right by Rodes's division of Ewell's Confederate II Corps arriving from the north, and the Union line began to reel. Howard's XI Corps came up on the I Corps's right flank to bar Rodes's division, but was then struck in its own right flank by Early's division of Ewell's corps coming into town from the northeast.

Much of the Union force that had been engaged so far then collapsed and fled through town, allowing the Confederates to capture well over 4,000 prisoners. Lee had this day managed to collapse his Napoleonic fan on two extended and vulnerable Union corps, finally overwhelming them with a series of flank attacks that made their positions untenable. Some 27,000 Confederates had smashed 23,000 Union soldiers, destroying their organizational structures by killing, wounding, capturing, or driving their men through town.[7] The men in blue fled south of town and climbed up on Cemetery Hill, where Howard had left a fresh brigade of infantry and two artillery batteries of twelve guns. These fired on the Confederate pursuers as Union soldiers flooded up the rise, where they were halted and deployed defensively.

In the wake of the Union collapse, Lee had ordered Ewell to continue the pursuit south of town and "if practicable" to take Cemetery Hill, where the Union soldiers were attempting to reassemble and establish defensive positions. Many words have been written that argue both sides of what Ewell should have done that evening, arguments that will not be repeated here. Ultimately, however, he did not launch a major attack against either Cemetery Hill or Culp's Hill that evening.

At around five o'clock on the evening of July 1, Longstreet arrived on Seminary Ridge and he and Lee discussed their situation, as they had often done in the past. Longstreet said that it would be too dangerous to attack the Union army in the defensive positions they were preparing and proposed a sweeping movement to the south and east instead, thus forcing the Yankees to attack the Confederates in a strong defensive position of their choosing.

Lee rejected this idea, and when he told Longstreet that he planned to attack the federals in their positions on Cemetery Ridge the next day, it was the subordinate who protested. If Meade and his Union army were there the next day, Longstreet said, it would be because they wanted Lee to attack them there. Then he protested that such a plan was at variance with a promise Lee had supposedly made to Longstreet at the outset.

This alleged promise was that, while the invasion would be strategically offensive, Lee had agreed to do any actual fighting on the tactical defensive, that he would force the Yankees to attack the Confederates in a defensive position rather than the reverse. Longstreet made these comments rather strongly and even showed some anger to his commander. But Lee paid no attention to these words and told Longstreet that he would devise a way to attack the Yankees in their position the next day.[8]

This strong opposition from Longstreet was somewhat of a surprise to Lee, and it did not sit well with him. Major G. M. Sorrel, Longstreet's chief of staff, captured the tension between the two men well:

*He [Longstreet] did not want to fight on the ground or on the plan adopted by the general-in-chief. As Longstreet was not to be made willing and Lee refused to change or could not change, the former failed to conceal some anger.*[9]

This unfortunate banging of rhetorical swords seems to have somewhat soured the relationship between Lee and Longstreet for the following days of the Gettysburg campaign, as Coddington has well stated:

*Anxiety, probably resulting from the loss of Jackson and the absence of Stuart, and uncertainty about Meade's intentions were quite another thing than unreasoning rashness, which Longstreet charged had taken possession of Lee. Much of Lee's uneasiness undoubtedly rose from Longstreet's rather truculent attitude and obvious unwillingness to attack. Lee had affectionate respect for his most experienced corps commander, and he depended on him to smash the enemy's position with well-timed blows or effectively smother Union attempts to break the Confederate line. All during the campaign the two generals had freely and constantly consulted each other on the basis of mutual confidence, and although Longstreet in no way*

*replaced the dead Jackson, the close relations between him and Lee fre-*
*quently attracted notice and favorable comment. Now, as Lee began plan-*
*ning for the next day's operations Longstreet's violent objections to his*
*proposals must have come as a shocking surprise. Although disturbed, the*
*commanding general nevertheless kept his temper.*[10]

After Longstreet had left, Lee returned to his headquarters tent, where he very studiously and laboriously developed his plans, weighing everything, down to the smallest detail. But it seems apparent that, after this rather brusque meeting with Longstreet, he would avoid, at least in the short term, seeking his advice and counsel.

That night of July 1, Custer and his brigade of cavalry camped at Heidlersburg, Pennsylvania. The scouts he had sent out returned with the news that Buford had found Lee and fought him all day. Infantry had come up to help Buford, the I Corps and the XI Corps, but they had been cut to pieces by the Confederates and were driven back through the town of Gettysburg. Union forces were still arriving, and they were well entrenched on high ground behind town for the night. It looked like the big battle might come on the next day.[11]

At sunrise on July 2 the men of the Second Brigade were ready to go, but they had to wait for orders. Then, after an hour of mounting anxiety, a courier delivered the orders to Custer: he was to proceed with all haste to Gettysburg, which was still nine miles away.

They moved down the Harrisburg Pike until they got to Rock Creek. They were stopped there with the loud noise of battle coming from somewhere to their north, where Howard's Union XI Corps and part of Ewell's Confederate II Corps were engaged in a fierce fight. Still in formation on a road close to Culp's Hill, Custer was told to deploy his troops facing northeast in such a way as to guard against the Confederate cavalry trying to get in behind him and turn the Union right wing. But while battle flared nearby all afternoon, the flame never reached them, and Custer's men did not fire a shot.

In midafternoon, Custer was ordered to move north and try to cut into Ewell's rear, to at least slash at his lines of communications, to do anything that might distract him from the savage beating he was delivering to Union forces. Custer quickly mounted his men and moved north several miles, crossed over the York Pike, then over the railroad line. Finally, he turned back south on a main road, thus making a loop that would bring his force back toward Gettysburg. But he hoped they were well behind Confederate lines.

They were on a dirt road now, which silenced their horses' hoofbeats, and within a short time, Custer would find a force of Rebel cavalry with which he would start a major fight. This engagement would be of very small scale relative to the much larger battle going on at Gettysburg on the same day, and it has been recorded by most historians who have noted it as a great blunder by Custer. But anyone who says that simply fails to understand what he was trying to do, let alone how well he carried it off.

As they approached the rural village of Hunterstown, scouts came rushing back to report Confederate horsemen there. Custer himself rode forward to investigate, ever careful that they not take notice of him or any of his men. A short distance southwest of town, he rode up over a wooded rise and looked down across wide fields that spread before him. The road went forward down the slope, then turned to the right as it leveled off and ran through an open area until it reached another rise nearly a mile away, where it disappeared into the trees. No more than a few hundred yards in front of him on the right and at the edge of the road stood a wooden house and a large wooden barn on stone footings. Beyond those buildings, the open plain spread, perhaps a half mile wide and covered by lush green fields of corn and wheat. The road ran straight ahead, dividing the crops in half, until it reached the far tree line.[12] Under those trees, Custer saw many men in gray, and he studied them through his field glasses.

It turned out to be a mass of Southern horsemen, most of whom had dismounted and were taking their ease at the edge of the woods, and he had no doubt that there were more Confederate horsemen beyond those he could easily see. A picket line of cavalry, some dismounted, was posted across the road a few hundred yards on his side of the larger Confederate group at the edge of the wood line, but as he watched them they didn't seem to notice his presence.

Slipping back into the trees, Custer remounted and rode back to his men, now only a few hundred yards away and on the other side of the rise that blocked them from Confederate view. He wasn't sure how big this Confederate force was, but it was part of Jeb Stuart's Invincibles, that much seemed certain, and his brigade had slipped up behind them, apparently undetected.

The road that led to the men in gray was bordered by what looked like solid, sturdy fences and was thus wide enough for perhaps only three or four horsemen to ride side by side. Once you got to the open area beyond the corn, the fields on either side were also crossed by numerous fences. That fact alone would preclude any major, sweeping cavalry attack by either side, so Custer was limited in the scope of any surprise attack he might deliver. But with those restrictions and the Confederates apparently not yet aware that he was at hand with two thousand of his own horsemen, the question he posed himself was how he could best deliver a stunning blow.

He knew he could not get his entire force down that narrow road to attack the Confederates with any effect, because they would have to move in a narrow column. This meant that before the full weight of their numbers could smash into the unsuspecting enemy soldiers they would be alerted and probably counterattacking, thus eliminating any advantage of surprise. But if he prepared a killing ground up here by the barn, how could he draw a sizable number of Rebel horsemen onto it?

He knew the answer right away, no doubt drawn from the famous Battle of the Cowpens that was fought in the Revolutionary War on January 17, 1781, a battle he had studied at West Point. There, General Daniel Morgan and a mixed force of about a thousand irregular militia and regular Continental soldiers took on twelve hundred British regulars under Lieutenant Colonel Banastre Tarleton. And there can be little doubt but that Morgan got his idea from Hannibal's triumphant victory at the Battle of Cannae in 216 B.C., as he followed its format closely.

The first American line at the Cowpens was made up of a few hundred militia on the crest of a small rise. These men stood up and yelled insults at the British, which caused them to deploy and attack, a line of redcoats advancing with Brown Bess muskets and cold steel bayonets. These were among the most feared soldiers in the world, but the militiamen were still untouchable by them at long range, and they continued to hurl verbal insults at the English. When the redcoats got to within musket range, the militiamen fired two or three volleys at their approaching formation, then turned and ran back to a second line manned by another hundred or so militia.

And there, once again, the same thing happened: American militiamen hurled verbal insults, then fired two or three volleys against lines of red-clothed infantrymen advancing toward them, only to once again turn and run as the King's men got close.

When the militia got back to the third line of five hundred Continental soldiers, formed in a shallow horseshoe, they were being pursued by tired and angry British soldiers who had already left a large number of their fellows bleeding on the ground behind them. The redcoats were milling like a mob by this time, and they plunged right onto Morgan's chosen killing ground. And once they were in the trap, they were fired upon from the front and both flanks by American regulars, the Continental soldiers who would not run. But they had no need to run.

Suddenly stunned and stopped, the British collapsed as a unit, and some of the survivors turned and tried to run themselves. But they were cut off by several hundred American cavalry, and most of the English infantry force quickly surrendered. Only Tarleton and his staff as well as some three hundred mounted dragoons got away.

That day, Morgan killed 110 British soldiers and took another 800 British prisoners, of whom 224 were wounded, while his own losses were 12 killed and 61 wounded. One of the few American victories during the Revolutionary War, this was precisely the sort of thing Custer had in store for that large body of Confederate cavalry at Hunterstown, gray horsemen whose precise identity was still unknown.

Custer quickly formulated his plan and, without sharing it with anyone, began to deploy his troops. The farm belonged to the Felty family, and it included a large house and barn very close to the road. Custer put three companies of the Sixth Michigan inside the barn, facing the road with their Spencer repeating rifles. He deployed the rest of the regiment on foot in the trees and bushes along the road on the sides of the barn, and he had the men of the Seventh Michigan dismount and hide in the cornfield across the road. Both these forces deployed on foot from the wood line on the crest of the ridge, and with the house and barn and the high corn, they would have remained hidden from the Rebels while they moved into position. The Confederate pickets stationed across the road nearly a mile away might have noticed some movement by a handful of Yankee cavalry, but given the lay of the land, the cornfield, and the large barn and house that obscured their vision, they couldn't have seen much more.

Once he had stationed the Sixth and Seventh Michigan cavalries on either side of the road, Custer closed off the U behind them with the First and Fifth cavalries arrayed across the road near the wood line along with his artillery battery. These guns were commanded by Lieutenant Alexander Pennington, a man who would truly shine on July 3. Still only a lieutenant, he had graduated from West Point one year ahead of Custer, and while he would eventually rise to the rank of brigadier general, on 2 July 1863, his moment was not yet at hand.[13]

The mission of both regiments would be to fire at the Confederate cavalry, but their fire was not to be directed at them down the road, where they were then resting. Rather, Custer intended to stir up the hornet's nest on his own, then get a large number of the gray horsemen to chase him back down the road and onto his chosen killing ground, under the guns of his waiting regiments and his artillery battery. It was in following the bluecoats that the mounted Rebels would make such easy short-range targets, galloping by right in front of the dismounted Union riflemen and into the mouths of Pennington's canister-spewing cannon. Custer had arrayed his men so as to make this road a true murderers' row.

Other historians have said that Custer led the charge without arranging his men as described above, that such an array just sort of "happened" on its own after Custer had left with "A" Troop (which is the technically proper designation of a company in the cavalry, though the terms are interchangeable) of the Sixth Michigan. But it is important to note that when the commander of a brigade of four regiments is about to enter combat with a small element of one of those regiments, only he would have had the authority to have moved the remainder of his brigade into any position. Had he said nothing before he rode off with "A" Troop of the Sixth Michigan, the four regiments and the artillery battery would have just stayed in formation on the road on which they were traveling. None of the regimental commanders would have been able to move his own or any of the other regiments, for only the brigade commander, the man responsible for the brigade, had that authority.

These arrangements took only a few minutes, and when everyone was in place, he had "A" Troop of the Sixth, commanded by Captain Thomson, form on the road in front of the barn. As these sixty-odd men were lining up, he casually mentioned that there couldn't be many Rebels down there, trying to calm their nerves for the death-defying ride in front of them. Then "A" Troop was ready, and Custer rode to their front, raised his sword, and said, "Come on, boys, I'll lead you this time!" He turned and dug in his spurs, and they galloped behind him, riding an emotional high like they had never known.

The Confederate force in the woods was the Cobb Legion of Hampton's brigade, which at that time in the war was the equivalent of a regiment numbering about 330 men. Custer's attack was totally unexpected, and he first drove in or scattered the Cobb Legion rear-guard element. But then this small Union force found itself counter-attacked from three sides by a howling mass of wild men in gray. Hampton himself was on the field, and he quickly ordered both the Phillips Legion and the Second South Carolina Cavalry, two of his other regiments, to strike this surprising blue arrow in the side of the Cobb Legion.

Custer's force turned around as quickly as it could and beat a hasty retreat, with fully half their number unhorsed or hit. Custer's horse was shot and went down, and suddenly he found himself on foot. But he was rescued by twenty-two-year-old Private Norvill Churchill, who pulled him up on his horse behind him and galloped back down the road to the Felty farm.[14]

Custer had guessed correctly: fully four companies of the Cobb Legion, more than two hundred horsemen, came racing down the country road after Custer's men, mad as hornets and furious to draw blood in revenge. But when they reached the Felty farm and passed the barn, they were cut down by slashing rifle fire from troopers of the Sixth and Seventh Michigan cavalries concealed on either side of the road. Those who got past the barn confronted six artillery pieces that slashed their ranks with canister. Five of their officers went down, and the continuing cannon and rifle fire soon drove the survivors back the way they had come.

After the gray riders got back to their own lines, a few Confederate guns were brought up to the edge of the field and traded fire with Pennington. Then, as night fell, both units moved farther apart.

On the main battlefield of Gettysburg this second day of July, Lee had made two attacks against Meade's army. The main assault had been by Longstreet with two of his I Corps divisions led by Hood and McLaws and Johnson's division borrowed from A. P. Hill's III Corps, while Ewell had later launched a second attack by three brigades of his II Corps against Culp's Hill. This last effort failed utterly, though Longstreet, for his part, drove Union forces out of the Wheat Field and the Peach Orchard and back to a strong defensive line on Cemetery Ridge. His attack against Little Round Top on his far right wing, however, though a very closely contested fight, also failed. Confederate forces pulled back at dusk while the Union soldiers built ever-stronger defenses along Cemetery Ridge, from Cemetery Hill in the north to Little Round Top in the south. Longstreet's attack especially was a desperate struggle from about four o'clock until about six o'clock, and blood had flowed heavily there from both sides.

AT HUNTERSTOWN, Custer had suffered thirty-two casualties in his attack against a force of seasoned Confederate cavalry. But it appears certain he had drawn heavier enemy blood, though the numbers are difficult to quantify because official Confederate casualty reports did not distinguish the fight at Hunterstown from other actions. One of Hampton's biographers says that "Cobb's Legion lost sixty-five killed and wounded, including nearly every officer,"[15] while a Custer biographer reports that "twenty-two dead Confederates littered the route of their retreat."[16] In his Official Report, Union General Kilpatrick said the "Second Brigade (General Custer) fought most handsomely. . . . The conduct of the Sixth Michigan Cavalry and Pennington's battery is deserving of the highest praise,"[17] while in his Official Report, Confederate General Hampton says: "The Cobb Legion, which led in this gallant charge, suffered quite severely, Lieutenant Colonel Delony and several other officers being wounded, while the regiment lost in killed quite a number of brave officers and men, whose names I regret not being able to give."[18]

Custer's command stayed in place near Hunterstown until about eleven that night, when they were ordered to move to Two Taverns, some five miles southeast of Gettysburg. They spent four miserable hours in the saddle before finally dismounting for a brief sleep.

It had been a stunning day for all the men in Custer's command. He no doubt committed some errors in leading that attack, having intended only to attract pursuit and not to so badly bleed "A" Company of the Sixth Cavalry. Still, every man in the brigade now knew that, despite his youth and fancy uniform, their new commander was a man whose raw personal courage was almost frightening to behold. But that courage made the blood of every man race: this was not some old man doing his best to survive while sending young men to face their deaths; he was leading them into the very teeth of danger, and showing them how to fight with his own personal example. What soldier wouldn't do anything for such a leader, what man would deny him full commitment up to and including the very sacrifice of his own life? This had been, despite the friendly blood spilled, the most exciting day in the history of the Michigan Cavalry Brigade. But on the morrow, they would know greater risk and—yes, the term fits—greater glory as well.

# 11

# Gettysburg, Day Two

IN THE EARLY AFTERNOON of July 2, well before Longstreet's attack in the Wheat Field and Peach Orchard, Stuart reported to Lee at Gettysburg. Much has been made of the emotional reactions supposedly displayed by both men when they finally met, though there was no contemporaneous recording of that moment. But since the fact of a harsh reception by Lee might be seen to damage the credibility of any theory I propose about Stuart's importance to a larger Confederate offensive plan for July 3, it seems fair to review the stories about that reception in some detail.

In *Bold Dragoon,* an excellent biography of Stuart, author Emory Thomas says that Stuart rode ahead of his column and found Lee on Seminary Ridge in the afternoon. He then condenses the reception as follows:

> *"Well, General Stuart, you are here at last." This and no more, according to legend, was Lee's greeting.*

Thomas cites as a source for this *Lee's Lieutenants* by Douglas Southall Freeman. On page 139 of volume III of that work, we find the following:

*It was afternoon on the 2nd when Stuart, riding ahead, reached his anxious chief on Seminary Ridge. No record of the exchange between them is known to exist. The tradition is that Lee said "Well General Stuart, you are here at last"—that and little besides.*

As a source for this, Freeman cites *Jeb Stuart* by John W. Thomason, on page 440 of which we find:

*Jeb Stuart goes to the Commanding General, to report. "Well, General Stuart, you are here at last!" says Lee, austerely.*

Thomason, however, has no footnotes in the entire work, and the reader, apparently, is supposed to just trust his veracity. But on the very next page, 441, while discussing the cavalry fight on East Cavalry Field on July 3, he says:

*On the third day came the cavalry fight, off to the northwest, beyond the Hanover Road. Pleasonton has Gregg, Buford, and some of Kilpatrick. Stuart has Fitz Lee, Hampton, Chambliss, and Jenkins.*

But Buford's force, having sustained heavy casualties while delaying Heth's division on the Chambersburg Road on July 1, had been sent back to Westminster on July 2 to guard the Union army trains.[1] Consequently, they were nowhere near East Cavalry Field on July 3. Given that error in his narration immediately after he tells us that Lee greeted Stuart "austerely," and with the realization that Thomason gives the reader no reference as sources for any of his information, I would tend to dismiss his narration of the meeting between Lee and Stuart that day as little more than rumor without foundation.

There are other stories, however, of Lee's somewhat rough and angry greeting of Stuart that day. On page 334 of his biography *JEB Stuart, the Last Cavalier,* Burke Davis tells us what he thinks happened:

> Stuart rode up to face Robert Lee. Major McClellan and Colonel Munford, among others, witnessed their meeting. "It was painful beyond description," McClellan thought.
>
> Lee reddened at sight of Stuart and raised his arm as if he would strike him. "General Stuart, where have you been?"
>
> Stuart seemed to "wilt" and explained his movements to Lee.
>
> "I have not heard a word from you for days," Lee said, "and you the eyes and ears of my army."
>
> "I have brought you 125 wagons and their teams, General," Stuart said.
>
> "Yes, General, but they are an impediment to me now."

Davis attributes this story to an account found in the Anne Bachman Hyde Papers at the University of North Carolina library. He says that the story is based on 1915 diary entries by Mrs. Hyde after a conversation she allegedly had with Colonel Thomas Munford.

Colonel Thomas Munford commanded the Second Virginia Cavalry in Fitzhugh Lee's brigade during the Gettysburg campaign, but it is unclear whether a diary entry recording a conversation between Colonel Munford and Mrs. Hyde exists. There is, however, a letter from Colonel Munford to Mrs. Hyde dated July 24, 1915, that is in her papers at the University of North Carolina and a copy of which is preserved in the archives of the Gettysburg National Military Park. The letter apparently is in response to questions Mrs. Hyde had asked Colonel Munford about his service during the Civil War, in which he says:

> Major McClellan told me he witnessed Gen'l R.E. Lee's reception of Stuart—and that it was painful *beyond description, raising his arm, he*

*said, "Gen'l Stuart where have you been? Not one word from your command has been heard by me! Where have you been?" Gen'l Stuart "wilted" after informing Gen'l Lee; Stuart added "I have brought you 150 wagons and their mule teams." "Yes, Gen'l, but they are an impediment to me now! Let me ask your help, we will not discuss this matter longer."* [2]

Mrs. Hyde added a postscript to this letter along the margin, which reads:

*Gen. Munford told me that Major McClellan told him that Gen. Lee added "I have not heard a word from you for days, and you the eyes and ears of my army." And showed wrath at first and then great tenderness.*

Munford was born March 28, 1831, and in 1915, he would have been eighty-four years old when writing a letter about events before a battle that had been fought fifty-two years in the past. But age and the passage of time, while important factors, are not necessary, for the details of his letter are easily refuted.

First of all, we know from his letter that Munford did not witness this reception, but says he heard of it from McClellan. But McClellan says nothing of this meeting between Lee and Stuart in his detailed Civil War memoir, *I Rode with Jeb Stuart*. In *Lee's Lieutenants,* Freeman says: "It was afternoon on the 2nd when Stuart, riding ahead, reached his anxious chief on Seminary Ridge."[3] In *The Union Cavalry in the Civil War,* Stephen Starr also says that "Stuart had ridden south from Carlisle in advance of his men, and, in the early afternoon of the second, reported to General Lee on Seminary Ridge."[4]

That seems to indicate that, when he met with Lee later that day, Stuart was alone, and Major McClellan could not have witnessed the meeting between his commander and Lee. But even if McClellan had accompanied Stuart when he reached Gettysburg, no staff officer would have moved forward to a position close enough to Lee and Stuart to have heard their conversation. That just wasn't done with Lee. Unless specifically invited for some reason having to do with their personal knowledge, insight, or other information, staff officers simply did not accompany their commanders when they had conferences with him, and Lee was a stickler for correct behavior by his subordinates.

Second, if Lee ever did rebuke one of his generals, he virtually never did so in public. This would include his treatment of General McLaws after that man had failed to attack Sedgwick at Chancellorsville, a failure that we know Lee thought crucial and which a few close aides suspected angered him greatly. But he never gave any notice of that anger by his words in public, either to General McLaws or to anyone else.

Third, when Lee gave Stuart permission to ride around the Union army on his way into Pennsylvania, this authority is stated in his orders of June 23. We find therein the following statement: "In either case, after crossing the river, you must move on and feel the right of Ewell's troops, collecting information, provisions, &c."[5]

What could be plainer? It is true that Stuart was delayed because of Hooker's army moving between his force and the Potomac, thus necessitating a wide sweep around them to the east. But Lee knew that delays are predictable in war. The important thing is that Stuart did arrive and he brought with him a wagon train filled with supplies that were no doubt of the greatest value to Lee, who was running low on many army necessities.

Munford graduated from the Virginia Military Institute in 1852, and he not only resented West Point graduates, he actively disliked them in some cases. For instance, he thought Stuart was as "ambitious as

Caesar," and was not shy about expressing his concern that favoritism was shown to West Pointers:

> *I was not a West Pointer, I graduated at the Virginia Military Institute. . . . I do not say this unkindly, but our army had to supply places for graduates of West Point of the old army, and some of them had better been at home.*[6]

Since his brigade commander, Fitzhugh Lee, had graduated from West Point in 1856, as had his cavalry division commander, Jeb Stuart, in 1854, it is easy to see that he may have bridled a bit under their command. But it also should be noted that, before the Civil War, Munford was a "planter aristocrat," while both Stuart and Lee had spent their time since graduation serving in the army. In addition, Stuart was well known to Robert E. Lee from his days as a cadet, and Fitz Lee was Robert E. Lee's nephew. These facts, coupled with the sterling individual performance of Stuart and Fitz Lee in the early days of the war, readily explain their rapid rise to high command.

I believe, despite rumors to the contrary, that Stuart was pleasantly received by Lee when he returned on July 2 and that the two men then studied their position on the Hotchkiss map and discussed how to turn the flank of Meade's army and so defeat it. And it seems clear in retrospect that at Gettysburg Lee sought a complete victory.

Lee knew that, given the industrial advantages of the North, coupled with the population disparity and the increasingly effective naval blockade of southern ports, it was only a matter of time before the South was suffocated. But if he could destroy the Army of the Potomac at Gettysburg, he would then be left with his powerful Confederate force poised above a helpless Washington, Baltimore, even Philadelphia, for no other Union army was within several weeks' march.

And indeed, if he were to destroy the Army of the Potomac—not simply defeat and drive off to fight again another day, but kill, capture, or scatter its soldiery—what Union force would want to take the field against him? Such a resounding victory was the sort of military coup that might eliminate all other political questions and bring about a hurried armistice and recognition of the Confederate states as an independent nation.

The ridgelines in the Gettysburg area run generally north-south, and if we start west of Gettysburg on Seminary Ridge and come east, the next ridgeline is Cemetery Ridge. In another mile we pass Culp's Hill, then it is another mile to Wolf's Hill. A mile east and nearly two miles north of that is Brinkerhoff Ridge. Moving to the east another mile or so, we come to Cress Ridge, somewhat more than three miles east of the town of Gettysburg.

Hanover Road runs east-southeast from Gettysburg, and passes a mile south of Cress Ridge. But just to the west of Cress Ridge, a country road leads southwest from Hanover Road for another mile to the Baltimore Turnpike, intersecting it three-quarters of a mile or so southeast of the Union rear behind Culp's Hill. Unbeknownst to Lee, this road, known then as Bonaughton Road (pronounced "Bonnietown" and since submerged under the man-made Heritage Lake), had been used by Union horsemen and wagons ferrying supplies to Gregg's two brigades of cavalry posted on Hanover Road at the bottom of Brinkerhoff Ridge, the true end of the Union right wing. From there, a line of Union cavalry pickets stretched to the southwest and ended south of Wolf's Hill, connected there with Union infantry units.

The Baltimore Pike comes up from the southeast well behind this picket line and Culp's Hill, and it was the Union's supply route, the only open door into the federal rear area. If he wanted to get into the Union rear, then Stuart would have had to use Bonaughton Road, as it was the fastest and only practicable way of getting around the Union right flank and intersecting with the Baltimore Pike just three-quarters of a mile southeast of Culp's Hill. The closest Union troops to the Baltimore Pike would have been infantry units posted southeast of Culp's Hill and a half mile or so east of the Baltimore Pike, facing away from it and connected to the cavalry picket line to their east-northeast.

We know from many of his interlocutors that Lee had hoped to win a major victory in Pennsylvania. But an added touch is given by Confederate Major General Isaac Trimble. On June 25, 1863, Trimble was passing General Lee's tent when that man came out and spoke to him: "You are the very man I wanted to see. Come to my tent and let us look over the map." There followed a lively discussion about potential battlefields in Pennsylvania, with Trimble saying that there were many good locations because of the generally rolling countryside. Lee told him that, as the Union army approached, he intended to attack it with overwhelming force and crush it, defeating it in detail. Then he laid his spread fingers over the map between Gettysburg and Emmittsburg and said:

> Somewhere hereabout, we shall fight a great battle, and if successful, will secure our independence and end the war.[7]

A bold thought, this, one that encompassed not just victory on the battlefield but also a victory so convincing that it would have brought about an end to the entire war, regardless of Union successes then occurring in the West. But Lee was a bold thinker, and I believe this was the overriding reason why he wanted to take his army into Pennsylvania.

Stuart's actions after meeting with Lee on the afternoon of July 2 are obscure, but they certainly would have involved meeting with his brigade commanders to tell them of his latest orders from Lee, just so they were informed in the event he was killed or wounded in the interim. Stuart was just too good a general not to have done this.

We also know that, as dusk approached on July 2 of the Battle of Gettysburg, a brief flurry of fighting occurred on Brinkerhoff Ridge. The Stonewall Brigade of Johnson's division in Ewell's Confederate II Corps was strung out from near Wolf's Hill northeastward to the Brinkerhoff Ridge north of the Hanover Road, a distance of about two miles. The Second Virginia was the regiment posted the farthest out that line, and they were just southwest of Brinkerhoff Ridge, filling the flank guard role normally performed by cavalry. Gregg's men were the right flank of the Union line, just southeast of that ridge.

Brinkerhoff is crested by a small stone wall, and around dusk elements of the Second Virginia Regiment suddenly raced for that wall from the southwest. They were seen and quickly opposed by Union soldiers from Gregg's Second Cavalry Division, men who, armed with breech-loading carbines, dismounted and ran up the ridge from the southeast. The federals won the footrace, but only by about twenty yards or so, and were then able to put out a great storm of fire with their carbines. The Rebels, armed with muzzle-loading rifles, put out a smaller volume of fire. And although their rifle fire was more accurate than that of the Union carbines, at this short range it did not matter much.

There was some jostling back and forth for position, and quite a bit of fire was exchanged. The Rebels did turn the right flank of the Union line, but the forces did not close with each other, for this was never intended to be a fight to the death. As flank security units, neither force had any real interest in a serious fight. They only wanted to have some rough idea of where each of their flanks were so that they would be able to warn higher command of any major advance by their opponent that might come from that direction. That, after all, was their purpose: to be watchdogs, not attacking lions.

As darkness fell, therefore, the Yankees drew off Brinkerhoff Ridge, having suffered sixteen wounded and one fatality, as compared with the eleven wounded suffered by the Stonewall Brigade. The Union cavalry was withdrawn all the way to Two Taverns, some five miles southeast of Gettysburg on the Baltimore Pike, while the Second Virginia and the rest of the Stonewall Brigade were pulled back to the base of Culp's Hill.

But as they were maneuvering against the Rebels to their west, feeling them out to learn their position, Union cavalrymen saw a group of what looked like Confederate scouts watching them with binoculars from a quarter mile or so to their northwest. General Gregg, to whom these Confederate horsemen were pointed out, ordered artillery fire, which scattered them. Gregg said in his report that they must have been from Johnson's division, a speculation that, as it turned out, was wrong.

Instead, this was probably either Jeb Stuart and a group of his aides or Fitzhugh Lee with his own entourage of aides and couriers. But what were these two doing there, far out on the left wing of the Confederate line? The only reasonable answer is that they were looking for the true right wing of the Union line. And on Brinkerhoff Ridge, defended by Gregg's cavalry, they had found it.

Quite some time before the skirmish on Brinkerhoff Ridge started, an interesting figure appeared on the scene. Campbell Brown was a cousin and stepson of, and staff officer for, General Richard S. Ewell, commander of the Confederate II Corps, which held the left of Lee's line at Gettysburg. On the afternoon of July 2, Brown and two couriers were sent to the extreme left of the line, where he was told to find General Stuart. He was to send a courier back when he found him, then wait for a few hours and watch the Union soldiers there to see if they could determine anything about their movements. After this, he was to return to Ewell and report in person.

Brown rode out the Confederate line until he came to the last Confederate infantry unit, the Second Virginia. Brown tells us that regiment, some 350 men, was concentrated on the western or southwestern slope of Brinkerhoff Ridge, and that he found Stuart with a small group of horsemen at the northern end of that ridge.

Stuart told Brown his men were coming up on their left rear, but he didn't expect them for a while. Stuart and his staff and couriers, along with Brown and his, stayed there for an hour or so. They were watching through their binoculars as some Yankee cavalry units—apparently what turned out to be the Tenth New York and the Third Pennsylvania—maneuvered back and forth in the open fields they could see on the southern and eastern side of Brinkerhoff Ridge. Brown noted that the area to the east of Brinkerhoff Ridge was level and "much cut up by roads, fields & patches of woods—well calculated at once to admit & to conceal the movements of large bodies of Cavalry."[8]

The Confederate Second Virginia Infantry was still out of sight of the Union cavalry, with the two units separated by Brinkerhoff Ridge, and there had as yet been no exchange of gunfire. Then, suddenly, a squadron of Union cavalry turned and advanced directly toward them. Stuart and his men, along with Brown, were dismounted at the time, and they thought they were concealed by trees and brush. But they quickly remounted and were prepared to ride away when the Second Virginia sent some sharpshooters up to their position to protect them. But before a shot was fired the Union squadron turned and rode away; apparently, the Confederates had not been seen.

Soon thereafter, they saw a small Yankee cavalry unit emerge from a clump of woods to the southwest and open fire at something off to their left. Soon after that, a piece of horse-drawn artillery came forward out of the same trees and opened fire in the same direction. Looking toward the burst of the artillery round, they noted Fitzhugh Lee and his entourage of aides and couriers just coming onto the field to their north. Those men quickly pulled back into cover, and then the Union gun retired with the horsemen and melted back into the woods to the south.

As soon as the gunfire started, Stuart had spurred off to join Fitz Lee. Brown stayed in place, but he saw no more fighting, and after an hour or so, he tells us, he went back to report to Ewell.[9] The firefight at dusk between the Second Virginia and the Tenth New York referred to above obviously happened after Brown had left.

Brinkerhoff Ridge, of course, is north of the Hanover Road and nearly a mile west of its intersection with the Bonaughton Road. But this intersection, as well as that of the Bonaughton Road and the Baltimore Pike, are clearly visible on the Hotchkiss maps. And that explains what Stuart was doing with a handful of horsemen on Brinkerhoff Ridge on the late afternoon of July 2: he was looking for the true right wing of the Union army, which he found there in Gregg's cavalry. But he was also looking for the intersection of the Bonaughton Road and the Hanover Road, and a concealed way in which he could approach it with his entire force, then move down it and eventually turn the Union right wing. Given Lee's entire military career, such a move is easily predictable: that's what he had done at Second Manassas and won a triumph, and that's also what he had done at Chancellorsville and won another triumph. Now, at the most important battle of the war, one that could win it all for the Confederacy, are we really supposed to believe that he willingly risked everything on Pickett's charge against the center of the Union line by 13,000 of his 63,000 troops while the rest stood by and did nothing?

I think that accepting such an idea is to fail to understand Lee as a leader. The Union left flank was being tested on July 2 by Longstreet, and it was not promising as a way to defeat the Army of the Potomac. But sending all his cavalry up the Baltimore Pike and into the Union rear behind Culp's Hill to roll up the Union right flank—that was a tactic worthy of Lee that would explain Stuart's July 2 presence on Brinkerhoff Ridge.

I believe that when Stuart rode off to confer with Fitzhugh Lee, it was because he had ordered him to be there. Then he and Lee, and probably Hampton and Chambliss, his other two brigade commanders, as well, would have gone north to near the York Pike and made a wide circle to the east, coming down on Cress Ridge a mile or more *behind* the ongoing fight between the Second Virginia and the Tenth New York cavalries. From Cress Ridge, they would have looked south over a mile of open fields.

Although you cannot see the end of the Bonaughton Road, or even much of Hanover Road, from Cress Ridge because of trees and undulations in the ground, Stuart probably would have been able to believe, given the absence of Union forces visible to him from there, that the way was clear. Indeed, aggressive reconnaissance leader that he was, he may well have ridden down onto what we now call East Cavalry Field and found it devoid of Yankee presence. He then would have gone to Lee's headquarters to tell him what he had learned and to receive his orders for the next day. He would have told Lee about the Union cavalry force east of Brinkerhoff Ridge, which might be a threat to his movement down Bonaughton Road to come up Baltimore Pike behind Culp's Hill the next day, but when Lee moved the Second Virginia and the rest of the Stonewall Brigade to one base of Culp's Hill after dark, it seemed reasonable that the Union cavalry would follow them, perhaps as far as Wolf's Hill, just to stay in contact with the true left wing of the Confederate line. And if they did that, they would necessarily leave access to Bonaughton Road from Hanover Road wide open for Stuart and his men.

The conventionally accepted version of events says that on Day Three, Lee gave Stuart the only cavalry brigade he had, Jenkins's brigade, and sent him out to his left wing, where he was simply posted, we are to believe, as flank security. And it is curious that Lee would have sent his entire cavalry force—Stuart's three brigades plus that of Jenkins, a force of some 6,000 men—out to cover the left flank, while he sent no cavalry at all to cover his right flank. And the position that Stuart took for this supposed flank security, on Cress Ridge, was roughly two miles northeast of the left-most unit in the Confederate line, the Stonewall Brigade of Johnson's division, which, as mentioned earlier, had been pulled back from Brinkerhoff Ridge to the bottom of Culp's Hill during the night.[10] But for any military leader to have taken such action without an underlying plan for the use of this force beyond that of flank security would have been the height of folly. Union deployments during the battle called for cavalry divisions to cover both flanks. And yet we are to believe that Lee sent all 6,000 of his horsemen to cover only his left flank, and so far beyond his true left flank as to be useless in that role?

If Stuart's force had constituted a true flank guard on the left flank, it would have been stationed in a position where it would have been physically connected to or within short visual distance of the last infantry unit on the left flank of Lee's army, which was then near the base of Culp's Hill. Instead, it was stationed two miles away across rolling, wooded ground in a position where it could not possibly have even seen, let alone covered, Lee's left flank infantry unit.

This means that, on July 3, both Lee's flanks were entirely uncovered. Had the Union army wanted to move the entire VI Corps (their reserve that was then held behind the Round Tops) around either Confederate flank, they could have done so with complete impunity, for there is virtually no chance at all that they would have even been seen by Confederates before they were well into their rear area. For that matter, any Union force operating west of Brinkerhoff Ridge would have been concealed from Stuart's men on Cress Ridge, and given the lay of the land, their placement there as flank security simply makes no sense.

While we do not know any of the specifics of Lee's reception of Stuart, we know that the two men met and talked and no doubt discussed future plans. Now that Lee's most trusted subordinate general had returned, the man who had taken over for Jackson after that general's fatal wounding at Chancellorsville and used his artillery and infantry so expertly, Lee had a most important mission for him. Napoleon famously spoke about using all of one's forces in battle:

> *When you contemplate giving battle, it is a general rule to collect all your strength and to leave none unemployed. One battalion sometimes decides the issue of the day.*[11]

Upon considering Lee and his life experiences to date, it is readily apparent that he was a consummate military strategist and tactician. When he defeated McClellan in the Seven Days, Pope at Second Manassas, Burnside at Fredericksburg, Hooker at Chancellorsville, and, despite the fact that the Union force was nearly twice the size of his own, fought McClellan to a draw at Antietam, Lee never left any of his forces inactive at the critical moments of those battles. I believe it frivolous and professionally insulting to think that Lee did not have some major plan in mind for Stuart as well as for the rest of his army during Pickett's charge by 13,000—less than 20 percent of his available force—against the heart of Union defenses on July 3.

# 12

## Plans for Day Three

ON THE EVENING OF JULY 2, Lee knew that Pickett's division would arrive in the morning and his Army of Northern Virginia would then number about 63,000 men. Meade's Army of the Potomac would field about 80,000, but for Lee, based on past performance, these were very good odds. And as he clearly knew, the success of his venture north and probably the final outcome of the war would depend on the plans he would come up with for all his forces that day—all of his plans for all of his forces. Heavily outnumbered and deep in the North, a true foreign country for the Army of Northern Virginia, he had to make very judicious use of his forces. Clearly, Lee could not afford to risk so much on the actions taken that third climactic day by a small portion of his army. So what was he to do?

Lee was confident that Meade and his forces were self-locked into their fortress and would wait for him to make the first move. Given the lackluster record of the Union army against Lee to date—no wins, many losses, and perhaps only one tie at Antietam—they could not have been very hopeful. Lee was quite confident, therefore, that they would not take any risks, especially not that of coming out of their defenses to attack his forces.

And indeed, Meade and his Army of the Potomac took no offensive action of any significance during the three days of battle at Gettysburg, or even on July 4, the day *after* the failure of Pickett's charge. Instead, despite the fact that Lee had to be low on ammunition and manpower, Meade refused to direct or even authorize a counterattack by his own massive infantry forces—even by the fresh, untouched VI Corps—of any kind. Instead, the Union commanders merely kept their men hunkered down in their defensive positions and waited for Lee to either attack again or simply disappear. On the night of July 4–5, they got their wish as Lee's army crept away and headed back south.

So how, making his plans on the night of July 2, was Lee to defeat them? He couldn't just nibble at their lines or bombard them with artillery; he had to deliver a resounding knockout blow that would stun the nation and the world. This was the opportunity he had sought, a climactic battle in which he could truly destroy the Army of the Potomac as an effective fighting force. And how, exactly, could he do that?

Of course, as an intellectual fully cognizant of the battlefield actions of all the military masters of history before him, and as a consummate tactician, one would expect that he would have tried to use the principles of war that had been used to triumphant effect in similar battlefield situations by the Great Captains. One would expect that he would have drawn from the greatest examples with which he was most familiar, those of Hannibal, of Frederick the Great, and mostly of Napoleon.

The question he faced was how he could use military principles, the principles of war, to apply the mass of his forces against Union weak points and so wreck his enemy's cohesion inside its defenses. How could he use deceit to envelop and/or divide the Union army and defeat it in detail? How could he attack the federals in their redoubt so as to totally destroy their structure, capture those who surrendered, and drive off in terror the shattered remnants of the Union's Army of the Potomac?

The Army of the Potomac was arrayed in a strong defensive position, running from Little Round Top north along Cemetery Ridge to Cemetery Hill several miles away, then turning to the east for another mile and ending on Culp's Hill. Seen from above, the Union defensive positions look like a giant fishhook, and that became their common description in later times.

I believe Lee's final plan becomes abundantly clear if we look carefully. Lee was a most secretive man, of course, and he left no written record of his thoughts and plans before the Battle of Gettysburg beyond the bland information to be found in his Official Reports to President Davis and the Confederate government. But while Lee had a very close relationship with Davis, it is also clear that he did not share all of his military thoughts and decisions with him.

We know that on the evening of Day Two, Lee had told both Ewell and Longstreet to continue, or renew, their attacks in the morning.[1] But before that happened, it would have been expected that Stuart would have reported to him and told him what he had found: that the Union right wing was covered by cavalry on Brinkerhoff Ridge, a force that had withdrawn to the south at night but could be expected to return to that position the next morning. And it would have been very normal for him to have reported to, or been called by, Lee the next morning for further orders.

I think Lee and Stuart then looked at Hotchkiss's map, which clearly shows the Bonaughton Road connecting the Hanover Road and the Baltimore Pike. As they studied the map, Lee probably asked Stuart if he remembered Napoleon's smashing victory over Wurmser at Castiglione in 1796. Remember, in their day, Napoleon was the great battlefield master without equal, and both men were military professionals who had studied him not only at West Point but all through their lives.

His exploits in Italy in 1796 would have been common knowledge to both of them, and this question I posit Lee asking of Stuart would be comparable to a college professor of English literature being asked if he was familiar with one of Shakespeare's plays.

But all this theory, unfortunately, sounds dry and is perhaps confusing. In order to put flesh and bones on the page, therefore, let us look at the Battle of Castiglione, one of the first battles in which Napoleon used his *manœuvre sur les derrières* to win a victory in Italy in 1796.

In the summer of that year, France and Austria were at war. Napoleon was in northern Italy with the 23,000 soldiers in his Army of Italy, and elements of his force had been fighting off and on over the past few weeks with parts of the Austrian armies led by Quasdanovich and Wurmser. One of Napoleon's divisions finally smashed a division from the force of Quasdanovich and sent it reeling in retreat. And this seemed like a good idea to Quasdanovich, who collected the rest of his 18,000 men and retreated to the north. Now, finally facing him alone, Napoleon wanted to totally destroy Wurmser's force.[2]

On August 5, just south of the town of Castiglione, Napoleon faced Wurmser and his 24,000 men, a force arrayed in a strong defensive line to his southeast. Wurmser's left was the weakest on low, unfavorable terrain, but it was bolstered by most of the Austrian cavalry as well as by massed artillery on an isolated hill known as Medalono. He was hoping to be reinforced by 5,000 men coming up on his right under Bajalich while another 5,000 under Meszaros were supposed to pin 5,000 French under Fiorella far to the south. But unfortunately for him, Meszaros missed Fiorella, who was streaming north that morning to join Bonaparte, his movement screened by a regiment of dragoons. He would arrive on the battlefield within hours behind Wurmser's left wing, a fact that remained unknown to the Austrian commander until its explosion in his rear.

Napoleon formed his troops at dawn and had Masséna and Augereau deliver limited attacks across the entire front while holding Despinoy and his cavalry under Beaumont in the rear as part of his reserve. But these offensive moves were meant merely to pin Wurmser's men and keep their attention focused on their front line. Since these attacks were not launched as strong, crushing blows, however, but rather were not much more than feelers, it did not take long for Wurmser to reject them and start to counterattack. The French troops, under Napoleon's orders, responded by gradually giving ground, fighting while retreating. The Austrians seemed to be winning the day and were even trying to turn Napoleon's left when a courier arrived and told him that Fiorella was in position in Wurmser's left rear. And that was the moment that Napoleon had awaited.

His first action was to have Masséna's and Augereau's divisions turn around and once again press the attack on the Austrians—a very difficult maneuver that only well-trained troops of high esprit can manage. He also sent much of his artillery and a brigade of cavalry around the Austrian left flank. The artillery went into action first, enfilading and firing on the Austrian guns atop Medalono at very close range, followed by an attack of grenadiers that swept over the hill and cleared it of enemy forces. The cavalry, meanwhile, went around the entire left flank and hooked up with Fiorella, who then proceeded to crash into Wurmser's rear.[3]

These stunning developments caught Wurmser by surprise, and he immediately pulled troops from his line and rushed them to the rear to confront these surprising strikes. But Napoleon was waiting for that and he threw Augereau and Masséna against the Austrian center and right, then hurled Despinoy in to turn the Austrian right. Soon both wings of the Austrian defensive line were giving way while Fiorella's infantry and Beaumont's cavalry in Wurmser's rear were shredding everything in their paths.

Although this was a major shock, Wurmser was an excellent battlefield leader, an old soldier who had been in a lot of fights. But this time he was desperate for survival, and he quickly committed his infantry reserve, then led several cavalry charges himself in an effort to give his men time to withdraw to their right rear. Even so, he probably would have been trapped by the wings collapsing on him if Bajalich and his 5,000 men had not come up to rescue his right wing at the last moment. He was thoroughly beaten in any case and barely got the bulk of his force away, leaving 20 guns, 1,000 prisoners, and 2,000 dead and wounded on the smoking field.[4]

This battle was early in Napoleon's career, but it provides rather stunning evidence of the effectiveness of a *manœuvre sur les derrières*. In future years, he would polish application of certain elements of this envelopment operation, but it is important to note that, at the age of twenty-six, he already had all the necessary components in place in his mind, and all he lacked was their refined application.

I believe that, on the evening of July 2, Lee told Stuart that he wanted to convert the fight at Gettysburg into another Castiglione. In the late afternoon of July 2, Longstreet's attack against the Union left had been so powerful that it forced Meade to send troops there from other parts of his defensive position, in particular the XII Corps under Slocum from Culp's Hill. Six of the seven brigades in that corps were sent to prop up Longstreet, leaving only one brigade under Greene in place. Johnson's attack against Culp's Hill started at about six o'clock that evening, but his three brigades made little headway against the well-entrenched men under Greene, who had been stiffened by some eight hundred more men from Wadsworth's I Corps. Around nine o'clock, elements of the XII Corps, some 5,000 men, began to reappear on or near Culp's Hill and ended any hope of Johnson's three brigades taking the hill. But Lee would have told Stuart, on the night of July 2, that Longstreet and Ewell would continue their attacks on the morning of July 3.

It was important that Ewell not attack Culp's Hill on the morning of

July 3 before Longstreet launched his attack. This was because Lee hoped the large Union unit he had learned was moving down onto Cemetery Ridge from Culp's Hill (the XII Corps) to stave off Longstreet's attack on July 2 would stay there, or be brought back down there, thus weakening the defenses on the Union right wing. If that happened, Lee had already arranged for the three Confederate brigades in Johnson's division at the bottom of Culp's Hill to be reinforced to seven brigades, or some 10,000 men. And with that force attacking from the front, even if some or all of the XII Corps had returned to Culp's Hill, he thought he could take Culp's Hill.

But to be sure the plan worked and the Union right wing would fall, Lee wanted Stuart to play the role of Fiorella at Castiglione and come up behind the Union right wing while it was being attacked from the front by Ewell. Lee told Stuart that timing was most important, that he had to let the attack mature until he got the signal from Lee. When that happened, he was to move down off Cress Ridge, follow Bonaughton Road to the Baltimore Pike, then turn right and race up to the rear of Culp's Hill.

Lee was leaving both his flanks naked, unprotected by cavalry. But Lee knew his adversary, and he was certain Meade was more worried about surviving a Confederate attack than formulating one of his own. He was confident, in other words, that his two open and unprotected flanks would not be tested by a major Yankee flank attack.

To carry off this flank maneuver, Lee would give Stuart command of his only other cavalry unit, Jenkins's brigade of some 1,000 mounted riflemen. These were mountain men from what would become West Virginia armed with the latest Enfield rifles and sword bayonets imported through the blockade from England. If needed, all 6,000 of Stuart's horsemen could attack Culp's Hill from the rear, in which case it would quickly collapse. But there was also the possibility it would take much less to tip the scales.

As an initial blow, this force of Jenkins's mounted infantry would dismount behind Culp's Hill and attack the Union defenses on top of it from the rear. With a thousand howling and firing Rebels attacking from the rear while ten thousand attacked from the front, he was confident the Union line would collapse and that he could then roll up the Union right wing. But if more was needed, Stuart had another five thousand men to throw in, though just having them gallop by screaming while Jenkins's men mounted their attack might do the trick. That would be up to Stuart.

As the barbed end of the Union Fishhook began to collapse thereafter, he would have Stuart's other three brigades of cavalry, some 5,000 mounted men, just move down the Union line and attack the Union troops on Cemetery Hill and between Cemetery Hill and Culp's Hill from the rear while they were attacked from the front by Early's division, then by Rodes's division, and eventually by all three divisions of A. P. Hill's corps. And as they moved along the rear of the Union line, one of the first things they would have done would be to kill or drive away from their guns the artillery crews, an easy task for a mounted man who came up behind them armed with carbine, saber, and revolver, all the more so since artillerymen wore no side arms behind friendly lines.

Stuart could then bring the crews from his own guns with him and use them to handle some of these guns. It would take only three or four men for each gun, and they would lower their muzzles and fire canister into the rear of the waiting Union infantry manning the defenses all along the line. Lee and Stuart would also have discussed the psychological power of six thousand Confederate cavalry crashing through the Union rear, filling the air with gunfire, explosions, and the high-pitched Rebel Yell that shook Yankee souls, all this occurring in what the Union soldiers would have thought was their safe and protected rear area. Such a surprise for the Yankees should have a stunning, heart-stopping, paralyzing impact.

The effect of these thousands of shooting, screaming horsemen loose in the Yankee rear would be far greater than that brought on by the few Guides and four bugles Napoleon had gotten behind Austrian lines at the Battle of Arcola, a small force that panicked them into fleeing to the rear. But the Union army in the hook of the Fishhook, attacked front and rear, would have nowhere to go, and mass surrender would be their only option. The result would be the elimination of the northern half of the Army of the Potomac.

Meanwhile, the three divisions of Longstreet's corps would have been attacking the Union's left wing, just as they had done the day before. But this would only be a pinning or holding attack, just to make sure the Union forces in front of them—hopefully including the bulk of the XII Corps, drawn down from Culp's Hill the day before—didn't flood north to rescue the men in blue who would quickly be going under.

Meade's troops were all deployed on the Fishhook line, save only the VI Corps. This was a fresh unit, Meade's reserve, and he kept it behind Little Round Top. If all these attacks occurred at once, the VI Corps probably would be used to stave off Longstreet's corps, which had been the greatest threat on July 2. Thereafter, as the Union troops at the northern end surrendered and their conquerors turned south, the other half of Meade's army would now suddenly be heavily outnumbered and would have, in their turn, either surrendered or scattered.

Lee might have told Stuart to inform his brigade commanders in general outline of what lay before them on the morrow, and he would have told Ewell and Johnson of his planned front-and-rear attack on Culp's Hill. But no one else could know anything, and such secrecy was quite common with Lee.

Remember Chancellorsville, where he told Jackson to make a long flank march around the Union right, but told no one else about this proposed flank attack. Because this meeting and Lee's orders to Jackson were never published anywhere or shared with anyone else in the Army of Northern Virginia, articles about Jackson's independence and tactical brilliance at Chancellorsville, claiming that the flank march had been his idea that he had carried off on his own, appeared in southern publications after the war. These allegations, however, spoke so poorly of Jackson's generalship that Lee broke his postwar silence on the conflict only that one time to correct that error. And he did that only to maintain the highest military reputation of the by-then-dead Stonewall Jackson.

If this high-risk venture didn't work for some unexpected reason, then no one other than Lee and Stuart and Ewell and Johnson, and perhaps a few brigade commanders and staff officers, would have known about it. And since it would not benefit the South to announce a flank attack attempted by Lee at Gettysburg, a high-risk flank attack that had failed, it would never be heard of again.

This flank attack by Stuart, of course, would have been a far less risky venture than Jackson's flank attack at Chancellorsville had been. In the worst case possible, if the attack failed, Ewell's seven brigades had only to go back down Culp's Hill and Stuart's horsemen had only to ride back down the Baltimore Pike or across the Fishhook to join A. P. Hill's corps on Seminary Ridge. If a cavalry attack on infantry failed, in other words, it would be easy for the mounted men to simply ride away.

We also know that on the night of July 2–3, Lee had ordered Ewell to once again attack Culp's Hill in the morning, but with his attack to coincide with that of Longstreet. For that purpose, Ewell's left-most division under Johnson had been reinforced—necessarily at Lee's command—by three brigades, and one of his brigades had been brought in from its position covering their left flank. This brought his attacking force up from three to a total of seven brigades, some 10,000 men.[5]

So I believe Lee's proposed attack would have been three-pronged, the first element of which would have been Longstreet's renewed attack against the Union left. The second element would have been Ewell's attack on Culp's Hill with seven brigades of infantry, but that would have been triggered by the activation of the third element: Stuart's arrival with his cavalry force in the rear of Culp's Hill.

As for the third part of this three-pronged attack I believe Lee ordered, we will not find the words coming from Lee's mouth, in the Official Records or anywhere else. Why not? Because this key cavalry attack, enabling the success of the other two, failed. It was never really even launched, and any mention of it could only embarrass Stuart, who failed to launch it. Lee simply would not do such a thing, particularly since it would have served no purpose whatever, save only to perhaps redeem his image in the eyes of those who might blame the loss at Gettysburg on Lee's faulty decisions on troop commitments. And about his own reputation relative to that of any of his loyal subordinates, Lee cared not at all.

But although we find no record of the actual orders from Lee, we do know from the Official Record that Lee ordered the third part of his three-pronged offensive, Stuart's attack from the rear that would have enabled Johnson's men to take Culp's Hill from the front and begin to roll up the right wing of the Union infantry line. This is contained in the Official Report of the man who failed Lee, Jeb Stuart.[6] Here we find the order Lee had given him to take his three brigades of 5,000 cavalrymen, to which Lee had added the 1,000 mounted infantrymen of Jenkins's brigade, out the York Pike to the northeast several miles, then turn south to the top of Cress Ridge. Lee was thus sending his entire cavalry contingent out on his left wing under Stuart.

A fuller understanding of the use of mounted troops puts the lie to any claim that Stuart was sent out to Cress Ridge simply to cover the Confederate left wing or to watch for and then pursue retreating Union soldiers. And in any case, they certainly would not have needed Jenkins's brigade of mounted infantry to perform the purely cavalry task of pursuit. So why did Lee attach them to Stuart's three brigades of cavalry?

Although the use of cavalry was not identical to the later use of tanks, they had a similar use to their commanders as mobile strike forces. I find Heinz Guderian, a well-known German tank commander from World War II and a respected authority on armor and battlefield theory, most instructive on this point:

> *Red and Blue are at war. Each side has 100 infantry divisions and 100 tank battalions. Red has split up its tanks among its infantry divisions. Blue has massed them in Panzer divisions under the direct control of supreme headquarters. On a front of, say, 300 miles, 100 are tank-proof, 100 are difficult for tanks, and 100 are good tank country. So in battle the following picture emerges: Red has deployed a sizable proportion of its divisions, along with their tanks components, opposite the Blue positions in country where tanks cannot operate and are therefore useless, while a further proportion are in difficult tank country where, though not entirely wasted, their chances of successful action are small. Whatever happens, only a fraction of Red's tank forces can be employed in the country for which they are suited. Blue, on the other hand, has collected all its armor in the one place where a decision can be reached and where the ground can be made use of; he therefore has the opportunity of going into battle with at least double his adversary's strength while assuming the defensive along the rest of the front against Red's very small-scale tank attacks.*[7]

I believe that Stuart's force was sent out on the left wing as a high-speed, deep-strike force. His mission was to come down off Cress Ridge, cross Hanover Road and take the Bonaughton Road southwest to Baltimore Pike, then turn up it and race into the Union rear. Union cavalry had been deployed and fought over the Brinkerhoff Ridge, one ridgeline and nearly a mile west of Cress Ridge on Day Two, and Stuart had seen this Union right-wing flank guard in action. So when he went out the York Pike on the morning of Day Three, in conformity with his orders from Lee, Stuart went to Cress Ridge, one ridge *farther* to the east. He did that because he hoped to get *around* the far right wing of the Union army, which would then have allowed him to slip behind them down to Bonaughton Road and thence to the Union rear behind Culp's Hill.

# ≈ 13 ≈

## The Final Plan

A S T H E   F I G H T I N G on Culp's Hill ended the night of July 2, Steuart's brigade of Johnson's division in Ewell's Confederate II Corps had taken certain Union trenches on the slopes of Culp's Hill. It stayed there overnight, but was to be rudely awakened just before dawn on July 3. During the night, troops of the Union XII Corps under Williams had returned to the Culp's Hill area. Only three Union brigades actually occupied Culp's Hill facing Johnson's Confederates— those of Greene, Candy, and Kane, some 3,000 men. The other brigades of XII Corps, another 3,000 to 4,000 men, were a half mile off to the west or south and were not in a position to confront Johnson's seven brigades of 10,000 men.[1]

But the Union had artillery, while their gray adversaries did not. The terrain east of Culp's Hill, as it turned out, proved too rough and too steep for them to have brought cannon across Rock Creek in hopes of being able to fire in support of their infantry. But Williams had assembled twenty-six artillery pieces, and at about four-thirty in the morning these guns opened up a ferocious barrage on Steuart's brigade of Johnson's division.[2]

This artillery attack lasted only about fifteen minutes, and since the men who were its targets were fortunate enough to be in trenches, they suffered few casualties. But that was followed up by infantry firefights between blue and gray regiments.

On the morning of July 3, Lee heard the fight from Culp's Hill erupt at dawn. But he heard nothing from his right flank, where Longstreet's corps was also supposed to launch an attack. Somewhat concerned, he rode down to meet with Longstreet and learn what had happened to disrupt the orders he had received the night before. But Longstreet surprised him by saying that he had sent his scouts out during the night to try to find a position from which to get around the southern end of the Round Tops and establish a strong defensive position, and that they had been successful.[3]

This must have truly stunned Lee, for he had discussed the same issue on the evening of July 1 with Longstreet, when he had emphatically rejected his corps commander's idea to move south and east around the Union left flank and assume a defensive posture. Ordinarily, Longstreet rode to Lee's headquarters after every day of battle to discuss what had happened and formulate plans for the morrow. But on the evening of July 2, this did not happen. Longstreet said he was too tired after the long day of battle to make the ride and instead simply sent a courier to Lee with a summary of that day's events. Lee, for his part, simply sent an order to Longstreet to recommence the attack on the next morning.[4]

On that morning of the third day of battle, Longstreet had not only failed to attack the Union left wing as he had been ordered to do, he had even assumed the authority to send scouts out to reconnoiter the area to the south and east of their position. And now, as Lee arrived at Longstreet's headquarters, he was in the act of issuing the orders to his divisions to move off in that direction, despite repeated specific orders from Lee, his commanding general, that this idea was not accepted and would not be enacted.[5] This, according to the standard operating procedure of any army of that or any other time, was a cardinal sin: Longstreet was not only failing to obey Lee's direct orders, he was embarking on a plan of his own making that would have, if implemented, frustrated the orders he had been given by the army commander. It is not difficult to understand that Lee might have been angered by these actions. But in his Official Report on the campaign written in January 1864, we read only the following:

> General Longstreet's dispositions were not completed as early as was expected, but before notice could be sent to General Ewell, General Johnson had already become engaged, and it was too late to recall him.[6]

Back on Culp's Hill, meanwhile, the brigades of Jones, Steuart, and Nichols responded to the Union cannon fire by charging up the hill, but made little headway. Around eight that morning, O'Neal's and Steuart's brigades attacked on a slightly different route, but with no more success. Finally, around nine-thirty, the brigades of Steuart, Walker, and Daniels went up the hill at nearly the same time. But they charged into the teeth of the Union defenses, complete with cannon fire that slashed through their ranks, and the effort was soon thrown back.[7] It should be noted that much of this fighting raged back and forth at the company or regimental level with little central control by commanders on either side.

Finally, around ten in the morning of July 3, Ewell received an order from Lee to stop trying to take Culp's Hill, and telling him that his troops were to await Longstreet's attack before they attacked again.[8] By ten-thirty or eleven o'clock, the Confederates pulled back and the fight for Culp's Hill was over. Or was it just a pause?

For Ewell to have made an unsupported attack on Culp's Hill with Johnson's seven brigades at the same time as Pickett's Charge would probably have been repetitive, pointless, and foolishly suicidal. In fact, Ewell never launched all seven brigades at once in a unified attack, as the nine brigades in Pickett's Charge were sent forward together at once. Why not? Why were all Rebel attacks made piecemeal by only a few brigades at a time? Because the triggering event of Stuart's arrival in the rear of Culp's Hill with thousands of whooping and shooting cavalrymen that would have signaled an attack by all seven brigades at once never occurred. But had that happened, the right wing of Meade's army on Culp's Hill would have been rolled up by attacks front and rear while the bulk of Stuart's column raced on to hit the rear of the Clump of Trees as Pickett's Charge hit the front.

What happened between Lee and Longstreet later that morning has been reported in several different formats by Longstreet. The version most supported by others has Lee conducting a small leaders' conference on Seminary Ridge. Present were A. P. Hill, Longstreet, and other staff officers, including Colonel A. L. Long, postwar author of the *Memoirs of Robert E. Lee*.[9]

The conference was conducted in sight of the Union lines, which Lee would occasionally peer at through his field glasses. Since Longstreet had not launched his attack at dawn, Lee's hope of throwing simultaneous attacks against both wings was now gone. That was most unfortunate to Lee because he truly believed that a simultaneous attack on both wings would have worked, that the Union line would have buckled and collapsed.[10] The attack in the rear by Stuart's cavalry that I have alleged was part of his plan only adds to the possible destruction of the Army of the Potomac. But Longstreet had not acted on time and was still not ready to act by midmorning, so Lee had to completely revise his plan. He also had to get Johnson's force disengaged so that he could save it for later use, so he sent a message to Ewell telling him that Longstreet would not attack until ten, and that he must delay his own attack until that of Longstreet had been launched.[11]

Lee then discussed matters with his generals and finally decided that, rather than attacking the Union left wing with Longstreet's corps, he would have that force attack the center of the Union line at the Clump of Trees. This was a wide-open spot that had seemed weakly defended the day before when he had watched Wright's brigade of infantry burst through what there was of a Union line there. But that attack had been made by only one brigade; in this attack, he would send all three of Longstreet's divisions, eleven brigades in all, in a wedge formation: they would start from Seminary Ridge in a line more than a mile long. As they moved toward the Union defenses, however, they would focus in so that they would hit a front no more than a few hundred yards wide.

When Longstreet heard this, he was almost distraught, saying:

*"General, I have been a soldier all my life. I have been with soldiers engaged in fights by couples, by squads, companies, regiments, divisions and armies and should know, as well as anyone, what soldiers can do. It is my opinion that no fifteen thousand men ever arrayed for battle can take that position" pointing to Cemetery Hill. General Lee, in reply to this, ordered me to prepare Pickett's Division for the attack.*[12]

Longstreet reported essentially the same conversation in "Lee's Right Wing at Gettysburg,"[13] so there is little doubt that he said it. And in the event, he was proven correct. Longstreet was Lee's senior corps commander, and many believe he was his most trusted subordinate at Gettysburg, although I would put Stuart ahead of him in that regard. But Lee had even more experience than did Longstreet, and like him he must have seen ahead of time that Longstreet's attack alone, even with Pickett's fresh division, would be doomed. So why didn't he listen to Longstreet and cancel the attack? Because, I believe, it was just one part of the three-part attack. Longstreet already knew Johnson had been ordered to attack, so why didn't Lee tell him about Stuart?

To understand this, we must realize that, strictly speaking, Longstreet had no need to know about Stuart's attack. Perhaps more important, however, was the surliness Longstreet had shown toward Lee over the past few days. Not only had he been inappropriately insistent, arguing the same point repeatedly, but he had finally started to launch his own maneuver in defiance of Lee's orders to the contrary, a troop movement that would have been highly frustrating to Lee's overall plans for the battle. This was a highly irregular performance by a corps commander, and I expect that, even if only temporarily, at that moment Lee had lost his trust and confidence in Longstreet and didn't want to start another endless argument with him. Moreover, this argument, had it occurred, might have ended like the last one—with Longstreet acting in a way to frustrate Lee's orders. So Lee told Longstreet nothing about Stuart's proposed attack on the rear of Culp's Hill.

After Lee announced Longstreet's proposed attack to the generals, Longstreet was able to convince him that the divisions of Hood and McLaws had been badly bled in the preceding day's fighting, and that he needed to leave them in place just so the Union would not advance and turn the Confederate right flank in mid-attack. Lee quickly agreed, but probably not because of fear of a Union turning movement. Rather, once his force had burst through Cemetery Ridge, he wanted to make sure that the Union forces stationed along the shaft of the Fishhook stayed in place where they were, as well as the fresh VI Corps Union reserve situated behind the Round Tops. A pinning attack by the divisions of Hood and McLaws would keep these Union troops, including the VI Corps, from mounting any sort of rescue for the northern half of the Army of the Potomac, which he planned to divide from the southern half and rather quickly defeat in detail.

Although he did not explain this to all of his generals, he obviously did not just want his men to move straight ahead and overwhelm the

Union line. With the weapons they used in those days, the deadliest attack by an infantryman was straight ahead, so that each soldier could shoot at the enemy right in front of him. If the Confederate line was to focus in as a wedge, however, that movement would eliminate fields of fire for almost all the men in that wedge. Lee would not have adopted that formation and given up that firepower without an offsetting advantage that would justify it. But what was it?

Quite clearly, the attack made in Pickett's Charge was not just a frontal attack. Rather, it was intended to effect a penetration of the Union line.

But why did Lee want a penetration?

So that the 13,000 men in that charge could meet up with 5,000 horsemen that Stuart would bring in from the other side. As the far end of the Union right wing was crushed, the 10,000 men of Johnson's division and the 1,000 of Jenkins's brigade would have just continued west along the bend of the Fishhook, rolling the blue units up as they reached them. Meanwhile, the 13,000 infantry of Pickett's Charge and the 5,000 horsemen of Stuart's command would have met at the Clump of Trees and routed the Union soldiers waiting there. Then they would have turned north and attacked Cemetery Hill from the south. This would have allowed them to attack the Union troops there from the rear while they were also being attacked from the north, northeast, and northwest by the divisions of Rodes, Early, and the two brigades of Pender's division that had not made up part of Pickett's Charge, possibly even by Anderson's division, which was Lee's only reserve on Seminary Ridge. And their right flank would eventually be attacked by Johnson's men, who would be coming at them from the east.

Lee shared this information only with those who would act on it: Stuart, probably Ewell and Johnson as well, but that's it. We know from page 341 in *I Rode with Jeb Stuart,* the memoir of Jeb Stuart's adjutant general, that he, Major Henry McClellan, also knew of this plan, since he says therein:

> *The result of this battle shows that there is no probability that Stuart could successfully have carried out* his intention of attacking the rear of the Federal right wing, *for it was sufficiently protected by Gregg's command." (emphasis added)*

It is probable that Ewell and perhaps Johnson may have shared the information with a few key subordinate officers, as Stuart clearly had done. But Longstreet's unruly behavior on the first days of this battle, as discussed earlier, probably affected Lee strongly and kept him from sharing information with him about the proposed flank attack by Stuart and Johnson. If it was successful, Stuart's troops would meet Pickett's men at or near the Clump of Trees, and whatever Longstreet knew or didn't know at that late point would be irrelevant.

But from all other Confederate commanders as well, I believe Lee kept this part of his plan secret, as was his habit (cf. Jackson's crucially important and Lee-ordered roundabout flank attack at Chancellorsville), and after he had decided on a course of action, planning the mechanics of the frontal attack followed. Longstreet was to send Pickett's fresh division from his corps, which would lead the attack. The charge would also include Heth's division from A. P. Hill's corps (because Heth had been wounded on July 1, his division would be commanded by Pettigrew on July 3) and two other brigades from Pender's division, also of A. P. Hill's corps.

Lee would have kept Anderson's division with him on Seminary Ridge as his only reserve. Other than they, all soldiers in the Army of Northern Virginia would have been involved in the effort to divide Meade's army and defeat it in detail.

And that inclusion in the battle applied also to the divisions of McLaws and Hood in Longstreet's corps, units that had been left in place facing Cemetery Ridge and Little Round Top. Although for many years after the Civil War Longstreet would not acknowledge that he had made any plans for them, he says something else in his *Memoirs*. In the event that Pickett's Charge had successfully broken through the Union line on Cemetery Ridge, he tells us there, he had already ordered Hood and McLaws to have their divisions ready to "spring to the charge" against the enemy line directly in front of them along the shaft of the Fishhook.[14]

As we learned earlier when discussing Jackson's actions at Chancellorsville, Longstreet would not have given such an order unless Lee had told him to do so, and especially not after Lee had just caught him about to deploy his divisions in a way that was at variance with Lee's orders. And this order for the divisions of Hood and McLaws to "spring to the charge," of course, would have been Lee's pinning attack to keep those Union troops frozen in place while he destroyed the other half of the Army of the Potomac.

After this leadership conference on Seminary Ridge ended, Lee's subordinates returned to their units to get them in motion. Lee no doubt returned to his own headquarters on Chambersburg Road, though he also had a habit of moving among his units and the headquarters of their commanders just to make sure that all was in order. It is certain that one of the commanders he visited, or had visit him, was Stuart.

There is no record, of course, that such a meeting ever took place on the morning of July 3, sometime between, say, nine and eleven A.M. But that meeting and the arrangements that came out of it are the only reasonable explanations for much that we know happened, including but not limited to Pickett's Charge. Unless we are able to discover some explanation other than Lee just having a very bad day, then Pickett's Charge was simply an incomprehensibly poor tactical decision made by the man widely renowned at the time as the master of Civil War battle-fields. And that just makes no sense at all.

If we are to attempt to recover the words that passed between Lee and Stuart at such a meeting, then we must necessarily depend on pure conjecture. But I think such projection of ideas into the minds and mouths of both Lee and Stuart might give us some new understanding of what really happened at Gettysburg.

At their meeting that morning, Lee and Stuart would have traced their plans on Hotchkiss's excellent map, where the country road we have been referring to as Bonaughton Road shows prominently. Lee would have told Stuart that things had changed, that the attack against both wings of the Union line would not take place, that there would be no further effort of replicating Napoleon's triumph at Castiglione in which Stuart's force would come up behind Culp's Hill and roll up the Union right wing. Instead, the new plan of attack would involve cutting the Union force in half and then defeating it in detail. Like Austerlitz.

The cutting force would be Pickett's 13,000 from the west and Stuart's 5,000 horsemen from the east. He would still drop off Jenkins's 1,000 men behind Culp's Hill, and the plan to roll up the Union right wing was still on. But now, that would be one part of separating the northern section from the southern and crushing it in short order. Mass surrenders should be expected as the attacks unfolded, for defending blue soldiers would be simultaneously attacked from front and rear, all along the line, and they would have had no place to run.

Lee also would have told Stuart that he was to take great care to silence the Union artillery on top of Cemetery Hill, well behind the infantry lines and seemingly safe. If possible, he should get his own crews in there to take some of the guns over and fire them into the rear of waiting Union infantry. This was important, for Lee no doubt expected that his infantry advancing from Seminary Ridge might be heavily punished by these guns, and it was therefore important that Stuart put as many of them as possible out of commission.

Lee would have told Stuart to get his men ready to move out to Cress Ridge, that he would give him the final signal to leave at the right time. Stuart would have been very easily able to move three or so miles on the York Pike and then down another mile into the woods atop Cress Ridge, a site Stuart had no doubt visited the day before with Fitz Lee and probably (as any good commander would have made sure to do) Hampton and Chambliss as well. Hampton and Fitz Lee's brigades were already out north of the York Pike, in good position to move down onto Cress Ridge, while Stuart had spent the night in town with the brigades of Chambliss and Jenkins. Lee would give him the word to begin moving those brigades and send couriers to alert the others well before he started his artillery barrage. Once Stuart had assembled his four brigades on Cress Ridge, he should keep them well concealed in the woods and signal to Lee by cannon shots that he had arrived and what his prospects were. This signal would give Lee important information on which the development of the rest of his battle plan would depend.

The signals agreed upon are open to conjecture, but we can say some things about the code that must have been involved. One shot would have meant nothing, for a single cannon being fired near an active battlefield could too easily have been fired by someone else and would mean nothing. The same might be true for two shots, or they might be a peremptory signal, like the simple fact that the York Pike was blocked or for some other reason Stuart could not make it to the top of Cress Ridge. Three shots would mean that Stuart had arrived at Cress Ridge, but his path to Bonaughton Road was barred by a strong Union force that seemed capable of keeping him from reaching it. And four shots would mean that he had arrived on Cress Ridge and the way was clear before him, that there was nothing apparent that might slow him down as he moved his men down the valley and headed them south on Bonaughton Road.

That last signal would be the best possible outcome, for it meant that from Cress Ridge Stuart had to move about one mile down to the junction of the Hanover Road and Bonaughton Road, another mile down Bonaughton Road to the Baltimore Pike, and then perhaps three-quarters of a mile up Baltimore Pike to the rear of Culp's Hill. That was a total of less than three miles, and Stuart's cavalry could cover that distance at a trot in less than twenty minutes. Stuart should save his horses over that stretch, for once he got behind Culp's Hill and Jenkins's brigade dismounted and reassumed their infantry role, the rest of his men would have dug in their spurs. They then would have descended like apocalyptic banshees on the back side of the Clump of Trees and Cemetery Hill, a fury of death and destruction striking the Union soldiers in the rear while their anxious attention would be riveted on Pickett's Charge to their front.

If Stuart reached Cress Ridge, found the way clear, and fired four shots, Lee would proceed with the rest of his attack. He planned to fire his artillery against Union gun emplacements and infantry positions around the Clump of Trees, a bombardment that would last for more than an hour, perhaps as much as two hours. But he would not open fire until he had heard Stuart's signal. If he heard four shots, he would launch the attack. If Stuart's signal was something else, that would mean he could probably not get through and Lee would have to consider other actions.

After the Confederate guns had fired for an hour or more, he would have them all stop. He expected the Union artillery to be answering his fire during this barrage, and they might stop when he did, but they also might not. But even if they did not stop, the Confederates would be firing about twice the number of cannon as the Union forces, so Stuart would note a dramatic lessening of explosions from the main battlefield.

By this time in the war, the soldiers in the Union Army of the Potomac were virtually all hardened veterans, men who could be expected to stick to their guns and fight. They had shown that on the third of May at Chancellorsville, when Jackson's men (led by Stuart that day after Jackson's wounding) had a very tough time with their Yankee counterparts. In fact, had Stuart not had two of the three Union corps he faced enfiladed by fifty guns on the high ground at Hazel Grove, and had the Yankees not begun to run out of ammunition, it's not entirely clear that the Confederates would have won that day. The men of this Army of the Potomac, Lee knew, would make it a tough fight, and they outnumbered his force significantly. So how could he offset this numerical advantage held by a hardened force?

Facing a larger army in strongly prepared defenses, Lee knew that, in the Battle of Leuthen tradition, he had to use some deceit and distraction as part of his plan.

After he stopped the cannon fire, Lee would have the nine brigades of infantry scheduled to make the attack remembered as Pickett's Charge brought forward, then line up at the edge of the trees on Seminary Ridge. Some would be very close to their starting positions on the ridge, others would take some time to get into place. Then they would pause while they unfurled their colors, dressed their ranks, and presented a stunning sight to the Yankees. This should take ten or fifteen minutes, during which time all eyes inside the Fishhook would be locked on Seminary Ridge, for if those men "over there" were to crash through the Union line, it would mean that, once again, the mythology of Lee's invincibility was proven to be true.

So the men in gray who would be dressing their ranks were also playing an important psychological role of distracting the attention of every soldier in the Army of the Potomac. But to those men aligned in formation before marching across the field, they were the only attack that would take place that day, and it was clear that they would meet fierce resistance on Cemetery Ridge.

Then the drums would beat, the bugles would ring, and the men in gray and butternut would march forward to meet their destiny.

This was to be the primary attack with which most Americans are familiar, "Pickett's Charge" that ended at the "high tide of the Confederacy" in the Clump of Trees. This attack was to be made by only nine of Lee's forty-three combat brigades, and virtually all Americans now believe that was truly the only attack there was to be that day. But if true, that means Lee was risking everything on an attack to be made by just over 20 percent of his army while the rest of his men sat idle. This would have been a rather shocking act by the man who had been the master of all Civil War battlefields before that day, and those nine brigades were a smaller proportion of his force than that with which McClellan had attacked Lee's forces at Antietam. McClellan, of course, had been outgeneraled and had failed there, and had shown himself repeatedly and irredeemably to be a hesitant battlefield incompetent. Are we to see Lee in that same historical light?

As they moved out into the field, depending on how effective the southern artillery bombardment had been, Union artillery would be expected to open up on them and rake their lines. But if things worked as planned, this would be about the time—twenty minutes after the end of the Confederate artillery barrage—that Jenkins would be attacking the rear of Culp's Hill and Stuart would be racing across the Fishhook. It was then expected that Stuart's men would silence many or most of the fifty-odd cannon on Cemetery Hill, as well as the dozen or so around the Clump of Trees. They also would have driven Union infantry out of their positions as the 13,000 Confederate infantry came pouring across the field and funneled through the break in Union lines.

Timing, of course, was all-important. Before launching Pickett's attack, Lee would have told Stuart he would start with a massive bombardment from more than a hundred of his own guns. Their targets would be Union artillery positions as well as the Union soldiers arrayed at or near the Clump of Trees, and Lee hoped to severely damage Union defenses, both artillery and infantry, with this fire.

The signal for Stuart to move down out of the woods on Cress Ridge and onto Bonaughton Road would be the end of the artillery barrage, which should last between one and two hours. During that time, it was most important that he carefully conceal his force from prying Union eyes, which meant keeping them hidden in the woods. But Lee and his cavalry commander also had to consider what might happen if Stuart fired four shots signaling that he was ready and the way was clear, and then a large Union force suddenly appeared and blocked him. In that event, Lee would have told him, he should simply use his head as they traced Stuart's possible movements on the map prepared by Hotchkiss.

If he was blocked by an infantry force, he could immediately move back up to York Pike and go a few ridges farther east, then come south all the way to the Baltimore Pike. This would take more time, but the cannonade would last at least an hour, perhaps two, and he could use that time to move and then try to conceal his force somewhere in the woods along the Baltimore Pike several miles short of Culp's Hill. But if this Union blocking force suddenly appeared when Stuart was supposed to be moving, after the end of the Confederate bombardment but before the Union artillery opened up on Pickett's men, then Stuart would have to try to go around the Union infantry and simply outrun them to the intersection of Hanover Road and Bonaughton Road.

If he was blocked by a cavalry force, that should prove a somewhat easier problem, since he would also have Jenkins's brigade with him. In the event that Stuart found his path blocked by a large force of blue horsemen, whether below Cress Ridge or even on Bonaughton Road, he should simply advance part of Jenkins's men, a force of mounted infantry, not cavalry. As they moved, Stuart should try to keep them out of Yankee sight if possible, until they reached a position between Gettysburg and the Union cavalry force. He would then have them dismount and form a north-south line, after which they would come out of cover, advance to the east, and take the Union cavalry force under fire. Facing that sort of surprise, no sane cavalry leader would stay in place while receiving rifle fire from a line of advancing infantrymen. Instead, they would simply use the mobility of their horses to ride out of range, probably off to the east.

But when that happened, Stuart's force would find itself between the Union cavalry and the battlefield, and it could no longer be stopped by them. This might cost Stuart the use of some of Jenkins's men, but that might be part of the cost of this flanking movement. One part of Jenkins's brigade, the Thirty-fourth Virginia Battalion, was 372 men strong, and their modern Enfield rifles should provide enough firepower to drive off several regiments of cavalry, perhaps even a brigade. In fact, it might even be a prudent move for Stuart, once his men were massed on Cress Ridge, to deploy a picket line of Jenkins's men on foot just south of Cress Ridge. If a Union cavalry unit were to stumble onto them, they might be easily driven off by rifle fire from what would then appear to be a Confederate infantry force.

But whatever the cost, once he had fired four cannon shots as a signal to Lee, Stuart had to get his men to the Fishhook within half an hour at all costs. The timely presence of his force there would be of crucial importance, and it might well mean the difference between victory and defeat.

This may seem like a very risky venture for Lee or any other Civil War general to have taken. But it was not nearly as risky as sending Jackson and 26,000 infantry down the Catherine Furnace Road on

May 2 at Chancellorsville and so separating themselves from Lee and the 17,000 men left in his army as they faced Hooker's looming 75,000 Union soldiers.

If Stuart's reconnaissance from the previous day was correct, then once he got his men on Cress Ridge they would be nearly a mile behind the line of Union cavalry pickets that covered the Union right flank out to Brinkerhoff Ridge. In fact, the Union horsemen might even have been brought in to face the true Confederate left wing the next morning somewhere between Culp's Hill and Wolf's Hill. But even if they weren't, they could be expected to return to Brinkerhoff Ridge where they had been the night before, and to once again stretch a line of pickets all the way down to Wolf's Hill.

And now it would all be up to Stuart. Once he got to Cress Ridge, he would signal his situation to Lee with an agreed-upon number of cannon shots. From then on, as Lee truly believed, the success or failure of Stuart's force would depend on God's will. As he told a German observer, J. Scheibert:

> *I plan and work with all my might to bring the troops to the right place at the right time; with that I have done my duty. As soon as I order the troops forward into battle, I lay the fate of my army in the hands of God.*[15]

On another occasion and in response to a question about the likelihood of success, Lee said:

> *I am not concerned with results. God's will ought to be our aim, and I am quite contented that his designs should be accomplished and not mine.*[16]

If we want to understand Lee here and how he thought, we must first recognize that he was a high-risk player all through the war. His biographer Douglas Southall Freeman perhaps captures Lee the best:

*His patient synthesis of military intelligence, his understanding employ-
ment of the offensive, his sense of position and his logistics were supplemented in the making of his strategy by his audacity. Superficial critics,
puzzled by his success and unwilling to examine the reasons for it, have
sometimes assumed that he frequently defied the rules of war, yet rarely
sustained disaster in doing so because he was confronted by mediocrity.
Without raising the disputable question of the capacity of certain of his
opponents, it may be said that respect for the strength of his adversaries,
rather than contempt for their abilities, made him daring. Necessity, not
choice, explains this quality. More than once, in these pages, certain of his
movements have been explained with the statement that a desperate cause
demanded desperate risks. That might well be written on the title-page
of his military biography, for nothing more surely explains Lee, the
commander.*[17]

And yet to say that "desperate cause demanded desperate risks" does
not fully do Lee justice. We should remember here the stories of his
actions in Mexico, of his raw personal courage to the point of seeming
fearlessness while he danced with death on the battlefield of Contreras,
in crossing the Pedregal, or in assaulting the heights of Chapultepec.
The Mexican-American War, in which Lee accompanied one of several American columns, did not present a desperate situation for Lee or
for American forces. Had they been unable to win at any of the three
aforementioned places, there were many options open to the American
commander, among which were setting up a defensive position and
sending for reinforcements.

Lee was the top adviser to General Winfield Scott, the American
commander in Mexico, and he was quite caught up in that war. As long
as he believed that he could personally find ways to overcome the
seemingly insurmountable barriers at Contreras, the Pedregal, or Chapultepec, he never even considered sitting and waiting to be rescued to

be a serious option. It would seem, then, that the risks he took, though perhaps well thought out and carefully measured, also displayed tongues of the fierce and ferocious fire that burned within him, an aggressive, competitive, unquenchable warrior spirit that defined him when he was fighting for his homeland in a war. In that regard, it was a sad moment indeed for the United States of America that, in 1861, he chose to cast his lot with his newly seceded state of Virginia.

## ≈ 14 ≈

# The Implementation

CUSTER'S BRIGADE had spent most of the previous night in the saddle, finally arriving around three A.M. at Two Taverns, a small crossroads on the Baltimore Pike some five miles southeast of Gettysburg. His men got a few hours' rest there, along with the troopers in Farnsworth's brigade, the only other brigade in Kilpatrick's Third Cavalry Division at Gettysburg. Gregg's Second Cavalry Division was a mile or so closer to Gettysburg, also along the Hanover Road, and Buford's First Cavalry Division had been sent off to guard the Union wagon train at Winchester.

This meant that, during the night of July 2–3, neither Union flank was covered by a sizable cavalry screen, the norm in those times. But this brief rest for the Union troopers had been badly needed, for all the troopers in Gregg's and Kilpatrick's divisions were exhausted, as were their horses. So far, to them this campaign had meant a lot of hard riding with, except for Custer's men at Hunterstown, precious little enemy contact.

The next morning, July 3, they awoke to learn that Pleasonton had sent orders to protect the Union flanks with cavalry: Kilpatrick was to move to cover the left wing, while Gregg moved to cover the right. Pleasonton had apparently learned of the Confederate withdrawal from Brinkerhoff Ridge to the base of Culp's Hill, and so he had ordered Gregg to the same place. At the time, Gregg had only two of his three brigades with him, those of Colonel J. Irvin Gregg (a distant relation) and Colonel J. B. McIntosh, each numbering from twelve hundred to thirteen thundred men. The brigades of Farnsworth and Custer in Kilpatrick's Third Cavalry Division, meanwhile, each contained about eighteen hundred men.[1]

If Pleasonton had moved Gregg to the base of Culp's Hill, of course, they might have been doing exactly what Lee wanted by moving to cover the true Confederate left wing between Culp's Hill and Wolf's Hill and so clear the way for Stuart to get down Bonaughton Road and up into the Union rear. But Gregg, who apparently had some keen prescience on this matter, wanted Pleasonton to amend his orders. On the previous evening, he had seen the wide-open expanse below Cress Ridge, almost a mile to his rear from Brinkerhoff Ridge. He had noted that it would be a perfect avenue for a large Confederate cavalry force to descend unnoticed, then use the Bonaughton Road—commonly used for Union troop movements and even supply wagons over the past two days—and so get into the Union rear. He urged Pleasonton, we are told, to send him back there instead of to Culp's Hill, and this time with reinforcements.

Pleasonton accepted Gregg's argument, and as Kilpatrick's division began the march toward the Round Tops, Custer (whose brigade was behind that of Farnsworth for this movement) received a peremptory order from General Gregg, under the authority of Pleasonton, to stop and move north with him to cover the Union's extreme right flank south of Cress Ridge near Hanover Road.[2]

We have here seen a very important decision by Pleasonton, apparently made at the urging of Gregg. If that is true, Gregg certainly deserves credit for his insightful prescience. But as we will see, Gregg does not have a spotless record for truthfulness.

After any winning battle, it is not uncommon for men in the victorious army who were not engaged, particularly commanders who were one or more levels above the actual combat, to try to find a way for themselves or their units to be credited for the successes of others. If we look at the after-action reports of some high-ranking Union officers at Gettysburg, that trait occasionally surfaces, unfortunately. But it is important that we see this at the outset, that we might better understand how the written records submitted by some men might not be a fair reflection of what they did or even of what actually happened.

The case in point is that of General David McMurtie Gregg, commander of the Second Division of cavalry. Custer commanded a brigade in the Third Division, but was attached to Gregg's command on this day. In his after-action report of the July 3 cavalry fight on East Cavalry Field that we are about to examine, Gregg said the following:

> *Our own and the enemy's loss during this engagement was severe. Our loss: Officers, 1 killed, 17 wounded, and 1 missing; enlisted men, 33 killed, 140 wounded, and 103 missing. . . . Brigadier-General Custer, commanding the First [Second] Brigade, Third Division, very ably assisted me in the duties of my command. Col. J.B. McIntosh, commanding First Brigade of my division, handled his brigade with great skill, and deserves particular mention for his gallantry and untiring energy throughout the day. The Third Brigade, Second Division, Col. J. Irvin Gregg commanding, was held in reserve upon the field.*[3]

That sounds like Gregg and the parts of his division on the field had a rough time, and Custer only "very ably assisted me in the duties of my command." But the casualties Gregg mentions include those of July 2 as well as July 3, and he also claims credit for Custer's casualties as if they were his own, something he is not supposed to do. The actual number of casualties for Custer's brigade on July 3 are: one officer and twenty-eight enlisted men killed, eighteen officers and 131 enlisted men wounded, and sixty-seven enlisted men missing (killed, grievously wounded, or captured). On July 3, Gregg's division on East Cavalry Field suffered casualties of none killed, seven officers and nineteen enlisted men wounded, and eight enlisted men missing. Total casualties on East Cavalry Field on July 3, then, were 219 for Custer's brigades and only thirty-four, with no fatalities, for the single brigade of Gregg's division that was engaged.[4]

Custer's after-action report was rather terse, in which he delivers only a short condensation of the actions of each of his regiments over the period of June 30 to July 25.[5] And each regiment gets only a few sentences for their action on a given day, as shown by one typical entry on one of the four regiments serving in Custer's brigade, the Seventh Michigan Cavalry:

*July 3,—Charged the advance line of the enemy's skirmishers at Gettys-burg. Held the field until the advance of the 1st Michigan Cavalry.*[6]

But as we shall see, the charge that day by the Seventh, a brand-new organization of just under four hundred men, was a rather ferocious experience that another man might have painted in much brighter hues.

At the time, the only medal awarded for heroism was the new Medal of Honor, though it was not widely recognized at the time as an appropriate award by men in uniform. Instead, notable courage in battle or other exceptional performance of military duty by an officer would be mentioned in dispatches from the commander on the field to higher headquarters. The 219 casualties of Custer's brigade accounted for more than 86 percent of those suffered on East Cavalry Field on July 3, but Gregg's report seems to imply almost the reverse: Custer is barely mentioned, while McIntosh is highly praised.

It is because of this very obvious attempt to claim the credit due Custer and his men for the victory they won on July 3 that I tend to discredit all that comes from Gregg in the written record, or at least to view it with some skepticism. But the reader should be aware that such shading of the truth, and sometimes bald-faced lies, too often fill the after-action reports of all battles.

This is not only because some soldiers are shameless liars, but also because, after the danger has passed, it seems an understandable human action to try to steer credit to oneself, sometimes to enhance a unit's reputation, but more commonly just for ego gratification, pure and simple. Not everyone wants to risk the dangers of combat or share the shame of defeat, but a great many people want to grab the glory of victory. And the shamelessness of some in that self-seeking effort can be quite surprising. But falsification of records is not always something done only by liars or cowards. Sometimes even the best and bravest of men fall victim to that siren, an unfortunate reality that only makes the historian's task more difficult.

A good example of this can be seen in the well-known July 2 infantry confrontation at Gettysburg between the Twentieth Maine under Joshua L. Chamberlain and the Fifteenth Alabama under William C. Oates. Vincent's Union brigade of five regiments on Little Round Top that day was attacked by Law's Confederate brigade, also of five regiments. The far right wing of Law's brigade was the Fifteenth Alabama, and they attacked the Twentieth Maine, which was the far left wing of Vincent's brigade—indeed, of the entire Union line. These two regiments slugged it out over several hours, with multiple charges going back and forth in both directions and no significant involvement in their fight by neighboring regiments in blue or gray. Eventually, depending on whom you want to believe, the Fifteenth Alabama either retreated downhill or was driven off by the Twentieth Maine.

Before the war, Chamberlain had been a professor at Bowdoin College and Oates a lawyer, while afterward, both eventually rose to become governors of Maine and Alabama respectively. Both men, in other words, having reached high public stations during and after the war, would have been expected to produce after-action reports that adhered to the highest standards of carefully measured fact. Yet Chamberlain reported that, during the Little Round Top fight, he captured four hundred Confederates, while Oates reported that his unit had only ninety men missing (some of whom would have been dead or wounded but not prisoners) from that battle.[7]

This anecdote is intended to illustrate the point that, in the Official Reports they wrote after a battle, commanders on both sides tended to inflate their successes and/or minimize their failures. This may mean added difficulty for people trying to investigate the facts of a given battle, but it is also a most unfortunate fact of human nature that should, in the search for historical truth, be recognized and accommodated.

Perhaps Gregg displayed amazing foresight on this day, for if he did argue that he and Custer be sent to Hanover Road rather than to the base of Culp's Hill, it was an act that may have saved the day for the Union. But brilliant though he may have been, it seems quite clear from the evidence we have that Gregg was neither much of a fighter nor a skilled or even competent battlefield commander.

When he was given eighteen hundred men under Custer to add to the twenty-five hundred then available from his division, he also had a requirement to post a picket line twelve hundred strong over a two- to three-mile distance, from Hanover Road to Wolf's Hill. A general officer since 1862 and a cavalry division commander at Gettysburg, Gregg by this time in the war should have developed a feel for the capabilities of his own subordinates and the ways of effectively commanding them. Custer and his men were complete strangers to him, and in a combat situation, an unknown unit placed under your immediate control right before a fight presents a very dangerous and risky situation for a commander.

A true fighter in that situation, or even any adequate commander, would have sent twelve hundred of Custer's troops to man the picket line and done the actual fighting with his own men. He then would have made sure that there was a minimal presence on the battlefield of the remaining six hundred new troops under Custer, troops whose behavior under the pressures of combat would have been completely unknown to him. This is because he would at least have known and been able to correctly manage his subordinate brigade and regimental commanders, he would have known the fighting experience and capabilities of the various units under his command, and therefore he would have known how and when to use them.

This would have been true even if the men filling his ranks were physically exhausted or brand-new or otherwise unreliable. At least under those circumstances, he would have known the strengths and weaknesses of his own command and would have known what to expect when he committed them to battle. If he was to rely on an unknown unit such as Custer's, however, he would have been completely in the dark.

So one may reasonably ask why Gregg did this, why he made sure that his men were absent on other conveniently justifiable assignments (picket line, flank guard, etc.) before the storm arrived. And the answer to that requires a sense of the psychological aura given off in the North by some Confederate leaders of the time.

Lee was the acknowledged master of the battlefield, a fact accepted since the Seven Days at the end of June 1862. But there was also a mounted monster loose in the fantasies of people safe at home in Ohio and New York, a man who, after Antietam, had struck like Genghis Khan, racing swiftly up into Pennsylvania with his wild horde of horsemen, unstoppable, uncatchable. Out of the dark and with no warning they had struck and were gone, leaving only fire and ash and death in their wake. This fiend was Jeb Stuart, the nightmare of Yankee boys and girls, and sometimes the "daymare" of Union generals, who feared his sudden, ferocious attacks. Stuart and his Invincibles had made such a grand *éclat* that tales of their prowess, inflated by the northern press, electrified the northern people, including some Union cavalry generals, to whom his image was quite edifying. Terrifying, even.

Gregg had crossed swords with Stuart before, most recently at Brandy Station, when his division had come out of the woods and surprised Stuart's nearly defenseless headquarters on Fleetwood Hill. But he had been hesitant in that assault as well, deterred from attacking by the fire of a single cannon until it had used up its few rounds of ammunition. And even when he did attack, the only impetuosity shown came from one of his brigade commanders, Kilpatrick, since promoted to command the Third Cavalry Division.

Now, at Gettysburg, he was very anxious at the prospect of his division of twenty-five hundred being posted alone on the flank, standing squarely in Stuart's path. And he tells us that he was convinced this would not just be a circumstance of two flank guards standing off and perhaps skirmishing but not engaging in any serious fight. No, this time, he was certain that Stuart intended to smash into the Union rear, and unless he could get reinforcements, only his division would stand in the way.[8]

Gregg had been able to get Pleasonton to approve sending Custer's brigade to assist him. But after Gregg's division and Custer's brigade had arrived at the intersection of Hanover Road and the Old Dutch Road, Gregg made sure that it was Custer's force that was put at risk by blocking Stuart's anticipated attack, not his own. He knew that, after Stuart had predictably blown through that supposed blocking force of blue cavalry, great shame and discredit would be heaped on some Union commander's shoulders in the aftermath that would arrive as early as the next day. But now, with this neat organizational move, he had seen to it that responsibility for the battlefield failure he could see coming would fall to Custer, not himself.

But after Custer had endured and rebuffed Stuart's attacks on July 3, as we shall see, that changed the game entirely. In his after-action report, as we know, Gregg rather shamelessly tries to steal Custer's thunder. Such behavior for a commissioned officer, let alone a general, can only be considered shameful. In remaking his cavalry force on June 28, Pleasonton had tried to get rid of weak commanders and replace them with men whose fearlessness in battle was widely recognized, men whose naked personal courage would be inspirational to the men they commanded. But he had failed to get rid of all weak leaders, and Gregg's actions in keeping his troops out of combat on East Cavalry Field and then trying to steal credit for the success won by Custer and his men are undeniable evidence of that fact.

There is more evidence of Gregg's reluctance to fight that we shall see, for while his two brigades were numerically superior to Custer's when the day began, he detailed so many of them to other duties that the remnants on the field when the fight broke out were about a third the size of Custer's command. And, through no fault of their own, even these few men did very little of the fighting and bleeding and dying.

Another issue that confronts us is the time at which certain events occurred. One reads time specifications from participants in different records that vary widely, and there seems little way to resolve many of these issues. However, we do know roughly what time the Confederate artillery bombardment of Union lines started, and we also know about what time it ended. Beyond that, we know that twenty to forty minutes after the fire from both sides stopped, the Union fire started again as the men conducting Pickett's Charge moved out into the open fields and became defenseless targets. We will therefore keep those times in mind and try to structure the action on East Cavalry Field in accord with them.

Stuart started his movement northeast up the York Pike in late morning, leading the brigades of Chambliss and Jenkins and having sent orders to Hampton and Fitz Lee to meet him with their brigades on Cress Ridge. But as he moved, unbeknownst to him, Stuart was being observed by men in Howard's XI Corps on Cemetery Hill. And as they watched the cloud of three thousand or so horsemen leave town, someone quickly put things together and sent a message to Pleasonton, who passed it on to Gregg around noon. The message said that thousands of Confederate horsemen were moving east-northeast of town on the York Pike and could only be moving into a position from which they would try to turn the Union right flank.[9]

Stuart's actions that day would have been of particular importance to the commanding general. If Lee did in fact send Stuart out to Cress Ridge just to act as a mounted cover for his left flank (with no such cover for his right flank), then Stuart did what he was ordered to do. But in that case, he would have had a very difficult task before him. That is because covering a flank at least means being able to see and warn of enemy forces trying to go around that flank. If a large body of Union troops had actually tried to go around that flank once Stuart was in position on Cress Ridge, then this supposed "flank guard" would probably never even have known about it. That is because his vision to the west would have been blocked by trees on Brinkerhoff Ridge and elsewhere, as well as by the undulations in the ground of the rolling countryside.

And if Stuart was truly sent out to be a flank guard on the Confederate left flank, one might ask why Lee had not simply divided Stuart's force in half and sent two brigades to cover each flank, both to be posted within easy visual range of the infantry farthest out on that flank. Why was it that Lee sent all of his cavalry out to a wooded ridge above an open valley far beyond his left flank?

And why, if they were on Cress Ridge just as flank guard or to await and descend on retreating Union troops, did Stuart's force repeatedly attack the Union cavalry blocking their way? Flank guards just didn't do that. Perhaps a little skirmishing, that might have been predictable. But they certainly would not have started any serious fighting with a Union force in front of them, fighting that might reduce their combat strength. This would be too big a risk, for as the main battle back on the Fishhook progressed, serious combat by the flank guard meant potential casualties that could threaten their organizational cohesion and thus their later ability to perform their missions.

The formal justification for Stuart's position on Cress Ridge is found in his after-action report, in which he discusses his position and its value:

> *On the morning of 3 July,* pursuant to instructions from the commanding general *(the ground along our line of battle being totally impracticable for cavalry operations), I moved forward to a position on the left of General Ewell's left, and in advance of it, where a commanding ridge completely controlled a wide plain of fields, stretching toward Hanover, on the left, and reaching to the base of the mountain spurs, among which the enemy held position. My command was increased by the addition of Jenkins' brigade. . . . I moved this command and W.H.F. Lee's [Chambliss's] secretly through the woods to a position, and* hoped to effect a surprise upon the enemy's rear, *but Hampton and Fitz.*

*Lee's brigades, which had been ordered to follow me, unfortunately debouched [came out] into the open ground, disclosing the movement, and causing a corresponding movement of a large force of the enemy's cavalry.*[10] (emphasis added)

But that is a highly misleading statement of the view from the southern end of Cress Ridge, which I have visited many times. It is true that the ridge "controlled a wide plain of fields," in that it is at a slightly higher elevation and one standing there at the southern edge of the wood line looks down over them. But one can see only details on the ground—such as people—for a quarter to a half of a mile or so. The rest of the fields beyond are obscured by tree lines and, again, undulations in the ground. It is true that one can see the tops of what Stuart would have called mountains as much as several miles in the distance, but only the tops and upper slopes of them, while the lower slopes are completely concealed from view by many trees and the natural rolling of the countryside in the foreground.

Hanover Road is now a paved road a mile away that carries a heavy load of traffic. But because of the trees and rolling terrain, from Cress Ridge one can catch only occasional glimpses of cars or trucks flashing by. One certainly would not be able to see a few thousand men and horses gathered near the intersection of Old Dutch Road and Hanover Road, and would not have been able to see them in July 1863 either.

I am confident of this because Dan Hoffman, the present owner and occupant of Rummel's farm who has lived there with his family for many decades, shared with me a period map of his farm and the area now known as East Cavalry Field. And sure enough, most of the same fields were bordered with tree lines, and other clumps of trees south of Rummel's farm obviously would have obscured one's view down that valley in July 1863 as much or more than they do today.

Farther on in Stuart's after-action report we find the following:

*During this day's operations, I held such a position as not only to render Ewell's left entirely secure . . . but commanded a view of the routes leading to the enemy's rear. Had the enemy's main body been dislodged, as was confidently hoped and expected, I was in precisely the right position to discover it and improve the opportunity. I watched keenly and anxiously the indications in his rear for that purpose, while* in the attack which I intended *(which was forestalled by our troops being exposed to view)*, his cavalry would have separated from the main body, and gave promise of solid results and advantages.[11] *(emphasis added)*

As will be shown, this entire paragraph is simply inaccurate and so misleading in many ways. But in it, Stuart also gives away some of what I believe to have been his true mission that day. In order to gain insight into what was really going on here, therefore, it would seem important to take a close look at his words to try to understand them.

First of all, as mentioned earlier, Cress Ridge is roughly two miles from the true end of the Confederate left wing on the east side of Culp's Hill. And from Ewell's position on that left wing, one's vision to the northeast in the direction of Cress Ridge is blocked by Wolf's Hill and Brinkerhoff Ridge as well as other rolling ground, vast tree lines, and even forests. Stuart's statement that he "rendered Ewell's left entirely secure" from Cress Ridge, therefore, simply could not have been true.

But perhaps even worse is the statement that Cress Ridge commanded a view of the "routes leading to the enemy's rear." That cannot mean Hanover Road, simply because it passes through the extreme right wing of the Union army, far from their center, and there were no other roads that would have given ready access to it from the Union rear area. Retreating Union troops would have been trying to move away from Gettysburg and Confederate forces, which would have meant to the south or southeast. Given that constraint, the best candidate by far for the role of main avenue of retreat would have been the Baltimore Pike, which also happened to have been the main resupply and logistics route for Meade's army. And that last factor alone means it would have been the natural first choice of a defeated Union commander trying to herd his forces out of danger.

As mentioned earlier, from Cress Ridge at the present time one might see occasional flashes of passing cars or trucks on Hanover Road a mile to the south. But Baltimore Pike is at least another mile or two farther south and so even more obscured from sight, a road one would not even suspect existed from that vantage point. In the event the Union army had been driven off in retreat on July 3, then, they clearly would have gone down the Baltimore Pike, not Hanover Road. And in that event, Stuart on Cress Ridge wouldn't have had any physical evidence that anything was moving on a road two to three miles to his south and totally obscured by small hills and trees. This is all the more true because in 1863 in Pennsylvania, paved roads were known as "pikes," of which the Baltimore Pike was one, thus eliminating even the possibility of a telltale cloud of dust raised by a retreating army.

For these reasons, Stuart could not have "watched keenly and anxiously the indications in his [Meade's Union army's] rear." He says he did, however, and I believe the only possible reason he does this is in an attempt to promote later belief that he had been posted on Cress Ridge by Lee only as a flank guard.

The next statement, however, betrays his true mission: that the "attack which I intended" was forestalled by Hampton's and Fitz Lee's brigades having come out of the woods and so alerted the Yankees to their presence there, which, Stuart believes, caused them to bring more of their own cavalry to the scene. But had he been able to make that attack, he explains, he would have gotten between the Union cavalry and the rest of the Union army—which eventuality "gave promise of solid results and advantages."

He gave another indication earlier in the report that, once he saw his way blocked by Union cavalry, he decided to try to drive them back with some dismounted men acting as infantry and then pass by them on their left with the great bulk of his horsemen:

> My plan was to employ the enemy in front with sharpshooters and move a command of cavalry upon their left flank, from the position lately held by me, but the falling back of Jenkins' men . . . caused a like movement of those on the left, and the enemy, sending forward a squadron or two, were about to cut off and capture a portion of our dismounted sharpshooters.[12]

If he had gotten between the Union cavalry and the main body, of course, he didn't just want access to Hanover Road, for that led only northwest toward Gettysburg and behind Confederate lines. But if by that separation he meant that he would have been able to go down Bonaughton Road, then that means he would have had access to Baltimore Pike, the rear of Culp's Hill, and the interior of the Fishhook. And in that case, yes, there was the very real "promise of solid results and advantages."

At a later point in his report, while addressing the major cavalry fight that ended the battle there, he says:

> Notwithstanding the favorable results obtained, I would have preferred a different method of attack, as already indicated; but I soon saw that entanglement by the force of circumstances narrated was unavoidable, and determined to make the best fight possible.[13] (emphasis added)

In his after-action report, of course, he is claiming victory on East Cavalry Field ("the favorable results obtained"). It was quite common, of course, for commanders on both sides to claim victory in their after-action reports, no matter the reality of the outcome. But once again, he indicates that he had a different attack in mind from the outset. What, other than the cavalry fight with the Union force he found in front of him which occurred, could that have been?

There is quite a bit of evidence from other sources that Stuart had been ordered, and fully intended, to make the flank attack upon Meade's army I have described, evidence that will be discussed in due course. But if we are looking for words from his own mouth, then I believe that three statements taken from his three-page after-action report on Gettysburg provide just that: "I moved these forces . . . and hoped to effect a surprise upon the enemy's rear"; "in the attack which I intended . . . his cavalry would have separated from the main body, and gave promise of solid results and advantages"; and "I would have preferred a different method of attack, as already indicated." But I will add more evidence to this as the story unfolds.

Custer and his men reached the intersection of the Old Dutch Road and the Hanover Road by mid-morning at the latest, where Gregg told them to deploy in the field at the northeast corner of that intersection. Open fields spread north from there for about a mile, and the breadth of this cleared land, known in modern times as "East Cavalry Field," is about a half mile. Custer set his men up in an L-shaped formation, with one leg, elements of the First and Fifth Michigan Cavalries, facing west toward Gettysburg, and the other, the Sixth and Seventh Michigan Cavalries, facing north toward open fields, with Cress Ridge off to the northwest a mile away. Next, he sent two parties of about fifty men each to scout beyond a line of trees that lay northeast of Cress Ridge and more than a mile to the north. One group was to scout to the northwest and the other to the northeast.[14]

Their independent missions were to investigate the wooded areas and whatever territory might lie beyond them. Custer also sent Captain Maxwell of the First Michigan with fifty men northwest to form a skirmish line along Little's Run, a north-south stream that flowed near the west side of the field. Finally, he sent scouts from the Sixth Michigan a mile or so out to the east and west along Hanover Road to cover his flanks, positions they would maintain throughout the coming battle. The rest of the Sixth he posted with Pennington's guns, to serve as their protection, along Hanover Road at the southern end of the open fields. He kept the First and Seventh Michigan Cavalry regiments mounted and drawn up in columns of squadrons south of Hanover Road, while he dismounted the Fifth Michigan and had them advance a short distance into the fields northwest of the Hanover Road–Old Dutch Road intersection.[15]

Custer's Fifth and much of the Sixth Michigan Cavalry were armed with Spencer repeating rifles that could fire seven rounds consecutively as they consumed metal-jacketed bullets stored in a cylindrical magazine in the stock. The First and Seventh Michigan were armed with single-shot carbines, but the men of all four regiments also carried sabers and Colt .44 caliber revolvers.[16] And as they waited in place, the Michigan brigade was ready to fight.

General David M. Gregg had followed Custer, and he placed McIntosh's brigade near the same intersection, while he directed Colonel J. Irvin Gregg to deploy his brigade in a long picket line that would stretch all the way to Wolf's Hill, over two miles to their southwest. This effectively removed Colonel Gregg's brigade from the looming cavalry fight, leaving General Gregg with only McIntosh and twelve hundred men and Custer with about eighteen hundred. And Gregg would soon send the First Maryland Cavalry off on a flank guard and scouting mission, further reducing McIntosh's force to around six hundred to eight hundred men.

Along with McIntosh's brigade, General Gregg brought Randol's battery of four three-inch guns. These, along with the six three-inch guns in Pennington's battery that was attached to Custer's brigade, would fight and win the artillery battle with Stuart's gunners, a battle whose salvos were exchanged over the heads of (though sometimes through) the waves of horsemen that would soon wash over the field.

Once Stuart had arrived on Cress Ridge around noon, he scouted the key valley below through his field glasses. His newly named adjutant general, Major Henry McClellan, was a Williams College graduate and a first cousin of George B. McClellan, the "Young Napoleon" who had captured so many northern fantasies early in the war but had proven himself to be utterly incompetent in battle. But unlike his Yankee cousin, Major Henry McClellan was to prove himself quite a cool customer under pressure, and he was a very valuable member of Stuart's staff.

McClellan was with Stuart that day, and he commented on what Stuart saw when he first rode to the southern edge of the wooded ridge and surveyed the open fields before him:

> When Stuart first reached this place the scene was as peaceful as if no war existed. The extension of the ridge on his right [Brinkerhoff Ridge] hid from view the lines of the contending armies, and not a living creature was visible on the plain below.[17]

This must have been close to noon, and it is certain that Custer and Gregg and their twenty-four hundred cavalrymen were a mile south of Stuart along Hanover Road at the time, and yet neither he nor anyone else in his unit could see them (so much for Stuart being in a position, as he said, that "commanded a view of the routes leading to the enemy's rear"). As the men of Chambliss's and Jenkins's brigades settled into the woods, Stuart's other two brigades under Hampton and Fitz Lee came down from York Pike, across a wide expanse of fields and then into a line of woods slightly north and east of Cress Ridge. McClellan tells us what happened next:

> While carefully concealing Jenkins' and Chambliss' brigades from view, Stuart pushed one of Griffin's guns to the edge of the woods and fired a number of random shots in different directions, himself giving orders to the gun.[18]

No one understood this action, Stuart volunteered no explanation, and even McClellan was mystified:

> I have been somewhat perplexed to account for Stuart's conduct in firing those shots; but I suppose they may have been a pre-arranged signal by which he was to notify General Lee that he had gained a favorable position; or, finding that none of the enemy were within sight, he may have desired to satisfy himself whether the Federal cavalry was in his immediate vicinity before leaving the strong position he then held; and receiving no immediate reply to this fire, he sent for Hampton and Fitz Lee, to arrange with them for an advance and an attack upon the enemy's rear. In the meantime, Lieutenant Colonel Vincent Witcher's battalion, of Jenkins' brigade, was dismounted and sent forward to hold the Rummel barn and a line of fence on its right.[19] (emphasis added)

Some have said that these cannon shots were aimed at Custer's unit and they brought on his return fire from Pennington, which destroyed two Confederate cannon. But these shots by Stuart were pretty clearly not aimed at Custer or anyone else, for McClellan, who was there with

Stuart, said that none of the enemy were in sight and that he received no immediate reply to his fire. But McClellan does not tell us from which edge of the woods Stuart fired those shots.

If McClellan was wondering whether they were a signal or exploration by fire, however, they must have been fired from the western side of the ridge, back toward Gettysburg. That would be the most efficient way to ensure that a cannon report was heard three miles away. Stuart knew there were no Confederates to his west closer than Culp's Hill who might be hit by his cannonballs, though he did not know if there were any Union troops in front of his gun as he fired. But he probably thought there was only empty woods and farmland out there, for he was far removed from the fighting lines, even those on Brinkerhoff Ridge of the day before.

In order to make some sense of this confusion, it is important to understand a little more about Civil War artillery. The guns Stuart had with him at East Cavalry Field were all muzzle-loaders. Their ammunition had to be rammed down into the cannon from the muzzle, and to simplify the operation and reduce the time it took to load and fire a round, the ammunition for these cannon was prepared ahead of time. Each consisted of one cylindrical round of charge and projectile that was wired or otherwise bound together and could be loaded and fired as a single unit.

That is, the proper amount of powder charge would be placed in a silk (though by this time in the war, the Confederates used other fabrics as well) cylindrical bag. On top of this would be placed a wooden "sabot" whose diameter was slightly less than that of the cannon and which was specially fitted to cradle a solid shot or other types of projectiles. This, finally, was topped by the projectile itself and the whole thing would be wired together or connected by other means. The result was one ammunition round for a muzzle-loading cannon that looked somewhat like modern metal-jacketed artillery ammunition. When the crew of a gun wanted to fire another round, they were no longer required, as in times past, to load powder and shell as separate items. Rather, the whole assembly would be fitted into the mouth of the cannon and rammed down as one unit.

What this means is that if Stuart had wanted to fire a certain number of cannon shots as a signal, he had to fire the entire round, not just the powder charge, for it was just too difficult to take them apart on short notice. In that case, wanting only the noise but stuck with the projectile, he probably would have told the gunners to fire at a particular clump of trees or a hill or some other prominent target. It is easy to understand, therefore, how someone might be confused whether an aimed round was fired as a signal or in an effort to stir up enemy activity.[20] But given his repeated desire for secrecy, I don't think Stuart intended to alert the Union army to his presence on Cress Ridge.

It seems appropriate here to once again quote from Stuart's after-action report, that we might understand a little better what was going on:

> I moved this command [Jenkins' brigade] and W.H.F. Lee's [a brigade now commanded by Chambliss] through the woods to a position, and hoped to effect a surprise on the enemy's rear.[21] (emphasis added)

If, as he said, he really wanted to "effect a surprise on the enemy's rear," it seems improbable that he was "exploring by fire" to locate Union forces. If his fire were to bring on a fight, that would eliminate any surprise, and he certainly did not want to do anything that might tie him down and alert Union forces to his presence way out there, several miles beyond the Confederate wing.

The only reasonable explanation is that he was signaling to Lee that he was safely on Cress Ridge with all his men, the way was clear, he had not run into any Union troops, and the valley below him seemed empty, thus enabling him to get to Bonaughton Road without any hindrance. After firing those signal shots, Stuart planned to wait with his men on Cress Ridge until he heard the artillery barrage end. From that moment, he would have twenty minutes to move his force one mile to Bonaughton Road, another mile to Baltimore Pike, three-quarters of a mile to the rear of Culp's Hill—less than three miles, all at a trot or canter in fifteen or twenty minutes.

McClellan tells us there was "no immediate reply" to this artillery fire, and Stuart began to busy himself with getting his unit ready to plunge into the Union rear. One of the first things he did then was to send the Thirty-fourth Virginia battalion of Jenkins's brigade forward on foot to occupy the Rummel barn and spread out along a stone fence on either side of it.[22] This unit of dismounted infantrymen would act as a combination picket line and, if the need arose, skirmish line. But for now, all Stuart had to do was wait.

About noon, Gregg received two messages. The first was from the XI Corps, warning him that a large body of Confederate cavalry had moved out the York Pike and looked like it was going to try to get around the Union right wing.

The second message was an order from Pleasonton directing Gregg to release Custer and send him to join Kilpatrick at the far left of the Union line, south of the Round Tops. When he got that order, Gregg had given orders to McIntosh to replace Custer's skirmish line with his own men. McIntosh sent elements of the First New Jersey, Third Pennsylvania, and Purnell Legion, perhaps two hundred men in all, forward to the north-south line along Little's Run still occupied by men from Custer's First Michigan under Captain Maxwell. From there, they could see a Confederate skirmish line developing on either side of Rummel's farm buildings, still several hundred yards away. McIntosh kept the larger part of these units—another four hundred men—half a mile away from the skirmish line, arrayed along the north-south edge of the heavy wood line on the eastern side of East Cavalry Field.

Custer, meanwhile, had heard back from the scouts he had sent north. They told him that a large body of perhaps thousands of Confederate cavalry had gathered in the fields beyond the woods a mile or so to the north, and that they had then descended into those woods and perhaps onto Cress Ridge as well. Soon after, as Gregg was passing on the orders from Pleasonton, Custer told Gregg what his scouts had seen. This information, in addition to the warning received from XI Corps, must have simply terrified Gregg.

The two brigades he had with him had originally numbered only about twenty-four hundred men together. But after he had been able to acquire Custer's eighteen hundred men to take on the main fight, he had farmed his own men out on other duties that would conveniently take them off the battlefield and so out of the line of fire of Stuart's men. But now, if Custer followed Pleasonton's orders to rejoin his own division on the far left Union wing, that would leave Gregg with only the nine hundred or so of his own men that he had not been able to conveniently get off the field to try to stem Stuart's tide, a seemingly hopeless situation.

It is probable that a somewhat desperate Gregg then pleaded with Custer to stay. Custer, ever eager for a fight, said that he would be happy to stay if Gregg would give him the order. And Gregg, no doubt relieved, did just that.[23]

Custer had not yet pulled Captain Maxwell's 1st Michigan Cavalry force back from their skirmish line posting, and he and Gregg could both see the Confederate skirmish line forming through their binoculars. Custer sent word to the Fifth Cavalry to dismount and be prepared to deploy forward on foot. Armed with Spencer repeating rifles, they would prove to be a fearsome infantry force able to put out a tremendous volume of fire.

Before we get to the cavalry battle itself, however, we need to gain some sense of the proportions of the two forces that confronted each other that day. It's important to know the specific units on each side and the number of soldiers in each who were probably engaged in the fight. The figures provided in *Regimental Strengths at Gettysburg* by Martin and Busey, which are themselves often only estimates, have been carefully weighed and judiciously made, and they are therefore probably the most accurate today.

The Union cavalry force was commanded by General David M. Gregg, and it included three brigades: those of McIntosh, Irvin Gregg, and Custer. Irvin Gregg's brigade of over twelve hundred men, however, was detailed by General Gregg to provide the picket line to Wolf's Hill and therefore was conveniently not available on East Cavalry Field.

McIntosh's brigade of thirteen hundred was broken up and parts of it sent elsewhere, so that in the eventual fight against Stuart, only the First New Jersey (199 men), Third Pennsylvania (355), and the Purnell Legion (66) were engaged, for a brigade total of 620 men.

When the fight opened, McIntosh also had with him the First Maryland, a regiment of 285 men that he held in reserve. Within the first hour of fighting, however, he learned to his great distress that General Gregg had sent the First Maryland off to act as a flank guard on the Union right flank, a position it would maintain all day and so never be involved in the fight against Stuart. It is a mystery why Gregg did this without even informing McIntosh, commander of the brigade to which the First Maryland belonged. It is all the more a mystery since Gregg must have known that Custer had already sent an element from his Sixth Michigan to guard the same flank, where that unit, too, would remain all day.

Custer's brigade consisted of the First Michigan (427), the Fifth Michigan (about 500),[24] the Sixth Michigan (477), and the Seventh Michigan (383), for a total of about 1,800 men.

The total number of Yankee cavalry soldiers who would be engaged in combat on East Cavalry Field, then, was about 2,400.

The Confederate force was commanded by Jeb Stuart, and it consisted of the brigades of Hampton, Fitz Lee, Chambliss, and Jenkins.

Hampton's brigade was made up of regiments from four different states, including the First North Carolina (407), the First South Carolina (339), the Second South Carolina (186), the Jeff Davis Legion from Mississippi (246), and the Cobb Legion (330) and the Phillips Legion (238), both from Georgia. Hampton's brigade, then, was able to field about 1,740 men.

Fitz Lee's brigade included the First Maryland Battalion (310), the First Virginia (325), the Second Virginia (385), the Third Virginia (210), the Fourth Virginia (544), and the Fifth Virginia (150). This gives us a total of around 1,920 men.[25]

Chambliss's brigade consisted of the Second North Carolina (145), the Ninth Virginia (490), the Tenth Virginia (236), and the Thirteenth Virginia (298), for a total of about 1,160 men.

Jenkins's brigade had left one of its regiments, the Seventeenth Virginia, in Gettysburg to perform other duties such as guarding prisoners. Its commander, General Jenkins, had been wounded by artillery the day before, on July 2, and brigade command was passed to a Colonel Ferguson. Lieutenant Colonel Vincent Witcher, commander of the Thirty-sixth Virginia Battalion, may have been the brigade commander that day, as it is not clear that Ferguson accompanied them to East Cavalry Field. Its units on East Cavalry Field, then, were the Fourteenth Virginia (265), the Sixteenth Virginia (265), the Thirty-fourth Virginia Battalion (372), and the Thirty-sixth Virginia Battalion (125), which means they had just over 1,000 men on Cress Ridge.

Stuart's force was initially accompanied by a battery of Green's Louisiana artillery of four guns and sixty men[26] and another battery of Virginia artillery under Jackson, who had two guns and fifty-odd men.[27] The batteries of Breathed, with four guns and one hundred men, and McGregor, four more guns and another one hundred men, had been ordered to follow after they had replenished their ammunition, and they arrived late in the day.[28] On the Union side, Custer was accompanied by Battery M, Second U.S. Horse Artillery under Pennington, which had six guns and about 120 men.[29] Gregg also had Batteries E and G of the First U.S. Horse Artillery under Randol on the field, made up of four guns and another eighty men.[30]

If we include the artillery and then subtract perhaps fifty from the Union side and a hundred from the Confederates for broken-down horses and other miscellaneous losses, the total number of Union soldiers on East Cavalry Field that July 3 was probably about 2,700 facing 6,000 Confederates. That means Stuart had more than twice the number of Union soldiers standing in his path, men he would have to get past to perform what I believe was his secret mission from Lee.

# ⁓ 15 ⁓

# *Stuart Meets Custer*

SOMETIME NOT TOO LONG after noon, fighting broke out between Stuart's force and the Union soldiers who were blocking
him. It is not clear whether Jenkins's brigade exchanged fire with dismounted Union troopers along Little's Run to their front or artillery
fire erupted before that—McClellan says the first fire was an artillery
exchange,[1] while Stuart says it was small-arms fire between skirmish
lines[2] and Captain William Miller of the Third Pennsylvania Cavalry
says the same thing.[3] Colonel John McIntosh, commander of a brigade
in Gregg's division, had taken over the picket line duty from Custer
along Little's Run and facing the Rummel barn. He says that he initially posted the First New Jersey Cavalry, dismounted, along that line,
and they could see a Confederate skirmish line facing them a few
hundred yards to their front, which was no doubt the Thirty-fourth
Virginia. McIntosh would later describe how firing then broke out:

> The 1st N.J. becoming warmly engaged, two squadrons of the 3rd Penn.
> Cav. were sent in on their left. The enemy then ran out a battery on the
> knoll in front of the woods in which they had their forces masked and at
> the same time further strengthened their line.[4]

But whatever the case, this discovery of Stuart's force by an unknown force of Yankee cavalry caused a problem for Stuart. He had already fired his signal shots to Lee, a signal that would have informed him that Stuart and his force had arrived safely on Cress Ridge and were ready to move into the Union rear with no apparent hindrance. And now that he had been discovered, this force might try to block his way. He was confident he could blow through what looked like no more than a single large brigade, perhaps two thousand men. But that would take time. And if the federals sent for reinforcements, his passage might be effectively blocked by a combined infantry-artillery-cavalry force—what was he to do?

First of all, he had some time to kill before the end of the Confederate artillery barrage, which hadn't even started yet. The initial gunplay had started with Jenkins and the Thirty-fourth Virginia, some 370 men, exchanging fire with what looked to Stuart like a dismounted Yankee cavalry unit of unknown size—as we know, the fifty-man skirmish line from the First Michigan as well as small squadrons from the First New Jersey and the Third Pennsylvania, perhaps two hundred men in all. Stuart decided to drive them back, and if the Union commander thought he was facing a Confederate infantry unit, perhaps he would just have his men remount and ride away.

So Stuart ordered the Thirty-fourth to attack, and they went whooping down the slope after the men in blue. But despite being outnumbered, these men stood their ground. In addition to sabers (which would have been left with their horses) and Colt revolvers, the First New Jersey was armed with the Burnside carbine and the Third Pennsylvania and First Michigan with the Sharps carbine. Both weapons were single shot, but they were also breechloaders, which meant that reloading would take only a few seconds.[5]

The men of Jenkins's brigade also had sabers and revolvers, but their long-barreled weapons were all muzzle-loading rifles.[6] This gave a significant advantage in firepower to the Union force along Little's Run as they faced the ferocious onslaught of the Thirty-fourth Virginia, a unit with twice their number of soldiers. To the Confederates' great surprise, the Yankees held, spitting out a second volley within seconds after their first. After that, firing was largely individual, but the Rebels were held off by the speed with which the Yankees were able to reload.

Soon after the skirmishing started, Jackson's Confederate battery of four guns wheeled out into the open at the southern end of Cress Ridge and began to shell Custer's position a mile away. This was no doubt the battery McIntosh had seen, as mentioned above. Its fire was quite effective, Custer tells us, and he turned to Pennington. The answering fire was stunning in its accuracy: the first round fired hit the mouth of one of Jackson's guns and blew it apart; the second hit the wheel of another gun and destroyed its undercarriage as well as wounding or killing a half dozen Confederate gun crew members. Gregg, in his after-action report, said:

> The batteries commanded by Capt. A.M. Randol and Lieut. A.C.M. Pennington, Jr., rendered most effective service. The fire of the artillery during this engagement was the most accurate I have ever seen.[7]

At this point, there was a lull in the fighting, and both sides along the skirmish line grew quiet. Perhaps one-third of McIntosh's brigade was on the west side of the field near Rummel's farm, with the larger portion on the other side of the field and arrayed along the edge of the woods a half mile to the east. Then, around one o'clock, the Confederate artillery barrage exploded from the main battlefield to the west, quickly answered by Union guns. The roaring grew until the ground was reported by many to have trembled with the explosions.

After an extended pause, the Thirty-fourth Virginia opened the fight again, and they pushed their opponents far out into the field, some said all the way across it. But then, whether they were supplied with only ten rounds at the outset, as Stuart said, or they simply burned through a larger original issue, they had to stop and withdraw, all but out of ammunition and awaiting more. Witcher tells a somewhat harrowing tale:

> *We stubbornly holding our own, until about noon, when my ammunition being nearly exhausted, and I having failed to receive any from the rear, though I had made application after application for some. I fell back with my command to the fence and barn, and Major Norman having come out to us, I mounted his horse and rode back to the waggons [sic] and got some ammunition in some sacks, threw it across the horse and rode back and rejoined my command. (I shall never forget that fearful ride with death all around me, front and rear, and bullets as numerous in the air as hailstones in a storm.)* [8]

After the Thirty-fourth had gotten their supply of ammunition, it was reinforced by the dismounted soldiers from the rest of Jenkins's brigade and renewed the fight.[9] Witcher again tells us what happened next: "With a wild yell, the whole line dashed forward, retook the fence and swept the Federal dismounted men back."[10]

The small-arms fire heated up once again as Jenkins's brigade pressed forward. Despite their breech-loading weapons putting out a raging sheet of fire, the men in blue were just too heavily outnumbered and they retreated in the best order they could manage. The Yankees would occasionally pause to fire, but then kept going, and they were pursued well into the southern end of the field. But this open farmland, which has become known as the East Cavalry Field, was really a large number of individual farm fields bordering one another that were often separated by lines or clumps of bushes and trees that gave infantrymen some cover but would not have slowed cavalry.

Then Custer sent most of the Fifth Michigan forward on foot, adding perhaps four hundred more men to the Union side. They steadily pushed back Jenkins's brigade, who gave ground grudgingly but could not match the fire of those Spencer rifles. As the moving lines of fire got closer to Rummel's barn, however, about 150 sharpshooters from Fitz Lee's brigade came rushing forward on foot and attacked the Union line's right flank. The Fifth and remnants of the other Union regiments were now outnumbered once again, although the raging fire of their breech-loading carbines and repeating rifles kept the Confederates back for a while. Then Stuart sent in a mounted charge by the Ninth and Thirteenth Virginia Cavalries from Chambliss's brigade, and the Union force buckled and began to retreat.

In addition to the mounted attack, the Union force had already found that their rapid-fire weapons brought on an unanticipated problem, since they were consuming ammunition far too quickly. As the pressure from the howling fiends of Jenkins's and Chambliss's sharpshooters built up, hundreds of gray cavalrymen charged through their ranks, firing their pistols or swinging their sabers, and then they were gone. Soon enough, low on bullets and beset by Confederate horsemen, their retreat spun out of control.

Once again, the tables had turned and the Fifth Michigan was pushed back—routed, really—to the southern end of the field. Now what had started as an unintentional meeting between two dismounted cavalry forces had evolved into a running rifle-revolver-saber fight. And as the forces committed by both adversaries increased, there had been a certain washing back and forth across the field, east and west as well as north and south, of Union and Confederate lines.

But Custer would not allow the men of his Fifth Cavalry to be driven off so easily, and he launched the first Union-mounted attack of the day. Riding to the front of the Seventh Michigan Cavalry, fewer than four hundred new and nervous men, he drew his long Toledo

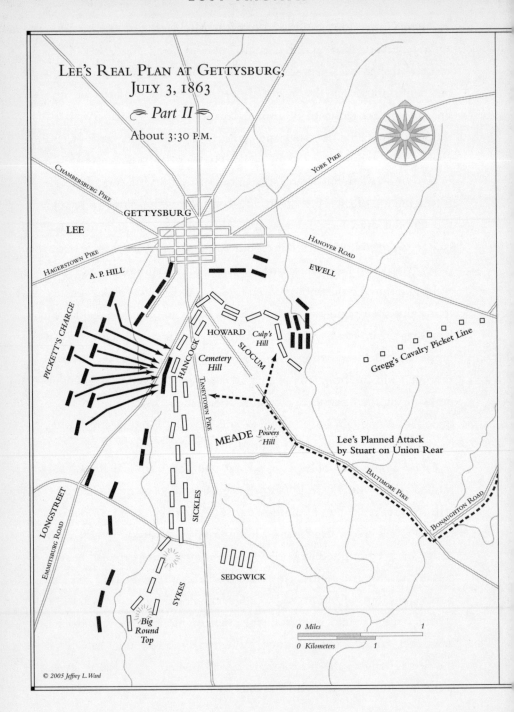

LEE'S REAL PLAN AT GETTYSBURG,
JULY 3, 1863

⮞ *Part II* ⮜

About 3:30 P.M.

YORK PIKE

CHAMBERSBURG PIKE

GETTYSBURG

LEE

HANOVER ROAD

HAGERSTOWN PIKE

A. P. HILL

EWELL

PICKETT'S CHARGE

HOWARD

Culp's
Hill

SLOCUM

Gregg's Cavalry Picket Line

HANCOCK

Cemetery
Hill

TANEYTOWN PIKE

MEADE

Powers
Hill

Lee's Planned Attack
by Stuart on Union Rear

LONGSTREET

SICKLES

BALTIMORE PIKE

EMMITSBURG ROAD

BONAUGHTON ROAD

SEDGWICK

SYKES

Big
Round
Top

0  Miles          1

0  Kilometers     1

© 2005 Jeffrey L. Ward

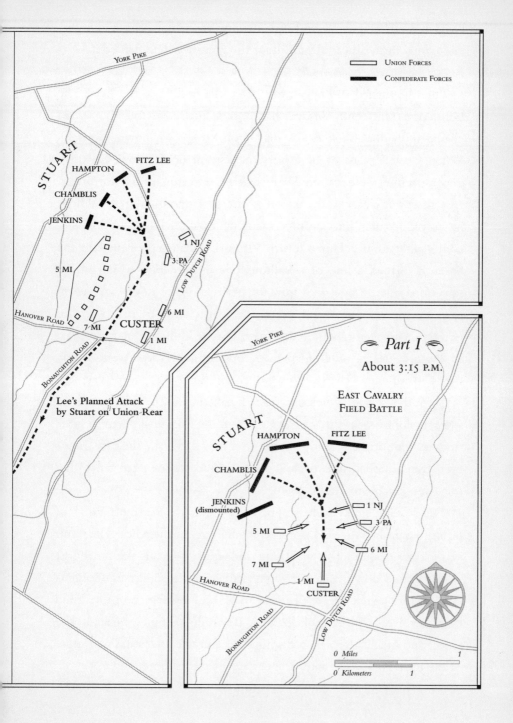

YORK PIKE

Union Forces
Confederate Forces

STUART

HAMPTON    FITZ LEE

CHAMBLIS

JENKINS

1 NJ

3 PA

LOW DUTCH ROAD

5 MI

HANOVER ROAD

6 MI

7 MI    CUSTER

1 MI

BONAUGHTON ROAD

Lee's Planned Attack
by Stuart on Union Rear

*Part I*

About 3:15 P.M.

EAST CAVALRY
FIELD BATTLE

YORK PIKE

STUART

HAMPTON    FITZ LEE

CHAMBLIS

JENKINS
(dismounted)

1 NJ

3 PA

5 MI

6 MI

7 MI

1 MI

CUSTER

HANOVER ROAD

BONAUGHTON ROAD

LOW DUTCH ROAD

0 Miles                1

0 Kilometers           1

blade and waved it above his head. Turning to them, he shouted loudly enough that it was heard by all above the gunfire which framed it:

*"Come on, you Wolverines!"*

Then he turned and began to trot up the middle of the field. The Ninth and Thirteenth Virginia had both splintered as their horsemen chased individual Yankees or small groups of them down the field. When Custer's mass of blue horsemen swept north, however, these gray horsemen were scattered before them, retreating to the northwest. As Custer got closer to the irregular line of dismounted gray soldiers, he moved his men into a canter. Lieutenant Colonel Vincent Witcher, commander of the Thirty-fourth Virginia Battalion, tells us that the Seventh formed a line of squadrons five ranks deep—which means squadrons side by side on a front of perhaps eighty horses arrayed in rows five horses deep—and swept down on clumps of men from his unit who had been caught in the open.[11] Some Union troopers stopped to capture groups of Confederates, but most of these were simply bypassed as the line charged forward, chasing after the gray cavalrymen.

Then the Seventh Michigan made a half-turn to the left in order to squarely confront and attack the Rebels in their original skirmish positions in front of the Rummel barn. After they had made the turn, however, they smashed unexpectedly into a solid wooden rail fence that they were unable to knock down.

The leading ranks were stopped dead, but the rearmost ranks of horsemen pushed forward, completely unaware of the fence. The result was a certain amount of smashing and squeezing, but the fence just would not go down, and as they pressed against its solid rails, Confederates on foot fired into their dense mass. Blue horsemen in turn fired their revolvers and breech-loading Burnside carbines through the fence, and finally a few men dismounted and tried to pull down some of the uprights so as to allow the passage of the mounted force.

Some people say they were successful, others that they were not. But while they were stuck behind that fence, they were attacked in the left flank by the Ninth and Thirteenth Virginia Cavalries from Chambliss's brigade, and the dismounted sharpshooters from Fitz Lee's brigade hit their right flank. The Seventh Michigan fought hard, but they were stuck in place, a stationary target being fired on from three sides, and they began to suffer heavy casualties. Finally, they were hit in the right flank by the mounted First Virginia, a blow they could not endure.

Custer finally realized they were trapped and must withdraw or be annihilated, and he shouted the word to his men. Then the entire unit that was still mounted turned and moved south, racing as best they could back to the protection of Pennington's guns. And as they ran, Stuart tells us, the First Virginia drove them hard from the east.[12]

On the west, they were pursued by the Ninth and Thirteenth Virginia, or perhaps it was by the First North Carolina and Jeff Davis Legion of Hampton's brigades—stories of southern participants in letters and unit histories written many years later vary. But this combined Confederate force, whatever its components, drove the Seventh Michigan almost all the way back to Pennington's guns near Hanover Road. Then these Confederates were hammered by canister from those six guns and in their turn were driven back to the north by the remounted Fifth Michigan Cavalry.

At this point, Stuart and Hampton tell us that the Ninth and Thirteenth were trapped by Union forces and had to be rescued. To that end, they say, the First North Carolina and the Jeff Davis Legion from Hampton's command were sent, but as they began their rescue effort, it unfortunately was expanded to encompass the entire brigades of Hampton and Fitz Lee.

This just happened, Stuart and Hampton would have us understand. One unit started to move, and with no orders other units moved sympathetically, and pretty soon . . .

But I don't accept these flimsy explanations and rather believe the

Union cavalry commanders, who tell a different story about this last, desperate charge by all of Stuart's as-yet–uncommitted troops. They were making, I believe, one last-gasp effort to break through the Union screen and perform their mission of hitting the Clump of Trees in the rear as Pickett and his men hit it from the front, thus cleaving Meade's army in half.

As will be discussed later, there are only two official after-action reports made by Confederate leaders, those of Stuart and Hampton. Stuart's report on this cavalry fight takes up only two pages out of the thirty he devotes to the entire Gettysburg campaign (June 16 through July 25), while Hampton's takes up only half a page out of a three-page report. But we can also learn the southern side of the story from fragments that appear in later regimental histories, private correspondence, and letters sent to Bachelder as he attempted to reconstruct the details of the battle more than twenty years after the fact.

Both Stuart and Hampton talk of the fight in loose generalities, claiming (as was the norm for both sides in most Civil War battles) to have punished their opponent and to have gained/retained valuable ground in the process. But to get the southern perspective, we have few other places to turn. In the interest of understanding what happened next on that day, therefore, the first place we will look is at segments of Stuart's report. Though his words are perhaps a bit flowery, important insights can be gained from them:

> My plan was to employ the enemy in front with sharpshooters, and move a command of cavalry upon their left flank from the position lately held by me, but the falling back of Jenkins' men . . . caused a like movement of those on the left, and the enemy sending forward a squadron or two [Custer and the Seventh Michigan], were about to cut off and capture a portion of our dismounted sharpshooters. To prevent this, I ordered forward

*the nearest cavalry regiment (one of W.H.F. Lee's) [Ninth and Thirteenth Virginia under the command of Chambliss here] quickly to charge this force of cavalry. It was gallantly done, and about the same time a portion of General Fitz. Lee's command charged on the left, the First Virginia Cavalry being most conspicuous. . . . Their movement was too rapid to be stopped by couriers, and the enemy perceiving it, were turning upon them with fresh horses. The First North Carolina and Jeff Davis Legion were sent to their support, and gradually this hand-to-hand fighting involved the greater portion of the command till the enemy were driven from the field. . . .* Notwithstanding the favorable results obtained, I would have preferred a different method of attack, as already indicated; *but I soon saw that entanglement by the force of circumstances narrated was unavoidable, and determined to make the best fight possible.*[13] *(emphasis added)*

That, of course, sounds like a hard-fought battle in which the Confederates finally drove the Union soldiers before them and ended up in sole control of the battlefield. But that, unfortunately, is the way many after-action reports read—favorably to the writer, no matter what the contrary realities may have been. But for a further look, let us see what Hampton had to say about the same fight:

*A short time after this, an officer from Colonel Chambliss reported to me that he had been sent to ask support from General Lee. . . . The First North Carolina and the Jeff Davis Legion were sent by Colonel Baker, and these two regiments drove back the enemy; but in their eagerness, they followed him too far, and encountered his reserve in heavy force. Seeing the state of affairs, I rode rapidly to the front to take charge of these two regiments, and, while doing this, to my surprise I saw the rest of my brigade (excepting the Cobb Legion) and Fitz. Lee's brigade charging. In the*

*hand-to-hand fight which ensued, as I was endeavoring to extricate the
First North Carolina and the Jeff Davis Legion, I was wounded and had
to leave the field.*[14]

As I said before, these are excerpts from the only two official after-
action reports by Confederate commanders on the cavalry fight on East
Cavalry Field. But there are some other writings made years later that
can help us understand what happened. One of these is McClellan's
memoir, *I Rode with Jeb Stuart,* written between 1880 and 1885,[15] in
which he says:

> *Up to this time no mounted men had been employed on either side; but
> now the enemy brought forward a body of cavalry [7th Michigan] which
> rode through the Confederate line, drove it back, and captured a number of
> prisoners. . . . The Federal Cavalry was in turn forced back, but being
> reinforced, the tide was turned against Chambliss, and he was driven back
> to his starting point. Just then Hampton arrived with his First North Car-
> olina and the Jeff Davis Legion, and the battle was renewed back and forth
> across the plain. . . . The impetuous attack of the Federal cavalry was,
> however, finally broken; and both parties withdrew to the lines held at the
> opening of the fight.*[16]

Before we leave this particular quotation, it is important to note that
McClellan says the "impetuous attack of the Federal cavalry" was broken. But when they arrived on East Cavalry Field, the Union cavalry
set up a skirmish line along Little's Run facing Rummel's barn, and
they never attempted to go beyond that line. Rather, they sought only
to keep Stuart from getting beyond them and into the Union rear. As
mentioned earlier, Gregg was well aware of the fact that the Bonaughton Road at the bottom of East Cavalry Field gave ready access to the
only open door into the Union rear behind Culp's Hill, and he believed

that was Stuart's goal. In his after-action report about the beginning of the fight, he says:

> *The enemy's cavalry had gained our right and were about to attack, with the view of gaining the rear of our line of battle.*[17]

Stuart said that the "greater portion of the command" was eventually caught up in this final cavalry fight, while both McClellan and Hampton say that only Hampton's brigade and Fitz Lee's brigade were involved. Both also say the Cobb Legion of Hampton's brigade was not involved, and McClellan says the Fourth Virginia was also not involved.

But Colonel William A. Morgan of the First Virginia Cavalry relates his experience in that battle in a letter to Bachelder. At the height of the hand-to-hand fight, he says:

> *Next the gallant dashing Young leading the Cobb Legion, rushed upon the scene, a very thunder bolt of war, waving his saber high in the air and cheering his men, and telling them to "charge and sweep them from the face of the earth."* . . . *I hastily reformed my men, and again advanced on the right of the Cobb Legion, who were now engaged in a hand to hand saber fight with the men of Gregg.*[18]

Hampton says that the First North Carolina and the Jeff Davis Legion had been sent forward and he was moving up to take command of them when he noticed the rest of his and Lee's brigades joining the charge. Stuart and McClellan simply say that those two regiments led the way. Stuart then says that the resulting hand-to-hand fighting "involved the greater portion of the command," while McClellan says that the battle was renewed back and forth across the plain until all of Hampton's and Fitz Lee's brigades were engaged. If we accept the word of Stuart, that means what it says—that the "greater portion of the command" was involved in this fight. If we accept the word of McClellan, however, the "detail" man as Stuart's adjutant general, that means that nine Confederate regiments made the final attack: the First North Carolina; the First and Second South Carolina; the Jeff Davis and the Phillips legions from Hampton's brigade; and the First, Second, Third, and Fifth Cavalry regiments from Fitz Lee's brigade, for a total of about 2,800 men.[19]

But Colonel R. L. T. Beale was the commander of the Ninth Virginia Cavalry in Chambliss's brigade. His regiment and the Thirteenth Virginia had been involved in the pursuit of the Seventh Michigan, only to be driven back to Rummel's barn themselves by the Fifth and Sixth Michigan. Beale wrote the history of the Ninth Virginia Cavalry, in which he talks briefly about the fight at Gettysburg. When Hampton's brigade was forming up to take the lead in the final attack, he and his men were nearby, and their blood was still up:

*The shout of Hampton's men now fell on their ears, and as he reached the barn all of our Brigade who have reached the field form upon his rear.*[20]

In analyzing this contradictory information, we must realize that Stuart and Hampton and even McClellan all have vested interests in making the number of southern units involved in the final attack smaller: since this last attack failed to break through, it becomes less onerous to them in history if they make their force appear smaller, or even to deny that they were trying to break through at all. They were just fighting for the sake of fighting, in this view, with no greater goal beyond maintaining their status as flank guard (though such protracted fighting would have seriously jeopardized this). Colonels Morgan and Beale, on the other hand, had no political aim whatever. One was trying to give all the facts to Bachelder, that the battle might be accurately remembered, while the other was simply attempting to record the history of the Ninth Virginia as accurately as he could for posterity.

So if Morgan says that the Cobb Legion was in the fight, and specifically states that he watched its commander, Colonel P. M. B. Young,[21] urging his troops on and then remembers fighting next to that unit, what are we to make of that statement? It does not smack of "special pleading" as the statements of both Stuart and McClellan do. In any case, it is an eyewitness statement that sounds more credible than Stuart's Adjutant General McClellan simply stating after the fact that the Cobb Legion was not involved.

Beale says all of the brigade that had reached the field formed on Hampton's rear, but what does that mean? At a minimum, I think, it would mean the Ninth and Thirteenth that had just come back from the pursuit of the Seventh Michigan formed on Hampton's rear, maybe the Second North Carolina and the Tenth Virginia as well, though we can never know for sure. But if, in the final analysis, my argument that Stuart was trying to break through and plunge into the Union rear to coincide with Pickett's Charge is accepted, then Stuart would have thrown every as-yet-uncommitted unit he had into the fray. And in that case, he would not have left the Fourth Virginia behind on the field doing nothing but watching. At any rate, I think it fair to say that Stuart's final attack was made by more than the nine regiments McClellan mentioned—perhaps, more accurately, by fourteen or fifteen.

After the Seventh Michigan was driven back in the engagement described earlier, the badly bled cavalry units from both sides began to withdraw to their own ends of the field. That was about three o'clock, and a number of Union leaders noticed that the artillery barrage from the main battlefield suddenly stopped. And if I am right that Stuart was expected behind Culp's Hill, his presence there would have been of crucial importance only twenty to thirty minutes after the artillery fire ended, which is when his clock started running. And at that exact moment, a number of Union soldiers looked north and saw something breathtaking, a sight they would never forget.[22] It was perhaps best described by Captain William Miller of the Third Pennsylvania Cavalry:

> About a half mile distant from the last-mentioned fence, where the cross-road passes through the woods on the Stallsmith farm, there appeared moving toward us a large mass of cavalry, which proved to be the remaining portions of Hampton's and Fitzhugh Lee's brigades. [This information on Confederate units involved necessarily comes from suspect Confederate after-action reports.] They were formed in close column of squadrons and directed their course toward the Spangler house. A grander spectacle than their advance has rarely been beheld. They marched with well-aligned fronts and steady reins. Their polished saber-blades dazzled in the sun. All eyes turned toward them.[23]

And if I am right that Stuart was trying to get down to Bonaughton Road and into the Union rear, this was his last chance. He had been unsuccessful in attempting to drive off the Union cavalry force with dismounted infantry from Jenkins's brigade so as to allow passage of his mounted force. Once the fight was begun, he had even had to supplement Jenkins's dismounted force with sharpshooters from Fitz Lee's brigade. When that failed, he had attempted to drive the Yankees off with a combination of mounted and dismounted attacks, but again, to no avail. Now his time was up, and Lee had ended the artillery barrage before launching Pickett's Charge. But if Lee's army was to have any chance of success, Stuart *had to* get to the Clump of Trees to facilitate the breakthrough. He knew that from the moment the artillery stopped, he had twenty minutes to go, maybe thirty at the outside. He knew he still outnumbered the Yankee force on East Cavalry Field at better than two to one, but he no longer had the time for a fight that would tie him down. What could he do?

When Stuart assembled his final force, he put Hampton's brigade at the front, then followed it with Fitz Lee's and, if we are to believe Colonel Beale, the commander of the Ninth Virginia Cavalry, ended it with part of Chambliss's brigade as well. At the time this column formed up and began to move south, the artillery barrage had ended within the previous five minutes. So Stuart still had fifteen to twenty-five minutes to get there, which he could do if he didn't stop or even slow down to fight.

If there had been more time available, of course, he could have easily driven these recalcitrant blue soldiers from the field. If we add to McClellan's nine regiments the four regiments from Chambliss's brigade, the Fourth Virginia from Fitzhugh Lee's brigade, and the Cobb Legion, then we come up with fifteen Confederate regiments, or about forty-eight hundred horsemen that it seems fair to assume he was throwing into this final attack.[24] If we then make allowances for a regiment or two that didn't make it into column, broken-down horses, and casualties suffered that day, then a rough number of Confederate cavalrymen in this final effort to break through the Union force would probably be around 4,000.

If Stuart had wanted to clear the valley of those few Union regiments, near and far, plus the scattered horsemen, all he had to do was form a line (as opposed to a column) of squadrons. If Stuart had chosen this formation, that would have meant the valley would be swept by a line with a front of between four hundred and five hundred horsemen arrayed eight to ten ranks deep. Such a front would have easily covered the entire half-mile width of East Cavalry Field and would have driven off or overrun all before it.

Remember, Witcher told us the Seventh Michigan had formed a

line of squadrons perhaps sixty horses wide and five ranks deep in their attack. But the valley was a full half mile wide, and only that fence near the northern end that had hung up the Seventh Michigan presented any sort of impenetrable barrier. Had that force of 4,000 swept down the middle of the valley, it would have bowled over the group of about six hundred under McIntosh near the middle of the field, then swept away the smaller group of some four hundred of the First Michigan at the southwest corner, and it would have routed the thousand or so disorganized remnants of the Fifth, Sixth, and Seventh Michigan milling around in the southwestern end of the valley. In fact, if Stuart had started down the valley with 4,000 horsemen arrayed in a line of squadrons, he would have felt confident that none of those smaller Union forces would have even hung around; they'd have disappeared like smoke.

But defeating or even driving off the Union cavalry force was not, and had never been, his goal. Now that the Confederate artillery barrage had ended, he couldn't afford the time it would take to fight any of those Union cavalrymen who did not instantly run as he approached. Besides, he just didn't have time to form a line of companies or squadrons, for once he got to the southern end of East Cavalry Field, he would have had to re-form into a column of companies or squadrons, a movement formation, just to be able to use the roads. And such a complete reorganization would have taken so much time that he would really have been cutting things too close for comfort.

But Stuart was confident if not cocky, and he must have believed that he didn't need to form a *line* of squadrons, all he had to do was form a *column* of squadrons, with which he would threaten the Yankees. He would take a calculated risk that they would run, but it was a risk that he felt he *had* to take, for time was running short. In any case, he was confident that, greatly outnumbered by the legendary Stuart and his Invincibles, when the Union cavalry leaders saw the size of his force approaching, they would pull their men back and let him pass, would play it safe against superior numbers and hope to fight again on another day when the calculus might be different.

After the fighting that had occurred so far, Stuart must have thought there was only one major barrier that could keep his force from getting through, and that was the group of what looked like five or six hundred Union cavalrymen, most of them on the eastern side of the field about halfway down. There were perhaps a hundred more of them stretched over the middle and on the western side of the field, and they seemed the most serious potential block to his movement. They had fought ferociously earlier on, but when driven back, they had not run south to the protection of Pennington's guns near Hanover Road. Rather, they had just withdrawn to the wood line on the eastern and western sides of the field, where they had held their ground. So those were fighters, men always to be accounted for if not feared.

If Stuart's column could push aside the few men in that unit who were in the middle of the field or on the western side, he hoped his unit would look massive enough that the larger group in the woods on the east would not try to come out and block his way. He knew they couldn't stop him, but a serious fight might delay his progress unacceptably.

Once he got past them, however, it looked like there was only one other cohesive unit left before him, maybe just a single regiment, no more than three or four hundred men down in the southeast corner of the field. They had been there all day, had not been used in the fight so far, and there must be some reason for that. Maybe they were new soldiers, more easily intimidated and thus held from the fray. But he was confident that if he was able to bluff his way past the first group of blue soldiers, an even smaller group would present no threat to him.

Other than that, there were a lot of blue troopers, a thousand or more, at the southwestern end of the field. But these men were scattered and disorganized, many of them dismounted. They presented no threat to Stuart, of that he was sure. Only the men closest to him, the five or six hundred horsemen who looked like an organized group of regiments, really worried him.

Time was the enemy now, and as soon as Hampton's brigade had formed, he signaled them to move out, then fell into the center of the First Virginia Cavalry in Fitz Lee's brigade.[25] Hampton and Fitz Lee and Chambliss and even Farnsworth or Witcher had all been fully briefed on what to do; they had even ridden this same field the evening before. Now all they had to do was get past these last blue soldiers, then they would race in from the rear to help Robert E. Lee split Meade's army in half and destroy it.

Unbeknownst to Stuart, the cavalry unit halfway down the field and mostly on the eastern side was the First New Jersey, the Third Pennsylvania, and the Purnell Legion, all from McIntosh's brigade. These were the only men from Gregg's cavalry division that stayed on the field when the serious fight with Stuart's men had started. The other units farther away were the First Michigan in the southeast corner, lined up in a column of squadrons, and the exhausted fragments of the Fifth, Sixth, and Seventh Michigan scattered around the southwestern part of the open farmland.

The men halfway down the field—McIntosh's brigade—were Stuart's first barrier. But as his massive column approached them at the trot, they did what he had expected and simply pulled back into the woods. The Union artillery was firing now and hitting them, tearing great rents in their formation. But his well-trained men simply closed ranks and kept moving south. The artillery was galling, but the guns could only fire one or two rounds each minute, and it wouldn't be long until they had left them behind. As they passed the First New Jersey, Third Pennsylvania, and Purnell Legion hiding in the woods on their left and right, they also drew some carbine fire, but nothing to slow their massive column. At this point, Stuart's confidence must have soared, for they had less than half a mile to go to the intersection of Bonaughton Road and Hanover Road. From there, they weren't ten minutes from the rear of Culp's Hill and enduring glory.

William Brooke-Rawle, then a lieutenant in the Third Pennsylvania, has also written a splendid description of this fight:

> *In close columns of squadrons, advancing as if in review, with sabers drawn and glistening like silver in the bright sunlight, the spectacle called forth a murmur of admiration. It was, indeed, a memorable one.*[26]

But as the men of McIntosh's brigade pulled back from danger, Custer also saw them coming—a column that was easily several thousand men strong, and he had only the First Michigan, four hundred veteran troopers, left uncommitted. What was he to do?

Long ago at West Point, he had studied such a circumstance. It was Alexander the Great with 47,000 men facing Darius with more than 200,000 Persians at the Battle of Gaugamela in 331 B.C. Darius had cleared a field on which he thought his scythed chariots would tear through Alexander's ranks, and he was able to get Alexander to face him across that prepared ground. Darius lumbered toward Alexander, his formation that of a bull's head, with elephants and the command group in the center, and the horns protruding far to the front on either side tipped by large cavalry formations. Then Alexander realized that Darius was trying to get him onto the cleared field, so he began to move his formation to the right.

It was difficult for the ponderous Persian army to retain its rigid structure as it also tried to move sideways so as to stay directly in front of Alexander's formation. By this time, 30,000 Persian cavalry were driving back the 6,000 cavalry Alexander had on his right wing, and he knew that wing would not be able to hold. But he quickly noted that the sideways movement had opened a great gap between the Persian left wing and its center. Before that door could close, he quickly organized an attack, leading his elite Companion Cavalry and five regiments of Macedonian infantry in a thrust into the Persian heart. Darius was right there, but terrified by this direct assault, he turned and ran with his entourage. He was immediately followed by the entire command structure in the center of the immense Persian formation, and then most of the left wing collapsed in turn.

Alexander's own forces washed forward and drove off the stunned Persians, causing an utter rout. The other wing of the Persian army that had been pushing Alexander's men back now saw their fate, and then they, too, turned and retreated. It turned out that a major force of Persian cavalry had made their way into Alexander's base camp and was destroying his baggage train during the main battle. After he had routed the main Persian formation, Alexander turned enough of his army around to drive off these predators. But at least their number had not been added to the main Persian attack, for who knew, that might have made the difference.

Darius was murdered that night by his courtiers, but Gaugamela is still remembered as an astounding triumph of Alexander the Great against a force that far outnumbered his own. And he won by surprising them with a bold and least-expected attack: right into their center, which was supposedly their strength.

As soon as Custer realized that Stuart was going to try to break through the Union cavalry force blocking his way, he knew what he must do. If he could somehow stop that column, then the other fourteen hundred men in his brigade might join his attack. They might still be outnumbered, but he was sure his eighteen hundred men could stop twice their number. And there were another six hundred men from

McIntosh's brigade, a force Stuart's column had already passed that, if Stuart's column was stopped, might pitch into the enemy flanks.

Custer raced to the front of his First Michigan Cavalry, drawn up in a column of squadrons near the intersection of Hanover Road and Old Dutch Road. Stopping in front of them, he drew his saber, threw off his hat so they could see his long yellow hair, and shouted the same challenge he had used with the Seventh Michigan:

*"Come on, you Wolverines!"*

Then he turned his horse and spurred him forward into a trot, the men of the First falling in behind him.

Some participants say there were two or more Confederate columns, so it is very possible that the First North Carolina and the Jeff Davis Brigade may have formed their own column and moved parallel to the one Hampton led. Similarly, the Ninth and Thirteenth Virginia as well may have been part of this separate column, or might even have formed a third column. At any rate, whether in one column or more, it seems clear that some 4,000 Confederate cavalrymen were about to try to burst through the last remaining blue barrier, the First Michigan cavalry regiment led by Custer.

Back in the Confederate column, Hampton was out in front of his brigade, a big man on an enormous horse. As he saw Custer approaching, he must have been sure this was just a feint, that as he got closer he would realize he was attacking a force perhaps ten times the size of his own and just veer off to the side. These men might put on a better show than that first group, which had done little more than run and hide. But however loud they might bark, they were now approaching in a threatening way that could only be a feint. They would soon veer off or be crushed, that much was clear.

When they got to within a few hundred yards of each other, Custer spread the front of his formation out to three times its original size and spurred forward into a gallop. He did this either to accommodate more than one Confederate column or to widen the front with which he would hit the lead Rebel element. The impact is described by a man who watched it, Colonel (then Lieutenant) William Brooke-Rawle:

*As the charge was ordered the speed increased, every horse on the jump, every man yelling like a demon. The columns of the Confederates blended, but the perfect alignment was maintained. Chester [Union artillerist] put charge after charge of canister into their midst, his men bringing it up to the guns by the armful. The execution was fearsome, but the long rents closed up at once. As the opposing columns drew nearer and nearer, each with perfect alignment, every man gathered his horse well under him, and gripped his weapon the tighter. Though ordered to retire his guns, toward which the head of the assaulting column was directed, Chester kept on until the enemy were within fifty yards, and the head of the First Michigan had come into the line of his fire. Staggered by the fearful execution from the two batteries, the men in the front line of the Confederate column drew in their horses and wavered. Some turned, and the column fanned out to the right and left, but those behind kept pressing on. Custer, seeing the front men hesitate, waved his sabre and shouted, "Come on you Wolverines!" and with a fearful yell the First Michigan rushed on, Custer four lengths ahead.*[27]

It seems clear that the lead ranks of the Confederate column did stop and turn right and left, "fanning out" as Brooke-Rawle described it. But they didn't do that because of the artillery fire that was hitting them, nor because they were afraid. Rather, they did it in response to a splendid trick Custer used. That is, as his men were galloping forward, he ordered them to change from a column of squadrons into a line of squadrons. That meant that their front rank grew from fifteen or sixteen into three times that number, between forty and fifty.

As they approached the Confederates, Hampton or his regimental commanders attempted to mimic the Yankees so that they could encompass this much smaller unit and keep it from streaking down the flanks of their formation, shooting and slashing as they careened down the column. But in order to "fan out," a rider must steer his horse to the left or right, and the harder the turn, the greater the reduction in that horse's forward momentum and inertia. Once the horses got to the outside, they could have once again turned and accelerated forward. But this took time, and apparently a lot of Rebel horses were all but standing still sideways when the blue mass crashed into them.

In 1886, Cassius M. Norton, an attorney in Iowa who had been a private in the First Michigan, wrote a letter to another lawyer, Amasa E. Mathews, a former captain in the First Michigan. Therein, Norton gives a rather detailed narration of the battle on East Cavalry Field, and that letter is now included in the Bachelder Papers collection. An excerpt illustrates much about this charge by the First Michigan that stopped the Confederate advance:

*We went out at a trot in columns of squadrons, think that is the term . . . at the time the command "charge" was given as we bounded from a trot to a gallop, the hill and its side toward us seem crowded with screaming advancing rebels, headed for us, 3 or 4 columns of them while beyond our right is the shattered 7th rallying as best they could here and there, numbers falling in with us, while we met many of the 5th and 6th dismounted falling back from the skirmish line, while way back behind us was many more of the same regts, having got to their horses was ready to join us . . . the "charge" was sounded, away we went, on they come they looked as if our less than 400 would be swallowed up, their columns in our front on our right and left seemed like a maelstrom just ready to open up to receive and then hide us from mortal view, but on we went. . . . To the front again, the 1st squadron obliques to the right the front of the 2nd is being exposed to the enemy, the 3rd Squadron (yes that was mine) received the command left oblique, it is done at a hard gallop . . . nothing but sabers being used, look firm as if cast in a mold, the oblique and front is made without a break or quaver in the line, the drill grounds of Fairfax C.H. [Confederate cavalry] have been outdone in the face of a charging enemy, that move whipped them, they stopped, their yell was silent . . . but the rebels, they have turned, and such a turn that they were crowded in great confusion the great grey mass reminding the Northern boy of a great crowd of sheep crowding upon a hole where they might get out . . .*[28]

Again, if there were multiple Confederate columns at the outset of the charge, it seems clear that they had all melded into one before they were punched in the nose and effectively stopped by Custer and the First Michigan. But the very idea of hitting a lengthy column of squadrons squarely in its front was something that even the experienced cavalry leaders in Stuart's formation didn't anticipate. An excellent description of the impact came from another observer, Captain William Miller of the Third Pennsylvania:

*As the two columns approached each other the pace of each increased, when suddenly a crash, like the falling of timber, betokened the crisis. So sudden and violent was the collision that many of the horses were turned end over end and crushed their riders beneath them. The clashing of sabers, the firing of pistols, the demands for surrender and cries of the combatants now filled the air.*[29]

After this sudden smashing together of galloping masses of horses, the long line of squadrons behind Hampton necessarily stopped. To Confederate horsemen far back in the formation, however, it wasn't clear what had happened. But the remounted troopers from the Fifth, Sixth, and even Seventh Michigan plunged into the western flank of the Confederate formation, while many from the First New Jersey and

Third Pennsylvania crashed into the eastern flank. Though they were still outnumbered, the steady arrival of more of these additional troops brought close to 2,000 into the fray for the Union, fighting to stop 4,000 Rebels. Soon the column formation broke up into individual saber and pistol fights, and Stuart realized that he had been stopped.

So Stuart's column got past McIntosh's brigade, and but for Custer's seemingly suicidal frontal attack, he might well have made it up the Baltimore Pike and into the Union rear, with unimaginable consequences. Many members of the Third Pennsylvania showed with their attacks on the Confederate flanks that they were not cowards, they had simply been ordered not to attack Stuart's column as it passed them. Miller makes that clear:

> *But Gregg, when he first arrived and looked over the field, had moved the 1st Maryland over to the Low Dutch Road, just north of the Hanover Road, in order to strengthen his right, and so failing to find his regiment where he had expected, McIntosh gathered up what loose men he could, joined them to his headquarters party and charged. My squadron was still deployed along the edge of Lott's woods. Standing in company with Lieutenant William Brooke-Rawle on a little rise of ground in front of his command, and seeing that the situation was becoming critical, I turned to him and said: "I have been ordered to hold this position, but, if you will back me up in case I am court-martialed for disobedience, I will order a charge." The lieutenant, always ready to "pitch in" as he expressed it, with an energetic reply convinced me that I would not be deserted.*[30]

Miller did lead the charge, with which he did quite a bit of damage to the Confederate column. But he was concerned about disobeying orders to hold those woods "at all costs." Another way to express defending woods is "You are forbidden to engage Stuart's cavalry." Who would have given such an order? There are only two possibilities:

McIntosh, his brigade commander, or General Gregg, his division commander.

But McIntosh, by immediately trying to bring his First Maryland regiment up to pitch into the fight—only to find that Gregg had sent it off to a safe location—and then immediately gathering whatever loose men he could find and mounting a charge into the Rebel flank, showed himself to be a fighter. Which leaves us with Gregg. And any general who would order a lieutenant to defend a piece of woods and not engage a large enemy cavalry force that only wants to get past them—as Gregg himself said was their intention in his after-action report—is a general who, fearing they will certainly be defeated, orders his men to avoid combat. And that sort of general shames his stars.

Within twenty minutes or so, the sound of an artillery barrage erupted once again from the Fishhook. This time it was all federal guns slashing at the ranks of Pickett's men as they came into range, a sound Stuart heard and understood. Realizing that he was still twenty minutes away even if he were free to move to the sounds of the guns, which he was not, he finally knew the game was up.

There was a lot of sword banging still to come, but eventually Stuart drew his men back up on Cress Ridge, and the Yankees stayed on the plain below. Stuart had tried to get past them, and failed. Whatever else might come, this "draw" between the two forces had been a big Union victory. Bigger, by far, than most of them realized then or would ever really understand.

Over on the Fishhook, Stuart never arrived, and Union artillery and rifle fire brutalized the nine attacking brigades of Pickett's Charge. By three-thirty, they reached the Clump of Trees, but could not hold. They retreated, bleeding, back across the open field, and Lee, it is said, was there to receive them, loudly telling one and all, "It's all my fault!"

But was it really?

# *Aftermath*

W HEN INVESTIGATING any military aspect of the Civil War, an important publication is *The War of the Rebellion: A Compilation of the Official Records of the Union and Confederate Armies* (Washington: Government Printing Office, 1889; hereafter O.R.). Stuart's after-action reports for the Gettysburg campaign ( June 16–July 24) run from page 679 to page 710 in volume 27, Part II of O.R. Within those thirty-one pages, he devotes less than two pages to the fight on East Cavalry Field on July 3. The report of one of his brigade commanders for the entire Gettysburg campaign, Wade Hampton, runs for less than five pages, of which less than one full page is devoted to the fight on East Cavalry Field.

After-action reports on the Gettysburg campaign submitted by all Confederate cavalry commanders appear in volume 27, Part II of O.R. In addition to reports by Stuart and Hampton, these ninety-three pages include thirty-two separate reports from various brigade, regimental, and battalion commanders under Stuart's command. But most of these reports concern the fights at Brandy Station, Aldie, Middleburg, and Upperville, or various other noncombat circumstances or experiences of those units and their commanders. Nowhere among these reports, save only in those of Stuart and Hampton as noted above, is there any mention of the July 3 Gettysburg cavalry fight on East Cavalry Field.

By way of comparison, the after-action reports on the Gettysburg campaign (June 14–August 1) submitted by all cavalry commanders in the Army of the Potomac are found in volume 27, Part I of O.R. (a different "part" or book than that containing the Confederate reports). Within those 118 pages, one finds ninety-six separate reports, in seventeen of which the fight at Gettysburg is mentioned.

Is that credible evidence that reports by Confederate cavalry commanders on the fight at Gettysburg were suppressed? I think that is the only reasonable interpretation of those facts one can make. But such a suppression would not be unprecedented: after Pickett had submitted his initial report on the Battle of Gettysburg, for instance, Lee rejected it because he was unhappy with its unknown content, and he told him to rewrite it.

Why, then, were these cavalry reports suppressed, and by whom?

I think there can be little question but that they were suppressed by order of General Robert E. Lee. Remember, as senior Confederate commander in the theater of Northern Virginia (which now included Pennsylvania), he was a stickler about keeping informed of everything that went on in his command, even down to details most observers would think insignificant. After Gettysburg, he would have had extended meetings with all his subordinate commanders, certainly to include Stuart, during which he would have learned all details of the battle according to them.

Since East Cavalry Field is not visible from Seminary Ridge, of course, Lee would have had to depend entirely on what he heard from Stuart and other participants in the battle to have learned what happened there. And even if one wants to believe that Stuart might have told him a story at variance with reality, Lee had an unfailing source of truth in the cavalry, for his nephew, Fitzhugh Lee, was one of Stuart's brigade commanders.

It seems reasonable to assume that Robert E. Lee discussed the cavalry fight on East Cavalry Field in great detail with Stuart, Fitzhugh Lee, and perhaps others as well. And as was indicated earlier, Fitzhugh Lee did not submit an after-action report on Gettysburg. He did write a letter to Bachelder in 1886, however, but it is very brief and says little that was not already public knowledge, save only that he apparently comments on Stuart's plan to attack the Union rear:

> *I infer from his [Stuart's] report that he must have moved first with Gen. W.H.F. Lee's brigade (under Chambliss) and Jenkin's* with the purpose of effecting a surprise on the enemy's rear. . . . *When* Stuart sent for Hampton and I to come to his position to see about making the movement to the rear, *not seeing Gen. Hampton anywhere, and thinking a fight was imminent at any moment, and not wanting to leave my command, and so remained with it.*[1] (emphasis added)

The Official Reports were normally written by commanders, but not until days, weeks, sometimes even months after a given battle. Stuart's report that mentions Gettysburg is dated August 20, 1863, while that of Hampton is dated August 13, 1863. Both, in other words, were submitted well over a month after the battle had taken place.

Why, then, did Lee want to suppress the truth about what happened there? Jeb Stuart's cavalry fought his Union counterparts to a standstill at Brandy Station on June 9, 1863, and none of the reports on either side of that fight were suppressed. Both Stuart and Pleasonton, in fact, claimed victory there, as they also did after the fights at Aldie, Middleburg, and Upperville. But all four of these fights have since been considered near things, and evidence of them has not been concealed in Confederate records.

On East Cavalry Field at Gettysburg, both sides fought hard, but at the end of the day, the Union still held the south end of the field, while the Confederates still held the north. This cavalry fight, too, like those at Brandy Station, Aldie, Middleburg, and Upperville, has generally been seen since as somewhat of a draw. So why did Lee want minimal mention of East Cavalry Field to appear in the official record or anywhere else?

If I am right that Lee had ordered Stuart to lead his men around the cavalry unit covering the Union right flank and then down the Bonaughton Road to the Baltimore Pike and thence up into the Union rear, then this suppression makes perfect sense. One is reminded of the old comedian's line: "If at first you don't succeed, destroy all evidence that you ever tried."

Lee, however, was very serious here. He had tried to get his cavalry into the Union rear and had even received the signal from Stuart—a specified number of cannon shots from Cress Ridge around noon—that the way was wide open and he was awaiting the next clearly audible signal from Lee, which was the end of the artillery bombardment, before proceeding up Baltimore Pike into the Union rear. Lee, reassured by this signal from Stuart that all was well, would have started the artillery barrage around one that lasted between one and two hours, then stopped it, waited ten or fifteen minutes, then launched Pickett's Charge. He expected Pickett's men to be met at the Clump of Trees by the thousands of gray cavaliers who also would have unhinged Culp's Hill while attacking it in the rear as Johnson's 10,000 attacked it from the front. Stuart's cavalry would also have ridden up behind and killed or driven off the gun crews that fired many of the Union cannon on Cemetery Ridge and Cemetery Hill, thus reducing the death rained on Pickett and his men. They—some of Stuart's gun crews brought along just for this purpose—might even have fired canister from some of these Union guns into the rear of waiting Union infantrymen, this just to spur a quick surrender by the surrounded and doomed Yankees.

But it didn't work, though Lee did not, at that moment, know why, particularly after Stuart's first signal with cannon shots that all was well. After he learned that Stuart had been stopped on East Cavalry Field, however, thus destroying the entire effort save only for the massacre of Pickett's men, such information was only poison for the Confederate cause. Nothing good for the South could come out of Lee admitting to anyone that he had tried to turn a Union wing with a cavalry-infantry combination, and then to cut the Union force in half and defeat it in detail, but that this effort had failed.

And the worst part of all was that it had failed because Jeb Stuart and his Invincibles, the flower of southern horsemen, had been stopped by a Yankee cavalry unit less than half its size. No, that was bad news no matter how you looked at it. And if it were ever made public, it would only boost the morale of Union forces while at the same time administering a major blow to that of Confederate forces. So Lee just swallowed it and never mentioned it to anyone.

After the battle, as always, Lee was not critical of the performance of his subordinates, such as Longstreet's long delay before battle on July 2. One of Lee's character strengths was that he never revealed any disagreements or the contents of private conversations he might have had with his subordinates. If those men saw fit to publish them in their own Official Reports or in any other forum after the war, Lee never even commented on them.

If others wanted to stretch the truth for egotistical reasons in Official Reports, Lee believed that was their decision, but he would never do so himself. He wanted, at all costs, to preserve the good name and honor of all Confederate soldiers, and if the exaggeration of a subordinate might be seen to reflect badly on his, Robert E. Lee's, name or reputation, he didn't care. The reputation of any of his veterans was more important to Lee than his own. He was a mature man who was comfortable with himself and his decisions, and he didn't care what other people thought of him.

He just didn't care.

And that is one of the reasons—probably the primary reason—that there is nothing in the Official Record, nor anything that has come from Lee's mouth or hand, that would reveal that he had ordered the attack by Stuart, a failed attack that was the key element of a three-pronged attack he ordered for July 3. Stuart's report, as will be seen, is quite defensive about a missed opportunity he had to slip by the Union cavalry below Cress Ridge. And although he never specifically mentions this planned attack, a careful reading of his report will show that he gives it away in several instances.

According to conventional wisdom, Lee's main effort on Day Three was to be the frontal attack by Pickett's Charge against Union defenses along Cemetery Ridge. And the failure of that charge is, with no question, how most Americans remember the Battle of Gettysburg. But there was more.

Lee was notoriously secretive about his plans, both strategic and tactical, and as we know, Gettysburg was not the first time this occurred.[2] That was standard behavior of the commander of the Army of Northern Virginia and his trusted subordinate commanders during the Civil War: give verbal operational plans only to those with a need to know, and give them only that part of the plan that they need personally. Lee had very nearly had his army destroyed after a copy of his written orders had been obtained by McClellan before the battle of Antietam, an event that only made him all the more reluctant to commit his orders to writing or to share information with anyone who did not have an absolute need to know.

Spreading such fragile information is dangerous, and there is nothing to be gained by it. If a regimental or brigade commander under Lee, or even a clerk or a courier, had known of Jackson's massive, daylong turning movement at Chancellorsville and been captured, or if written orders to that effect had been compromised, then that would have been the end of a key operation. Such plans, by their very nature, must be protected information, and their implementation must be made with great stealth and the use of surprise to gain maximum advantage.

Others, of course, including a number of the Union participants in the cavalry fight, have also proposed that Lee intended for Stuart to get past Gregg on July 3 and attack the Union rear. Stuart even admits as much in the following extracts from his after-action report:

> *"I moved this command and W.H.F. Lee's secretly through the woods to a position, and* hoped to effect a surprise on the enemy's rear"; "My plan was to employ the enemy in front with sharpshooters, and move a command of cavalry upon their left flank" [I believe Stuart here uses "upon" to mean "past" or "beyond"]; "Notwithstanding the favorable results obtained, I would have preferred a different method of attack, *as already indicated; but I soon saw that entanglement by the force of circumstance narrated was unavoidable, and determined to make the best fight possible"; and "I watched keenly and anxiously the indications in his rear for that purpose,* while in the attack which I intended *(which was forestalled by our troops being exposed to view),* his cavalry would have separated from the main body, and gave promise of solid results and advantages."* [3] *(emphasis added)*

Hampton also, though he attempts to cover up any larger plan, inadvertently gives it away with a few words:

> The disposition I had made of my command contemplated an entirely different plan for the fight, *and beyond this disposition of my*

*own brigade, with the subsequent charge of the First North Carolina and the Jeff. Davis Legion, I had nothing whatever to do with the fight.*[4] *(emphasis added)*

Although Chambliss submitted no after-action report on Gettysburg, he made a slip in his letter to Bachelder mentioned above:

*When Stuart sent for Hampton and I to come to his position* to see about making the movement to the rear. *(emphasis added)*

But in his after-action report, Stuart says only the following about calling Hampton and Chambliss:

*Having been informed that Generals Hampton and Lee were up, I sent for them to come forward, so that I could show them the situation at a glance from the elevated ground I held,* and arrange for further operations.[5] *(emphasis added)*

We have it from Fitzhugh Lee's pen that when Stuart said "arrange for further operations," that meant "see about making the movement to the rear," which obviously means into the Union rear, for at that point Stuart's force was in an attack mode.

Another key giveaway comes from Major Henry McClellan, Stuart's adjutant general at Gettysburg. In his memoir, *I Rode with Jeb Stuart,* McClellan makes several apparently inadvertent admissions. The first is when he is talking about Stuart's mission on the left flank. After the usual repetition of protecting the Confederate left flank and being prepared to attack retreating Union troops, he says:

*He proposed, if opportunity offered, to make a diversion which might aid the Confederate infantry to carry the heights held by the Federal army.*[6]

Remembering Alexander at Gaugamela and the Persian cavalry that was destroying his baggage camp during the battle, it is clear that no such attack on Union communication lines or supplies or anything else that did not directly and immediately affect the ongoing fight on the field of battle would have helped the Confederates "carry the heights held by the Federal army." Only a direct attack on the Union rear at the Clump of Trees would have done the trick, and this would have been a major "diversion."

McClellan next tells us what Stuart did after he had fired his cannon signal shots:

> . . . *and receiving no immediate reply to this fire, he sent for Hampton and Fitz Lee, to arrange with them for* an advance and an attack upon the enemy's rear.[7] *(emphasis added)*

And this is basically just a repetition of what Fitzhugh Lee said in his letter to Bachelder—that the proposed meeting on Cress Ridge between Stuart and his two brigade commanders who had just arrived on Cress Ridge was intended to go over final plans for an advance and an attack into the Union rear.

And McClellan tips his hand one last time in his memoir:

> *The result of this battle shows that there is no probability that* Stuart could successfully have carried out his intention of attacking the rear of the Federal right flank, *for it was sufficiently protected by Gregg's command.*[8] *(emphasis added)*

I think the slips or outright admissions of Stuart, Hampton, Fitzhugh Lee, and McClellan noted above, when combined with the abundant circumstantial evidence, make up a rather compelling argument that Stuart intended to launch an attack into the Union rear on

July 3. But did any of his Union army opponents suspect that at the time?

General Gregg, as earlier noted, says as much in his official after-action report:

> . . . *a strong line of skirmishers displayed by the enemy was evidence that the enemy's cavalry had gained our right, and were about to attack, with the view of gaining the rear of our line of battle.*[9] *(emphasis added)*

When Gregg says that, of course, he means the rear of the line of battle of Meade's army, not just of his cavalry force. And he goes further in an article he wrote in *Annals of the War*:

> *On the 3rd, during that terrific fire of artillery, which preceded the gallant but unsuccessful assault of Pickett's Division on our line, it was discovered that Stuart's cavalry was moving to our right, with the evident intention of passing to the rear, to make a simultaneous attack there.*[10]

Other Union cavalry officers seem to agree. For instance, William Brooke-Rawle, who had been a lieutenant in the Third Pennsylvania Cavalry, wrote an article entitled "The Right Flank at Gettysburg," which also appeared in *Annals of the War*:

> *It was Stuart's last reserve and his last resource, for, if the Baltimore Pike was to be reached, and havoc created in our rear, the critical moment had arrived, as Pickett was even then moving up to the assault of Cemetery Ridge.*[11]

Brooke-Rawle's imagination may have disserved him here, for if Stuart was successful in getting past Gregg, he would have wanted to do much more than just create "havoc" in the Union rear; he'd have wanted to assist Lee in the defeat and destruction of Meade's army.

Union Army Major Edward Carpenter seems to understand what happened:

> *The facts summed up, then, are these: Stuart, on the 3rd of July, attempted to reach the rear of the Federal line of battle, but, encountering Gregg's command, after a stubborn fight, in which the first mounted charge of Stuart's troopers was partially successful, he was utterly and entirely defeated, and, under cover of night, retreated from his position before his successful antagonist.*[12]

In fact, Pleasonton, the Union army cavalry commander, repeats a somewhat watered-down version of that in his Gettysburg after-action report:

> *About noon the enemy threw a heavy force of cavalry against this position, with the intention of gaining our rear. This attack was met and handsomely defeated by General Gregg, who reports several fine charges made by the First Michigan Cavalry, of Custer's brigade, and the First New Jersey and Third Pennsylvania Cavalry, of his own division.*

It would have been difficult for Gregg to praise his own men without even mentioning Custer, and he does a minimal sort of job of that. But Pleasonton's report went to Meade, the commander of the Army of the Potomac. In his own report, however, Meade doesn't seem to believe Gregg's statement that Stuart was seeking to attack the Union rear and Gregg stopped him and so saved the Army of the Potomac, for he simply ignores it:

> *At the same time, General Gregg was engaged with the enemy on our extreme right, having passed across the Baltimore Pike and Bonaughton Road, and boldly attacking the enemy's left and rear.*[13]

The perception of Gregg and Brooke-Rawle and Miller and Pleasonton of the importance of the July 3 fight on East Cavalry Field did not gain wide acceptance at the time, and even less so in the twentieth century. This is primarily because these were interested parties arguing that they, and their men, were the *real* heroes of Gettysburg, that it was only through their efforts that Lee was defeated. But exaggerated puffery in Civil War after-action reports was so common as to be almost expected. The claim made by Union cavalrymen that they were really the ones who saved the day for the Union at Gettysburg is quite obviously such special pleading that most veterans of the Civil War simply ignored these claims by Gregg et al.

This is especially true with serious historians. Douglas Southall Freeman, for instance, does not even mention the July 3 cavalry fight on East Cavalry Field in his two superbly detailed works, *R. E. Lee* and *Lee's Lieutenants*. Unfortunately, most other modern Civil War historians have also either ignored this cavalry fight or given it short shrift, dismissing it as unimportant, a side issue irrelevant to the main battle at Gettysburg.

There are a very few exceptions to this, of course.

In *Battle Cry of Freedom,* one major Civil War historian seems to have cracked the code. James McPherson comments on the potential of Stuart's force at Gettysburg:

> He [Meade] did know that Stuart was loose in his rear, but had not yet learned that a division of blue troopers had stopped the southern cavalry three miles east of Gettysburg—thus foiling the third part of Lee's three-pronged plan for Meade's undoing.[14]

The most accurate historian on this issue may be a man focused narrowly on blue horsemen. In *The Union Cavalry in the Civil War,* Stephen Z. Starr says:

*What was the result of the fight? Stuart's claim that he was only protecting the left flank of the Confederate army is not worth a moment's credence. The course of the battle from its beginning makes it evident that his objective was to brush Gregg out of the way and attack the rear of Meade's infantry on Cemetery Ridge at the same time that it was attacked frontally by Pickett. In this he clearly failed. In the sense that the battle ended with Stuart and Gregg occupying their original positions, it was a draw, but in a wider sense, it was a victory for Gregg and, more importantly, for the Union.*[15]

A few other historians have also mentioned almost in passing that Stuart may have been trying to reach and attack the Union rear.[16] But none of these authors has presented convincing arguments or even any evidence to support their claims, nor have they researched or developed that theme in any detail whatever. And since no compelling evidence is presented to support these statements, they appear to be nothing more than guesses without foundation in the record. They are educated guesses, of course, but no more than that. It has therefore not required much reflection on the part of their readers, both laymen and academics, before their suppositions that Stuart intended to attack the Union rear have been rejected rather uniformly. And clearly, in addition to the lack of evidence presented in support of those claims, one of the most important reasons for these rejections is the small number of casualties suffered by both sides in the cavalry battle on East Cavalry Field.

Stuart's casualties on that day were forty-one killed, fifty wounded, and ninety captured or missing, for a total of 181. But these figures do not include casualties suffered by Jenkins's brigade or by Confederate artillery on the scene. Both were heavily involved, and it does not seem inappropriate to attribute seventy casualties to them, bringing the Confederate total to about 250.

Union casualties were thirty killed, 149 wounded, and seventy-five missing or captured, for a total of 254 casualties

The total butcher's bill from East Cavalry Field on July 3, then, was probably around five hundred. For the entire three-day battle, on the other hand, casualties for both North and South are almost 50,000. Most people find it hard to believe, therefore, that a small battle three miles off to the east of the main battlefield, a fight that resulted in perhaps 1 percent of the total casualties for the entire battle, could have been so important as some of its participants claim. But history has shown us before that the failure of anticipated forces to arrive on a battlefield can have rather profound effects.

After abdicating on April 6, 1814, Napoleon had gone into exile on the isle of Elba in the Mediterranean. Back in France, the returned nobles had begun to grab back the title to lands that the peasants had been given after the revolution, and this was widely resented. Napoleon was bored by ten months of exile, and in February 1815, sensing the time was right, he sailed back to France, and soon after landing was enthusiastically welcomed by the army and the people.

Marshal Ney then told Louis XVIII that he would go south to confront him, capture him, and bring him back in an iron box. Instead, he fell under the emperor's spell and was among the leaders of the parade of glory that brought him back to Paris. Louis XVIII fled for his life, and Napoleon once again ascended the throne to oversee the last hundred days of life for the French empire.

Most of the people, particularly the farmers who had lost their lands and old soldiers who had been unceremoniously discharged, were delighted by his return. For their part, the nobles who had returned to France soon disappeared, while the men of the Grande Armée got out their uniforms and eagerly returned to the ranks. Once again, it would be Liberté, Egalité, Fraternité pitted against the crowned heads of Europe.

These royal families were united in their hatred and fear of the returned giant, and they quickly fielded armies to defeat him. After several months, the British and the Prussians had armies near Brussels, and the Russians and the Austrians were mobilizing in the east. Napoleon saw that he might be able to raise as many as half a million French soldiers, but he knew he would face twice as many Allies. Therefore, it would be best to strike the English and the Prussians first, and after he had crushed their armies the other European powers might be willing to talk peace rather than risk the same.

Accordingly, he began to concentrate his forces on June 6. His much-trusted chief of staff, Berthier, died under mysterious circumstances on June 1, but Napoleon had already appointed Marshal Soult to fill that post. As he moved north, his army was deployed in the formation he used when facing two enemy armies.

This consisted of a screen of cavalry out front, followed by two wings deployed left and right, forces of all arms each numbering about 35,000. The left wing was commanded by Ney, the "bravest of the brave," and the right wing by Grouchy, an experienced cavalryman. Napoleon remained behind and between these two wings with his reserve of about 50,000, including his powerful Guard formations.

As he moved north, he was aiming for a point between the Prussian and the English armies, and he expected to strike the British first. In that event, Grouchy's role would be to pin the Prussians in place while Napoleon defeated the English. If Grouchy found he did not need all his force to pin the Prussians, he might send as much as half of it to assist Napoleon.

As they grew closer to their target crossroads of Quatre Bras on June 16, however, they found only part of the English force was present on the left, while Napoleon was amazed to see the Prussians deploy what looked like their entire force on open ground near the village of

Ligny. As Napoleon approached, he found 76,000 Prussian infantry, 8,000 cavalry, and 224 guns arrayed in a line some seven miles long. This was an extensive line for an army that size to hold, and it was just too good a target for him to pass up. Accordingly, Napoleon turned his reserve force to the right behind Grouchy's wing and made the Prussian army his primary target of that day.

Ney, meanwhile, did not press forward quickly enough to take the key road intersection at Quatre Bras, and English forces that arrived there ahead of him halted his approach. At two o'clock, as his forces were about to attack the Prussian center, Napoleon sent a message to Ney ordering him to attack the forces to his front and after driving them back to then turn to his right and envelop the Prussian right flank.

But unbeknownst to Napoleon, Ney was already fighting hard to push back a smaller English force and making little headway. At 3:15, Napoleon's forces were pressing the Prussian center, commanded by Blucher, and he sent another message to Ney, telling him to maneuver immediately "in such a way as to envelop the enemy's right and fall upon his rear; the fate of France is in your hands." But he had no sooner sent the courier off than he learned that Ney was facing some 20,000 English soldiers. Clearly, Ney could not bring his entire force around Blucher's right flank. He then scribbled a note telling Ney to send only d'Erlon's corps of 15,000.[17]

It is not clear that Ney ever received this order, but a staff officer saw d'Erlon's corps moving north to join Ney and intercepted him, saying that Napoleon wanted him to come around his left and attack the Prussian right wing. D'Erlon immediately obeyed, but sometime after he had started east he says that he received a countermanding order from Ney to join him. He released one division of 4,000 for Napoleon, and then turned around and marched back to the west. The result was that his corps spent the entire battle marching between Napoleon and

Ney without helping in either fight. Even the single division that joined Napoleon's left wing was too small to envelop the Prussians.

Napoleon eventually broke through Blucher's center, his massed artillery simply devouring the Prussian regiments as they were fed into it. When the hole in the line gaped open at dusk, Napoleon began pouring his guard through it, and in a moment of desperation, Blucher personally led Zeiten's cavalry in a suicidal attack to try to stop them. But the cavalry broke on the Guard's squares and Napoleon's cuirassiers smashed and rode over the remnants. Blucher's horse was killed and he was trampled and lost for a time, though a loyal aide finally found his semiconscious form and carried him to safety.

Because d'Erlon's corps had not arrived, the Prussians were able to escape that night, but they had been soundly beaten. While Napoleon lost 11,000 casualties here, Blucher lost 35,000, including 12,000 desertions in the dark. Napoleon did not immediately pursue the Prussians with infantry, instead having some of his cavalry nip at their heels as they struggled to get away and reach safety.[18]

The next morning, the English army in front of Ney had withdrawn, no doubt having learned of Blucher's defeat, and French cavalry said they were moving north toward Brussels. Napoleon then had to decide which army to follow. He finally decided that he had hurt Blucher so badly that there was little to fear from him. However, he sent his right wing of 33,000 under Grouchy to follow the Prussians, telling him that at all costs he must prevent them from supporting the English army before Napoleon had destroyed it.

Around noon on the seventeenth, Grouchy started east and stopped at Gembloux, some six miles east of Ligny. From there, he sent cavalry out on all roads leading east and north, trying to learn where the Prussian army had gone. He was soon convinced that they had gone east toward Liège. In fact, what his cavalry saw and reported was only a mass of deserters, and instead, the Prussian army had gone north to Wavre, which was fifteen miles north of Ligny and only ten miles east of Waterloo. Grouchy had been duped, and confident that the Prussians were in Liège, he simply stayed in place with his force in Gembloux.

Napoleon, meanwhile, had followed Wellington north in a heavy downpour, and when he approached Waterloo, he saw an English line spread out near Mont-St.-Jean. Curious whether this was Wellington's main force, he sent cavalry forward. When they drew the fire of some sixty guns, he knew he had run his prey to ground. He reconnoitered English lines, took a brief nap, and was up again at one o'clock in the morning. Although it was raining again, he spent many hours checking his lines and reconnoitering as much as possible.

Grouchy had heard reports of Prussians in Wavre, and he began moving north around 10 in the morning on the eighteenth. After only a few miles, he stopped at Walhain when he heard from a local resident, who professed to be a former French soldier, that the Prussians had moved through Wavre to the northeast. He was delighted to hear this and sent Napoleon a note simply asking for orders on the nineteenth, then stopped his forces and stayed where he was.

The rain ended in the morning, but because the ground was so wet, Napoleon allowed it to dry before attacking in the afternoon. His first attacks tried to feel the English out, and a number of his subordinates failed to perform as well as he had hoped. Having received reports that the Prussians were moving toward him from the east, he sent a message to Grouchy to come up on his right and envelop the English left flank, but it did not get through.[19] He finally decided to smash through the English center, and his superior artillery soon pushed the English-Dutch forces back over the crest of the plateau. As Wellington threw forces into the center to reinforce it, Ney somehow thought the English were in retreat and threw his cavalry after them.

He was wrong, and the English formed some twenty squares, none of which, it was later loudly claimed, were broken that day. And Ney, of course, had failed to send infantry or artillery forward with the cavalry, the only sort of attacks that might have broken the squares and won the battle. Repeated cavalry attacks failed, of course, and they were eventually driven back to their own lines. By now Prussians had begun to appear on Napoleon's right, and he sent yet another desperate message to Grouchy to come up, yet another message that failed to get through.

Napoleon still had eleven battalions of Old Guard left, and he sent five of them forward to break through the center. But Ney seems to have gone mad, and as they came forward, he threw them in piecemeal, thus dramatically reducing their impact and resulting in their failure to pierce the line, the only time anyone could recall when the Old Guard had failed in such a mission. By this time, the Prussians were flooding the field, and Napoleon threw two more battalions of the Old Guard at them, which stemmed the tide enough to allow a less-than-orderly French withdrawal from contact and retreat toward Paris. But this time, it really was all over for Napoleon. Within a month, he was on Saint Helena, a lonely island in the South Atlantic, where, constantly monitored on land and guarded by circling British warships, he passed the remaining few years of his life.

The importance of Waterloo for our purposes, however, is just to show how the failure of a detached force to arrive on the battlefield can mean the difference between victory and defeat. If Grouchy had come up from the south on Napoleon's right and added his force to the attack on Wellington, all this before the Prussians arrived, his 33,000 men surely would have turned the British left flank and Napoleon would have won a resounding victory. And even if he had come up as the Prussians, reinforced back up to a level of some 85,000, were approaching Waterloo, an attack on their southern flank surely would have stopped them long enough for Napoleon to have brought his artillery and infantry forward to finish off the British squares. But as things worked out, even though Grouchy lost not a single man at the Battle of Waterloo, his failure to come up on Napoleon's right converted what would have been a bright victory into Napoleon's final defeat.

If I am right about Lee's plan, it did not come to pass as he had intended and ordered. And if fault can be ascribed to any southern commander for that failure, then it is Jeb Stuart who would be held accountable. But how does one fault him? Because he failed to get past a Union cavalry force half the size of his own?

When the Army of Northern Virginia had moved north in late June 1863, they were led by the cavalry brigades of Jenkins and Imboden and were supposed to be followed by the cavalry brigades of Jones and Robertson. Stuart, meanwhile, led the other three brigades around the Union army. But as soon as Lee crossed the border into Pennsylvania, he sent Imboden's brigade off on raids to destroy Yankee railroad track and telegraph wires and to gather up as much livestock from the countryside as possible.

Consequently, Imboden did not get to Gettysburg until the afternoon of July 3 and his unit took no part in the fighting there. That night, he was called to the commanding general's tent, but didn't actually meet with him until after midnight when Lee returned from visiting one of his corps commanders, General A. P. Hill. Imboden has recorded his conversation with Lee then, and some of his memories are important:

> *The moon shone full upon his massive features and revealed an expression of sadness that I had never before seen upon his face. Awed by his appearance I waited for him to speak until the silence became embarrassing, when, to break it and change the silent current of his thoughts, I ventured to remark, in a sympathetic tone and in allusion to his great fatigue:*

*"General, this has been a hard day on you."*

*He looked up and replied mournfully:*

*"Yes, it has been a sad, sad day to us," and immediately relapsed into his thoughtful mood and attitude. Being unwilling again to intrude upon his reflections, I said no more. After perhaps a minute or two, he suddenly straightened up to his full height, and turning to me with more animation and excitement of manner than I had ever seen in him before, for he was a man of wonderful equanimity, he said in a voice tremulous with emotion:*

*"I never saw troops behave more magnificently than Pickett's division of Virginians did to-day in that grand charge upon the enemy. And if they had been supported as they were to have been—but for some reason not yet explained to me, were not—we would have held the position and the day would have been ours." After a moment's pause he added in a loud voice, in a tone almost of agony, "Too bad! Too bad! OH! TOO BAD!"* [20]

Lee, of course, could not have shared his plan for a three-pronged attack with Imboden ahead of time, simply because that man was far away on a raid when the plan was finalized. Therefore, Imboden would have had no reason to report words that Lee did not actually say, especially if he didn't completely understand them. But what did Lee mean by them?

Surely he didn't mean that he had expected Pickett's men to have been supported by the other brigades in the charge, for Lee had watched them with his own eyes. Pickett's I Corps division consisted of three brigades, but six other brigades also took part in that charge, and at least four of them made it across the field and reached the stone wall near the Clump of Trees. In fact, men from some of those brigades claimed to have gotten *farther* than did Pickett's men, which may be technically true because of a sharp angle in the stone wall.[21] So when Lee says that they were not supported "as they were to have been—but for some reason not yet explained to me, were not," he surely means something other than the infantry brigades crossing the open field supporting each other.

Lee knew that his artillery fire had stopped and never really started up again because his guns were perilously low on ammunition, so that was no mystery to him. But what else could he have meant?

Stuart tells us that his cavalry force withdrew to the York Pike that night, and then he makes an interesting comment:

*During the night of July 3, the commanding general withdrew the main body to the ridges west of Gettysburg, and sent word to me to that effect, but his messenger missed me. I repaired to his headquarters during the latter part of the night, and received instructions as to the new line and sent, in compliance therewith, a brigade (Fitz Lee's) to Cashtown, to protect our trains.*[22]

Lee, of course, stayed in place with his army all the next day and did not leave Gettysburg until the night of July 4. But let's just assume that Stuart did not get the nights of July 3 and July 4 confused, because the fact remains that he says he went to Lee's headquarters "during the latter part of the night," and we can't be sure how late that would have been. However, Imboden tells us that he was called to Lee's headquarters at about eleven that night, and when he got there, he was told Lee was at A. P. Hill's headquarters a half mile away, so he went there. But Lee told him to go back to his (Lee's) headquarters and wait for him, which he did. Finally, around one A.M., he tells us, Lee returned and the above-quoted conversation occurred, to be followed by these words:

*We must now return to Virginia. As many of our poor wounded as possible must be taken home. I have sent for you because your men and horses are fresh and in good condition to guard and protect our train back to Virginia.*

*The duty will be arduous, responsible, and dangerous, for I am afraid you will be harassed by the enemy's cavalry. How many men have you?*[23]

At a later point in his story "The Confederate Retreat from Gettysburg," told in *Battles and Leaders of the Civil War*, Imboden says that he received instructions at his meeting with Lee that night on which roads to follow and various other details for the march. And at a later point in his narration of the retreat, he says:

*It was apparent by 9 o'clock [the morning of July 4] that the wagons, ambulances, and wounded could not be collected and made ready to move till late in the afternoon. Lee sent me eight Napoleon guns . . . and a Whitworth under Lieutenant Pegram. Hampton's cavalry brigade, then under the command of Colonel P.M.B. Young, with Captain James F. Hart's four gun battery of horse artillery, was ordered to cover the rear of all trains moving under my convoy on the Chambersburg road.*[24]

General Imboden outranked Colonel Young, and the last sentence above is important, for it indicates who was in charge and therefore who was first assigned the duty. And that means Lee met with Imboden before he met with Stuart, who says that, after meeting with Lee, he "sent . . . a brigade (Fitz Lee's) to Cashtown to protect our trains." The fact that he said Fitz Lee's brigade while it was actually Hampton's is no more than a slip, for Imboden, in his story of the retreat, makes frequent reference to Hampton's brigade under Colonel Young and the various activities in which it was involved.

And that suddenly explains Lee's words "if they had been supported as they were to have been—but for some reason not yet explained to me, were not—we would have held the position and the day would have been ours." Lee had not yet met with Stuart when he spoke, and

Stuart's failure to arrive behind Culp's Hill and the Clump of Trees that day was the only question left open for Lee—why had they not been "supported as they were to have been"? That interpretation explains everything and seems the only possible meaning of Lee's words to Imboden.

There are only two known general letters on his campaigns written by Lee after the war. One of these, to B. H. Wright of Rome, New York, is cautiously written and its later publication would have done no harm. The other was written on April 15, 1868, to W. M. McDonald, who was preparing a school history and had sent him a letter in which he made certain inquiries. Lee concludes his letter of response with a request: "I must ask that you will consider what I have said as intended solely for you."[25]

In that letter, Lee says:

*As to the Battle of Gettysburg, I must again refer you to my official accounts. Its loss was occasioned by a combination of circumstances. It was commenced in the absence of correct intelligence. It was continued in the effort to overcome the difficulties by which we were surrounded,* and it would have been gained could one determined and united blow have been delivered by our whole line. *As it was, victory trembled in the balance for three days, and the battle resulted in the infliction of as great amount of injury as was received, and in frustrating Federal plans for the season.*[26] *(emphasis added)*

But what was that "one determined and united blow . . . delivered by our whole line" whose absence, according to Lee, meant defeat but whose occurrence would have meant victory? Surely, it was not the assault referred to in modern times as Pickett's Charge, for that was simply an attack by 12,000 men while the other 50,000 men in Lee's army did nothing and played no role whatever. At least, that is the conventional understanding of Pickett's Charge, a perception with which, as stated above, I disagree. But if Lee had truly planned the three-pronged attack I allege, along with supporting attacks from outside the Fishhook while Stuart and his men had pierced it to its center, then that would have been "one determined and united blow . . . by our whole line." After Appomattox, Lee refused to discuss his battle plans during the Civil War with anyone. But here, in a letter written in response to an inquisitor, Lee may have unintentionally given away the fact that his full plan at Gettysburg was never implemented.

The major reason for the failure of this masterful plan is that Lee and Stuart both failed to consider the fighting power of Custer. Not that they might have known of him personally—a junior officer on Pleasonton's staff would not be familiar to them. But they failed to consider that some brash young Union cavalry leader might do the truly unexpected and throw his regiment of four hundred into the face of Stuart's oncoming column of some 4,000 horsemen. When that happened, Custer stopped their movement, and when they were then assailed in both flanks by his other three regiments as well as a few other Yankee units, Stuart and his men became fatally entrapped.

The heavy artillery barrage followed up by Pickett's Charge had been the only one of the three intended blows against Union forces to occur. But that did not disturb Lee, beyond his deeply felt concern for the men who had died or been injured. How, one might ask, could Lee send his men on a such a charge when he knew they were serving in large measure as a distraction? Was he really willing to pay the blood price of their injuries and deaths just for a chance to defeat the Union army?

But these questions answer themselves. A skillful chess player who faces an opponent locked in a strong defense will often tempt him by sacrificing a rook, or even his queen, just to get him to open up enough for him to send a knight in for a checkmate. And more pertinent still are the words of Napoleon: "The general who cannot look on a battle-field dry-eyed will cause the unnecessary loss of many lives."[27]

After that last Confederate column was stopped and broken up by Custer and his men, I think Stuart was whipped psychologically, and second thoughts would have flooded in—"If Pickett's unsupported attack fails, I've got to cover for the whole army, I can't risk losing the cavalry here . . ." "Maybe they don't really need me, maybe Pickett pulled it off on his own, or Johnson and Pickett together . . ." Even though he may have had the numbers—some 6,000 horsemen to Custer's 1,800, possibly reinforced by McIntosh's six hundred—he was obviously unwilling to try to force the issue. He could have realigned his superior mounted force at the northern end of the valley and tried one last, desperate all-or-nothing charge against a Union force at most little more than half the size of his own. But if he had done so, of course, he would have risked getting whipped a second time on the same day and perhaps, who knows, having his entire force destroyed by a larger Union cavalry force that, for all he knew, might have been down there somewhere hiding in the woods. . . . And finally, for Stuart, this proved to be an unacceptable risk.

As the young Union general who bested Jeb Stuart on the field of battle at Gettysburg, George Armstrong Custer truly marked himself for the first time as a Great Captain. Jeb Stuart's ride was ending, and his was just beginning. But in modern times, unfortunately, he is remembered by most Americans for one salient moment, "Custer's Last Stand," when he and his men were slaughtered by an enormous host of Sioux and Cheyennes on a bluff above the Little Bighorn River, a brief spate of combat about which we know virtually nothing.

That's more than just "too bad," and "unfair" doesn't quite fit, for life, as we all know, is unfair. But over the next two years of the Civil

War, Custer was promoted to major general and commanded a division of cavalry. And during that war, he became widely renowned as one of the best battlefield generals on either side. This view of his selfless courage and truly heroic and inspirational actions gives a better picture of the real Custer—a young man for whom risk and danger were almost aphrodisiac, whose greatest joy was leading a mounted charge against the enemy. No, this might not be the kind of man you would want to have in your home for a quiet dinner, but thank God he was there when this nation's survival hung in the balance.

Finally, after reading, sifting, and absorbing all the evidence, it is the reader who must make the ultimate choice. Did Lee just have a really bad day, as the current revealed wisdom would have it? Or had he in fact concocted a plan for a three-pronged attack that, if successful, would have stunned the world? If the latter is chosen, then it becomes apparent that, had Jeb Stuart carried out his task, it probably would have resulted in a smashing victory for Lee, a victory that could have won recognition and acceptance of the Confederate States of America as an independent nation, an outcome with truly unimaginable consequences.

Whatever the reader decides about Lee and his plans for the Battle of Gettysburg, our assessment today is unfortunately meaningless: even if I am right about Lee's full plan, it simply failed. There seems little doubt that Lee ordered Stuart to try to travel those roads at the bottom of Cress Ridge and "effect a surprise on the enemy's rear." But despite the fact that he had a much larger force, Stuart was simply unable to get past Custer. And so, if one accepts this view of Lee's full plans at the Battle of Gettysburg, that cavalry charge by Stuart's force that was blunted by Custer and his Wolverine Brigade was the more important high-water mark of the Confederacy.

If there was such a plan for a deep attack into the Union rear by Stuart's cavalry at the height of Pickett's Charge, Stuart would have smarted over his inability to carry it off. He would have carried that psychic wound for the ten months left in his life, until May 1864, when he was mortally wounded while fighting for his doomed country under Lee's command. It was a pistol shot that killed him, fired by a Fifth Michigan cavalryman at the height of battle at a place known as Yellow Tavern. And the Fifth Michigan, of course, was one of the regiments from Custer's Michigan brigade.

A loyal acolyte since his days at West Point, Stuart had provided reliable service to Lee over many years of hardship, often service that simply wasn't available from anyone else. And it was those things that Lee remembered and cherished about Stuart, not a single moment at Gettysburg when he was unable to carry out his orders. If all had worked out as Lee envisioned it, this Battle of Gettysburg would have been a magnificent victory—not unlike that of Austerlitz, with a little bit of Cannae and Leuthen thrown in for balance. Failing to see and accept this as Lee's goal is to fail to understand Lee as a bold man in thought and action, a daring gambler when the stakes were very high indeed. In fact, he was one of the boldest Americans of all times, something he showed the world every day of his wartime life. And Gettysburg, had his plans and orders been properly carried out, would have been his greatest triumph of all.

But preservation of the sterling military image and reputation Stuart enjoyed on both sides in the war would have been far more important to Lee than any personal satisfaction he might have gained from exposing Stuart's failure at Gettysburg. Not only was he one of the greatest military leaders ever produced in this country, he was also a noble, honorable, and kind gentleman to those who served him loyally and well. In the wake of his death under arms fighting for the Confederacy less than a year after Gettysburg, Lee would never have said or done anything to shadow Stuart's image. A true father figure to Stuart, Lee simply took that secret with him to the grave.

Finally, this battle really comes down to Custer and his seemingly suicidal attack on Stuart's column with the First Michigan Cavalry Regiment after it had already gotten past McIntosh and his two regiments. McIntosh, remember, commanded the only soldiers from Gregg's division still left on the field after he had managed to send the others off. And apparently, Gregg had ordered these men not to attack Stuart and his Invincibles as they rode by.

In that light, it seems very reasonable to say that, at Gettysburg, Custer truly saved the Union.

If Custer hadn't been there on July 3, it seems likely Stuart would have gotten through to the back of Culp's Hill and the interior of the Fishhook. In that event, it looks like Lee would have crushed Meade's army at Gettysburg, and to stave off further disaster, the Union would have recognized the Confederacy, with all that implies. Meade would have then become just another name on the long list of Union army commanders who had been thrashed and humiliated on the field of battle by Lee.

But that didn't happen, of course. Gettysburg has since been remembered as the turning point in the Civil War, a moment when Lee was finally outthought, outfought, and outgeneraled by a Yankee commander. This crushing Confederate defeat, therefore, has become widely accepted as having been brought about by Lee's faulty decision making on July 3, 1863.

But was it really?

# Acknowledgments

At the outset, I must thank my good friend Judge Eugene Sullivan, who has championed my ideas about Gettysburg over many years, especially early on, when I doubted them even myself. My deep gratitude also goes to John Bowman, editor of my first book (*Battles and Campaigns in Vietnam,* Crown, 1983) and a close friend who has endorsed everything I have ever written. A true professional, John was key to the actual structure of this work, and I cannot thank him enough.

As I began to formulate the thesis that underlies this book, I exchanged three sets of letters with Professor James McPherson, to whom I am also deeply indebted for his patient guidance. After I had answered his challenges and presented additional evidence, he gradually swung over to my side and now validates my argument in the foreword to this book, an affirmation I appreciate enormously. I am also grateful to three figures at the United States Military Academy at West Point, New York, for their unstinting support: Dr. Stephen Grove, the Academy's historian; Dr. Suzanne Christoff, the Academy's archivist; and Dr. Alan Aimone, the Academy's senior special collections librarian. Without their help, I could never have ferreted out the myriad documents that underlie this book. I salute my many West Point classmates who offered reasoned critiques as this story developed, and I thank them all with our old class refrain: "Fruit and Milk!"

I also thank Michael Phipps, a Licensed Battlefield Guide at Gettysburg, who gave generously of his time and deep knowledge about the East Cavalry battlefield, and Paul Shevchuck, another Licensed Battlefield Guide, who helped me in my investigation of the archives kept at Gettysburg.

And finally, I could never have produced this book without the enduring support of my most beloved wife and best friend, Jan, and of our two wonderful sons, Tommy and Jason, bright shining pearls each. To all of you here mentioned, and to the countless others who have helped me along the way, I give my heartfelt thanks. I accept, of course, full personal responsibility for any factual inaccuracies or other flaws found herein. But I also admit that researching and writing this book has been the most fun I have ever had.

# Notes

## Introduction

1. All figures on unit strengths at Gettysburg are drawn, in the absence of contradictory evidence, from John W. Busey and David G. Martin, *Regimental Strengths at Gettysburg* (Baltimore: Gateway Press, 1982).

2. *The Bachelder Papers: Gettysburg in Their Own Words,* 3 vols. (Dayton, Ohio: Morningside House, 1994–1995); © 1994 New Hampshire Historical Society.

## 1. In Mexico

1. Armistead L. Long, *Memoirs of Robert E. Lee* (New York: J. M. Stoddart, 1886), 52–54; Douglas Southall Freeman, *R. E. Lee* (New York: Charles Scribner's Sons, 1935), vol. 1, 237–41.

2. Thomas M. Carhart, *West Point Warriors* (New York: Warner Books, 2002), 24.

3. Freeman, *R. E. Lee,* vol. 1, 242–43.

4. Long, *Memoirs,* 52.

5. Winfield Scott, *Memoirs* (New York: Sheldon & Co., 1864), 450.

6. Long, *Memoirs,* 60.

7. Freeman, *R. E. Lee,* vol. 1, 272.

## 2. Building Up to the Civil War

1. Thomas Cooper, ed., *The Statutes at Large of South Carolina* (Columbia, S.C., 1836), vol. 1, 356–57, as published in *The Annals of America* (Encyclopaedia Britannica, 1968), vol. 5, 585–92.

2. Carl Sandburg, *Abraham Lincoln, the Prairie Years and the War Years* (New York: Harcourt, Brace, 1926), 138.

3. James M. McPherson, *Battle Cry of Freedom* (New York: Oxford University Press, 1988), 202–203.

4. Samuel E. Morison, *The Oxford History of the American People* (New York: Oxford University Press, 1965), 613.

## 3. West Point and West Pointers

1. Freeman, *R. E. Lee,* vol. 1, 98.

2. Oliver Otis Howard, *Autobiography of Oliver Otis Howard* (New York: Baker & Taylor, 1907), 54.

3. Freeman, *R. E. Lee,* vol. 1, 346.

4. *Register of Graduates and Former Cadets of the United States Military Academy, West Point, New York,* bicentennial edition, 4-38 through 4-44.

5. List of books checked out by Lee as a cadet, Special Collections, U.S. Military Academy Library, West Point, New York.

6. Morris Schaff, *The Spirit of Old West Point* (New York: Houghton Mifflin, 1908), 62.

7. Interview with Dr. Stephen Grove, United States Military Academy historian, November 26, 2003.

8. Stephen E. Ambrose, *Duty, Honor, Country* (Baltimore: Johns Hopkins University Press, 1966), 138.

9. Superintendent Bowman to President Lincoln, May 6, 1863, Special Collections, USMA Library.

10. William H. Harris to his father, April 4, 1858, William H. Harris Papers, New York Public Library.

11. Freeman, *R. E. Lee,* vol. 1, 356–57.

12. Ibid., 353–55.

13. Ibid., 357–58.

14. Antoine Henri Jomini, *Précis de l'Art de la Guerre* (Paris: Anselin et Laguyonie, 1838), vol. 2, 33–34, 246–48.

15. Burke Davis, *Jeb Stuart, the Last Cavalier* (New York: n.p., 1957), 17–28.

16. Emory M. Thomas, *Bold Dragoon* (New York: Harper & Row, 1986), 33–67.

## 4. Classic Battles of History

1. Paddy Griffith, *Battle Tactics of the Civil War* (New Haven, Conn.: Yale University Press, 1989), 189.

2. John Warry, *Warfare in the Classical World* (Norman: University of Oklahoma Press, 1995), 120; G. P. Baker, *Hannibal* (New York: Dodd, Mead, 1929), 126–49; Mark Healey, *Cannae 216 BC* (Oxford, U.K.: Osprey, 1994), 73–85.

3. Christopher Duffy, *Prussia's Glory* (Chicago: Rosemont Emperor's, 2003), 124–75; J. F. C. Fuller, *Military History of the Western World* (New York: Da Capo Press, 1955), vol. 2, 208–15.

4. David Chandler, *The Campaigns of Napoleon* (New York: Macmillan, 1966); Somerset de Chair, ed., *Napoleon on Napoleon* (London: Brockhampton, 1998); Vincent Esposito and John Elting, *A Military History and Atlas of the Napoleonic Wars* (New York: Frederick A. Praeger, 1964).

## 5. Infantry, Artillery, and Cavalry

1. John R. Elting, *Swords Around a Throne* (New York: Free Press, 1988), 207–25.

2. E.g., General John Reynolds, commander of the Union First Corps and considered one of the best generals in the Union Army, arrived on the battlefield at Gettysburg early on the first day with the leading infantry unit, but was soon spotted and killed from long range by a Confederate sharpshooter.

3. Griffith, *Battle Tactics of the Civil War,* 99–103.

4. Fairfax Downey, *The Guns at Gettysburg* (New York: David McKay, 1958), 178–81.

5. Ibid., 238–48.

6. Michael Howard, *The Franco-Prussian War* (New York: Dorset Press, 1961), 55–56.

7. Ibid., 155–57.

8. Chandler, *The Campaigns of Napoleon,* 144–46.

9. Griffith, *Battle Tactics of the Civil War,* 35.

10. Chandler, *The Campaigns of Napoleon,* 159–63.

11. Ibid., 184–91.

## 6. The Fighting Begins

1. Vincent J. Esposito, *The West Point Atlas of American Wars* (New York: Frederick A. Praeger, 1959), vol. 1, 20.

2. Thomas, *Bold Dragoon,* 79–81.

3. Official Records of the Union and Confederate Armies (hereafter O.R.), vol. 11, I, part 3, 140.

4. Ibid., vol. 11, I, part 1, 536, 43.

5. Ibid., 153, 198–99, 651, 914.

6. H. B. McClellan, *I Rode with Jeb Stuart* (Bloomington: Indiana University Press, 1958), 53–71.

## 7. Early Confederate Victories

1. Heros von Borcke, *Memoirs of the Confederate War* (New York: Peter Smith, 1938), vol. 1, 290–97.

2. McClellan, *I Rode with Jeb Stuart,* 154.

3. Von Borcke, *Memoirs,* vol. 1, 309.

## 8. Chancellorsville

1. Long, *Memoirs,* 253–54.

2. Vincent Esposito and John Elting, *A Military History and Atlas of the Napoleonic Wars* (New York: Frederick A. Praeger, 1964), 20–21.

3. Douglas Freeman, *R. E. Lee* (New York: Charles Scribner's Sons, 1935), vol. 2, 445–47.

4. Esposito, *American Wars,* vol. 1, 84–88.

5. Ibid., 91.

6. Esposito and Elting, *Napoleonic Wars,* 25.

## 9. Lee Moves North

1. Chandler, *The Campaigns of Napoleon,* 155.

2. Edwin B. Coddington, *The Gettysburg Campaign* (New York: Charles Scribner's Sons, 1968), 5–8; Douglas S. Freeman, *Lee's Lieutenants* (New York: Charles Scribner's Sons, 1942), vol. 2, 518.

3. Coddington, *The Gettysburg Campaign,* 5–8.

4. Most of the information on the cavalry battle at Brandy Station that follows is drawn from the following sources: Fairfax Downey, *Clash of Cavalry* (New York: David McKay, 1959); Thomas, *Bold Dragoon;* Davis, *Jeb Stuart.*

5. von Borcke, *Memoirs of the Confederate War for Independence,* vol. 2, 263–67.

6. O.R., vol. 27, I, part 1, 1046.

## 10. The Gettysburg Fight Begins

1. Coddington, *The Gettysburg Campaign,* 180.

2. Ibid., 220.

3. Ibid., 220–21.

4. James H. Kidd, *A Cavalryman with Custer* (New York: Bantam Books, 1991), 65–67.

5. O.R., vol. 27, I, part 1, 992.

6. Kidd, *A Cavalryman with Custer,* 132–33.

7. Coddington, *The Gettysburg Campaign,* 308–309.

8. James Longstreet, "Lee in Pennsylvania," in *Annals of the War* (Edison, N.J.: The Blue & Gray Press, 1991), 421.

9. G. Moxley Sorrel, *Recollections of a Confederate Staff Officer* (New York: Bantam Books, 1992), 167.

10. Coddington, *The Gettysburg Campaign,* 361–62.

11. O.R., vol. 27, I, part 1, 914–16.

12. Paul Shevchuk, "The Battle of Hunterstown," in *The Gettysburg Magazine,* no. 1 (July 1989), 99.

13. United States Military Academy, "Register of Graduates."

14. Shevchuk, "The Battle of Hunterstown," 100.

15. Manley Wellman, *Giant in Gray* (Dayton, Ohio: Morningstar Bookshop Press, 1988), 117.

16. Gregory J. W. Urwin, *Custer Victorious* (Lincoln: University of Nebraska Press, 1983), 70.

17. O.R., vol. 27, I, part 1, 992.

18. Ibid., part 2, 724.

## 11. Gettysburg, Day Two

1. O.R., vol. 27, part 1, 914.

2. A copy of this letter, written in longhand, can be found in the archives of the Gettysburg National Military Park in Gettysburg, Pennsylvania.

3. Freeman, *Lee's Lieutenants,* 139.

4. Stephen Z. Starr, *The Union Cavalry in the Civil War* (Baton Rouge: Louisiana State University Press, 1979), 431.

5. O.R., vol. 27, part 3, 923.

6. Robert F. O'Neill, Jr., *The Cavalry Battles of Aldie, Middleburg, and Upperville* (Lynchburg, Va.: H. E. Howard, 1993), 37.

7. *Bachelder Papers,* vol. 2, 926.

8. Terry L. Jones, ed., *Campbell Brown's Civil War* (Baton Rouge: Louisiana State University Press, 2001), 219.

9. Ibid., 219–20.

10. Freeman, *Lee's Lieutenants,* vol. 3, 130–32.

11. Esposito and Elting, *Napoleonic Wars,* 35.

## 12. Plans for Day Three

1. O.R., vol. 27, part 2, 320.

2. Esposito and Elting, *Napoleonic Wars,* 12–15.

3. Ibid., 15–16.

4. Chandler, *The Campaigns of Napoleon,* 191–201.

5. Busey and Martin, *Regimental Strengths,* 50–171.

6. O.R., vol. 27, part 2, 697.

7. Gerard Chaliand, ed., *The Art of War in World History* (Berkeley: University of California Press, 1994), 955.

### 13. The Final Plan

1. Harry W. Pfanz, *Gettysburg, Culp's Hill & Cemetery Hill* (Chapel Hill: University of North Carolina Press, 1993), map 16.1, 286.
2. Coddington, *The Gettysburg Campaign,* 454.
3. O.R., vol. 27, part 2, 359; James Longstreet, *Memoirs* (New York: Konacky & Konacky, 1992), 385; James Longstreet, "Lee's Right Wing at Gettysburg," in *Battles and Leaders of the Civil War* (New York: The Century Company, 1887), vol. 3, 342.
4. O.R., vol. 27, part 2, 320; Long, *Memoirs,* 287.
5. O.R., vol. 27, part 2, 359.
6. Ibid., 320.
7. Ibid., 504; Pfanz, *Gettysburg,* map 16.2, 301, map 17.1, 311.
8. O.R., vol. 27, part 2, 447–48.
9. Long, *Memoirs,* 288; Longstreet, "Lee's Right Wing at Gettysburg," 343.
10. Coddington, *The Gettysburg Campaign,* 457.
11. Freeman, *Lee's Lieutenants,* vol. 3, 143.
12. Longstreet, "Lee in Pennsylvania," in *Annals of the War,* 429.
13. Longstreet, "Lee's Right Wing at Gettysburg," 343.
14. Longstreet, *Memoirs,* 393.
15. Freeman, *R. E. Lee,* vol. 2, 347.
16. J. William Jones, *Personal Reminiscences, Anecdotes, and Letters of Gen. Robert E. Lee* (Harrisburg, Pa.: The Archive Society, 1996), 143.
17. Freeman, *R. E. Lee,* vol. 4, 174–75.

### 14. The Implementation

1. Busey and Martin, *Regimental Strengths,* 104–108.
2. Michael Phipps, *Custer at Gettysburg* (Gettysburg, Pa.: Farnsworth House, 1996), 32–33; Kidd, *A Cavalryman with Custer,* 72–74.
3. O.R., vol. 27, part 1, 957.
4. Ibid., 958.
5. Ibid., 997.
6. Ibid., 1000; Custer's entire report runs from 997 to 1001.
7. Chamberlain's report is found ibid., 622, while that of Oates is found ibid., part 2, 392.
8. Ibid., part 1, 956.
9. Ibid., 956.
10. Ibid., part 2, 697.
11. Ibid., 699.

12. Ibid., 698.

13. Ibid., 698.

14. Phipps, *Custer at Gettysburg,* 33–36.

15. Ibid., 33–36.

16. Busey and Martin, *Regimental Strengths,* 206.

17. McClellan, *I Rode with Jeb Stuart,* 338.

18. Ibid., 338.

19. Ibid., 338–39.

20. For this lesson in Civil War artillery given to me in a personal interview, I am indebted to General (retired) Harold Nelson, Ph.D., the former chief of military history for the U.S. Army and the author of a number of Civil War books. A man who started his military career in the artillery branch, General Nelson has become an impressive authority on the use of that arm during the Civil War.

21. O.R., vol. 27, part 2, 697.

22. McClellan, *I Rode with Jeb Stuart,* 339.

23. O.R., vol. 27, part 1, 956.

24. Although Busey and Martin tell us that the Fifth Michigan counted 646 men in its ranks, then-Major Trowbridge tells us on page 15 of his 1886 paper "Operations of the Cavalry in the Gettysburg Campaign" that one battalion of that regiment was away guarding a train, which probably accounted for roughly 150 men.

25. McClellan says, on page 340 of *I Rode with Jeb Stuart,* that neither the Cobb Legion of Hampton's brigade nor the Fourth Virginia of Fitz Lee's brigade was involved in the fight, but in the Bachelder Papers, members of both units say they were, and McClellan's comment seems to smack of special pleading on the order of "You may have beaten us, but we had fewer soldiers in the fight than you may think."

26. O.R., vol. 27, part 2, 497; Busey and Martin, *Regimental Strengths,* 162.

27. Phipps, *Custer at Gettysburg,* 37; Busey and Martin, *Regimental Strengths,* 199.

28. Robert J. Trout, *Galloping Thunder* (Mechanicsburg, Pa.: Stackpole Books, 2002), 291; Busey and Martin, *Regimental Strengths,* 201.

29. Busey and Martin, *Regimental Strengths,* 109.

30. Ibid., 110.

## 15. Stuart Meets Custer

1. McClellan, *I Rode with Jeb Stuart,* 339.

2. O.R., vol. 27, part 2, 698.

3. William Miller, "The Cavalry Battle Near Gettysburg," in *Battles and Leaders of the Civil War,* vol. 3, 402.

4. *Bachelder Papers,* vol. 2, 1123.

5. Busey and Martin, *Regimental Strengths,* 206; Henry Woodhead, ed., *Arms and Equipment of the Union* (Alexandria, Va.: Time-Life Books, 1996), 58–63.

6. Woodhead, *Arms and Equipment of the Confederacy,* 44–49.

7. O.R., vol. 27, part 1, 957.

8. *Bachelder Papers,* vol. 2, 1237.

9. Ibid., 1237–38.

10. Ibid., 1238.

11. Ibid., 1236–39.

12. O.R., vol. 27, part 2, 698.

13. Ibid., 698.

14. Ibid., 724–25.

15. McClellan, *I Rode with Jeb Stuart,* xi.

16. Ibid., 340–41.

17. O.R., vol. 27, part 1, 956.

18. *Bachelder Papers,* vol. 2, 1281.

19. McClellan, *I Rode with Jeb Stuart,* 346.

20. "Stuart's and Gregg's Cavalry Engagement, July 3, 1863," by David L. Ladd and Audrey J. Ladd, in *The Gettysburg Magazine,* no. 16 (January 1997), 100.

21. O.R., vol. 27, part 3, 1062.

22. Coddington, *The Gettysburg Campaign,* 522; William Brooke-Rawle, "The Right Flank at Gettysburg," in *Annals of the War,* 480.

23. William E. Miller, "The Cavalry Battle near Gettysburg," in *Battles and Leaders of the Civil War,* vol. 3, 402.

24. Busey and Martin, *Regimental Strengths,* 195–97.

25. Though Stuart did not say where he was or whether he was with his troops in any of the action this day, Sergeant Elliott G. Fishburne of the First Virginia Cavalry tells us in two letters he wrote to Bachelder after the war that he saw Stuart ride with the First Virginia in the final charge. *Bachelder Papers,* vol. 2, 1285, 1286.

26. Brooke-Rawle, "The Right Flank at Gettysburg," 481.

27. Ibid., 482.

28. *Bachelder Papers,* vol. 3, 1435–36.

29. Miller, "The Cavalry Battle near Gettysburg," 404.

30. Ibid., 404–405.

## 16. Aftermath

1. *Bachelder Papers,* vol 3, 1377.

2. Coddington, *The Gettysburg Campaign,* 6.

3. All segments of Stuart's after-action report appear in O.R., vol. 27, part 2, 697–99.

4. Ibid., 725.

5. Ibid., 697.

6. McClellan, *I Rode with Jeb Stuart,* 337.

7. Ibid., 339.

8. Ibid., 341.

9. O.R., vol. 27, part 1, 956.

10. *Annals of the War,* 378.

11. Ibid., 480.

12. Major Edward Carpenter, "Gregg's Cavalry at Gettysburg," in *Annals of the War,* 534.

13. O.R., vol. 27, part 1, 117.

14. McPherson, *Battle Cry of Freedom,* 663.

15. Starr, *The Union Cavalry in the Civil War,* 438.

16. Wellman, *Giant in Gray,* 121; Longacre, *The Cavalry at Gettysburg,* 221; Coddington, *The Gettysburg Campaign,* 520–21.

17. Chandler, *Campaigns of Napoleon,* 1007–95.

18. Esposito, *American Wars,* 156–61.

19. When he later asked Soult how many copies of the message he had sent and was told only one, he reportedly said, "Alas, my Berthier would have sent six!"

20. General John D. Imboden, "The Retreat from Gettysburg," in *Battles and Leaders of the Civil War,* vol. 3, 421.

21. John M. Priest, *Into the Fight: Pickett's Charge at Gettysburg* (Shippensburg, Pa.: White Mane Books, 1998), 86–159; Carol Reardon, *Pickett's Charge* (Chapel Hill: University of North Carolina Press, 1997), 151.

22. O.R., vol. 27, part 2, 699.

23. Imboden, "The Retreat from Gettysburg," 422.

24. Ibid., 422–23.

25. Freeman, *R. E. Lee,* vol. 4, 477.

26. Ibid., 476.

27. Esposito and Elting, *Napoleonic Wars,* 44.

# Index